Best New Media, K–12

Recent Titles in the
Children's and Young Adult Literature Reference Series
Catherine Barr, Series Editor

The Newbery/Printz Companion: Booktalks and Related Materials
for Award Winners and Honor Books
John T. Gillespie and Corinne J. Naden

Books Kids Will Sit Still For 3: A Read-Aloud Guide
Judy Freeman

Classic Teenplots: A Booktalk Guide to Use with Readers Ages 12–18
John T. Gillespie and Corinne J. Naden

Best Books for Middle School and Junior High Readers: Grades 6–9.
Supplement to the First Edition
John T. Gillespie and Catherine Barr

Best Books for High School Readers: Grades 9–12. Supplement to the First Edition
John T. Gillespie and Catherine Barr

War and Peace: A Guide to Literature and New Media, Grades 4–8
Virginia A. Walter

Across Cultures: A Guide to Multicultural Literature for Children
Kathy East and Rebecca L. Thomas

Best Books for Children, Supplement to the 8th Edition: Preschool through Grade 6
Catherine Barr and John T. Gillespie

Best Books for Boys: A Resource for Educators
Matthew D. Zbaracki

Beyond Picture Books: Subject Access to Best Books for Beginning Readers
Barbara Barstow, Judith Riggle, and Leslie Molnar

A to Zoo: Subject Access to Children's Picture Books. Supplement to the 7th Edition
Carolyn W. Lima and Rebecca L. Thomas

Gentle Reads: Great Books to Warm Hearts and Lift Spirits, Grades 5–9
Deanna J. McDaniel

Best New Media, K–12

A Guide to Movies, Subscription Web Sites, and Educational Software and Games

Catherine Barr

Children's and Young Adult Literature Reference
Catherine Barr, Series Editor

LIBRARIES
UNLIMITED
A Member of the Greenwood Publishing Group

Westport, Connecticut • London

Library of Congress Cataloging-in-Publication Data

Barr, Catherine, 1951–
  Best new media, K–12 : a guide to movies, subscription web sites, and educational software and games /
Catherine Barr.
      p. cm. — (Children's and young adult literature reference)
  Includes bibliographical references and indexes.
  ISBN 978-1-59158-467-4 (alk. paper)
  1. Libraries—Special collections—Video recordings for children. 2. Libraries—Special collections—
Children's films. 3. Libraries—Special collections—Children's software. 4. Video recordings for
children—Catalogs. 5. Children's films—Catalogs. 6. Children's software—Catalogs. 7. Children's web
sites—Directories. 8. Multimedia library services—United States. 9. Children's libraries—Collection
development—United States. 10. Young adults' libraries—Collection development—United States. I. Title.
  Z692.V52B37   2008
  011'.37—dc22   2008020191

British Library Cataloguing in Publication Data is available.

Library of Congress Catalog Card Number: 2008020191
ISBN 978-1-59158-467-4

First published in 2008

Libraries Unlimited, 88 Post Road West, Westport, CT 06881
A Member of the Greenwood Publishing Group, Inc.
www.lu.com

Printed in the United States of America

The paper used in this book complies with the
Permanent Paper Standard issued by the National
Information Standards Organization (Z39.48–1984).

10 9 8 7 6 5 4 3 2 1

Contents

CONTENTS

Major Subjects Arranged Alphabetically

Preface

Best New Media, K–12: A Guide to Movies, Subscription Web Sites, and Educational Software and Games is a new addition to the well-established Best Books series (*Best Books for Children, Best Books for Middle School and Junior High Readers,* and *Best Books for High School Readers*). *Best New Media* has been developed to help librarians and other specialists working with children and young adults to identify suitable new media — including software and computer games — for collection, access, and circulation.

General Scope and Criteria for Inclusion

Best New Media includes 1,326 entries, of which 1,156 are individually numbered entries and 170 are cited within the annotations as additional recommended titles, usually in the same series. It should be noted that some series are so extensive that only representative titles are included.

Most of the materials were published after 2000, but a number of the DVDs listed were previously available only in VHS format. Interestingly, many of the award-winning films issued in VHS format have not yet been reissued on DVDs.

Many journals, library catalogs, and Web sites were consulted during the compilation of this work. Most materials included received a positive review in one or more of the sources listed below. Others were mentioned in awards lists or recommended in other printed or online sources. Criteria such as availability, currency, accuracy, usefulness, relevance, and presence in library catalogs were also considered.

Reviews from the following library-related journals are cited following the annotations:

Booklist (BL)
Children's Technology Review (CTR)
Library Media Connection (LMC)

MultiMedia & Internet @ Schools (MM&IS)
Public Libraries (PL)
School Library Journal (SLJ)
Video Librarian (VL)
Voice of Youth Advocates (VOYA)

Uses of This Book

Best New Media is designed to help librarians and media specialists with four tasks: evaluating existing collections; building new collections or enhancing existing collections; providing guidance to young patrons; and preparing bibliographies and events. Many libraries are just beginning to build collections of computer games, and we hope this volume will prove a useful resource.

Arrangement

The arrangement of this volume corresponds roughly to that of others in the Best Books series. However, the contents of this volume are divided into two parts: Materials for Younger Readers (Grades K–3) and Materials for Older Readers (Grades 4–12). Materials that straddle the K–3/4–12 divide are placed in the older section. So a DVD on nutrition that is recommended for grades 2–6 (*The Lunch Lady's Guide to the Food Pyramid,* for example) will be found under Materials for Older Readers in the chapter on Health and the Human Body: Nutrition and Diet, which in turn is part of the section called Guidance and Personal Development.

The Table of Contents gives easy access to the arrangement of the subjects. Following the Table of Contents is a listing of Major Subjects Arranged Alphabetically, which provides spans of entry numbers as well as page numbers for easy access. Following the main body of the text are a Title Index and a Subject Index.

Materials — be they DVDs, software, computer games, or Web sites — can be found under the appropriate subjects throughout the book. The painting program *ArtRage 2.5,* for example, is under Drawing and Painting in the Crafts, Hobbies, and Pastimes section. *Math Baseball,* a program for Leapster users that integrates math and baseball facts for grades 1 to 3, is found in the section titled Alphabet, Concept, and Counting.

Computer games are harder to categorize. Many are clearly linked to a topic — an interactive science game is found under Science, a Harry Potter game under Fantasy, a baseball game under Baseball. Games that are more entertainment-oriented are placed in the Computer Games chapter in the Sports and Games section.

The Subject Index gives access to computer games by subject and by genre. The genres are explained here:

Action — usually for a single player, these games involve speed, dexterity, and quick reactions and usually include some violence as well as exploration challenges and puzzles to solve

Action/adventure — these games combine aspects of action games and adventure games, usually requiring both good reflexes and problem-solving, in both violent and nonviolent scenarios; the *Zelda* games are a good example of this genre

Adventure — players interact with characters in sometimes lengthy narratives that involve investigation, exploration, and puzzles to solve

Fighting — generally rated T (teen) because of their violence, these competitive games are very popular in tournaments and appeal particularly to boys

First-person shooter — even more competitive than the above, these games focus on skill with weapons and victory over the enemy, all viewed from a first-person perspective

Party — these multiplayer games often consist of a number of simple mini-games; those that involve moving to, or creating, music — sometimes called rhythm games — are often rated T because of the lyrics

Puzzle — logic, strategy, word skills, pattern recognition, and sequence solving are features of these games

Racing — a wide variety of games fall into this popular category that features both real-world and fantasy scenarios and equipment from go-karts to the fastest racing cars to air and sea vehicles

Role playing — players assume the roles of characters, often in an adventure setting, and make choices that shape the direction of the game; usually featuring various levels of play, these games require the player to acquire skills or earn points to advance from one level to the next

Simulation — simulating either real life or a fantasy environment, most of these games feature complex scenarios in which the player must make choices and control events

Strategy — combining elements of simulation and often adventure and role playing, these games require forward planning and strategic thinking, often with a war theme

Entries

The following materials are included in *Best New Media*: films and documentaries on DVD; software (in the form of CD-ROMs, online downloads, interactive books, and handheld devices); computer games offered in a variety of formats; and subscription Web sites accessed over the Internet. The following icons are used to denote format:

- ● DVD
- 🖳 Software
- 🎲 Game
- 🖱 Web site

DVDs

DVD entries usually give the following information:

> Title (grade level). Date of publication. Running time. Series title.
> Producer (with distributor if applicable). Price.
> Annotation (review citations).
> Award(s)

Additional bibliographic information may include notation of public performance rights (PPR), the presence of closed captioning, and ISBN. (Note that many DVD producers and distributors do not assign ISBNs to their DVDs — or if they do, this information is not readily available even on the relevant Web sites.) Review citations may refer to a previous VHS version and therefore may precede the date of DVD release. Similarly, awards may refer to the earlier format.

> **374** ● **Andy Warhol** (4–6). 2007. 24 min. Series: Getting to Know the World's Greatest Artists. Getting to Know. $29.95.
> An animated Andy Warhol describes his childhood, life, and career as a pop artist in New York City and shows reproductions of his work. (Rev: BL 11/1/07; SLJ 8/7)
> ☃ ALA ALSC Notable Children's Videos 2008

COMPUTER GAMES

Computer game entries usually give the following information:

> Title (grade level). Producer. Platform(s). Number of players. ESRB (Entertainment Software Rating Board) rating
> Descriptive annotation (review citations)
> Award(s)

Prices and dates of publication are not usually given for games as they can vary widely depending on the platform and the length of time since initial publication.

> **335** ▨ **Beyond Good and Evil** (8–12). Ubisoft. Windows, PlayStation 2, GameCube, Xbox. Players: 1. ESRB: T13+ (comic mischief, violence).
> Hillys, a planet in the distant future, is under attack. A reporter, Jade, seeks answers to the secrets of her past while defeating many enemies; players journey through high-tech cities and fantastic landscapes while seeking clues.
> ☃ YALSA Top 50 Core Recommended Collection Titles

The following platforms are cited in entries:

Windows
Macintosh
PlayStation 2
PlayStation 3
PSP (PlayStation Portable)
GameCube
Nintendo DS
Game Boy Advance
Xbox
Xbox 360
Wii

Ratings

Several organizations evaluate computer games. We have chosen to cite the ratings assigned by the Entertainment Software Rating Board (www.esrb. org/index-js.jsp):

E   Everyone
E10+ Everyone 10 and older
T   Teen
T13+ Teen 13 and older
M   Mature

A mature rating means that the game is only suitable for those who are 17 and older.

Ratings may be accompanied by content descriptors in parentheses that indicate elements in a game that may have triggered a particular rating and/or may be of interest or concern.

> 284 🎲 **Halo 3** (11–12). Microsoft Game Studios. Xbox 360. Players: 1–16. ESRB: M (blood and gore, mild language, violence).
> Choose humans or aliens and battle it out to the end. This very popular first-person shooter is set in the future and includes many high-powered and exciting vehicles and weapons that are needed to eliminate the enemy. The last installment in the Halo trilogy.
> 🎮 YALSA Top 50 Core Recommended Collection Titles

SOFTWARE

A typical software entry specifies the platform and gives similar information to that provided for other formats. Many are CD-ROMs that can be used both on Windows PCs and Macintosh computers or programs that can be downloaded from the Web and used on these computers. There are also examples of dedicated software for Leapster handheld devices.

> **363** 🖥 **Comic Book Creator** (6–12). 2007. Planetwide Games (dist. by AV Café). Windows. $29.99.
> A lot of fun for students with artistic abilities as well as those who can't draw at all. Using templates, they can add art (from online sources, the CD's collection, or their computer) and embellish their stories with speech balloons, graphics, and so on. (Rev: SLJ 9/07)

SUBSCRIPTION WEB SITES

Subscription Web site entries usually give the following information:

Title (grade level), Publisher, URL
Descriptive annotation (review citations)
Award(s)

> **1130** 🖱 **The African American Experience** (7–12). Greenwood Publishing.
> http://aae.greenwood.com
> A comprehensive research database that provides reliable information on African American life, history, and culture. Users can browse a wide range of subject areas, from "Arts and Entertainment" and "Business and Labor" to "Sports" and "Women." The Resources section includes the following headings: Title List, Timeline, Image Index, Primary Source Index, Landmark Documents, Slave Narratives, Classic Texts, and Audio Files. (Rev: BL 11/1/06; LMC 4–5/07; PL 11–12/06)

Many of the subscription Web sites will be used most often for research purposes. We have, therefore, added a new Reference section.

Acknowledgments

I would like to thank in particular the publishers of *Video Librarian* and *Children's Technology Review* for their help in the compilation of this volume. Janell Cipriani, Susan C. Olmstead, and Jim Gibson also made significant contributions. And, as always, I'm indebted to Julia C. Miller and Christine McNaull for their extensive knowledge about databases, design, and editing, and to Barbara Ittner of Libraries Unlimited for her support and guidance.

The coverage of this first edition will inevitably have gaps. Many reviewing journals have been slow to add sections on software and gaming; and the VHS format continued to be strong even after the introduction of the more durable DVD. We have no doubt omitted someone's favorite DVD, another person's favorite game. We aim to keep this book up to date with supplements and new editions and would be grateful to receive your suggestions.

Catherine Barr
barr@bogartandbarr.com

MATERIALS FOR
YOUNGER CHILDREN
(GRADES K–3)

Alphabet, Concept, and Counting

1 ⦿ **The A to Z Symphony** (K). 2004. 30 min. Classical Fun Music. $19.95.
Presents each letter of the alphabet in both capital and lower-case format, lists representative words, and pairs each letter with a classical music selection and brief video. (Rev: BL 11/1/04; SLJ 10/04)

2 🖳 **Alphabet Track** (K–6). 2006. Series: Track. Tool Factory. Windows, Macintosh. $69.95.
Students with dyslexia and other problems that make learning difficult will benefit from these attractively presented alphabet activities. Other programs in the series include *Eye Track* and *Phoneme Track*; the first improves visual perception and the second teaches phonemes.
⚱ ALA Notable Children's Software 2006

3 🖳 **Animal Babies ABC** (K–2). 2007. Capstone. Windows, Macintosh. ISBN 978-1-4296-1135-0. $26.95.
Users can "play" this book by Sarah L. Schuette with a simple click, viewing text and pictures of baby animals and hearing the text read aloud. (Rev: SLJ 3/08)

4 🖳 **Bajo las olas 1, 2, 3: Vamos a contar la vida marina/Under the Sea 1, 2, 3: Counting Ocean Life** (K–2). 2007. Capstone. Windows, Macintosh. ISBN 978-1-4296-1133-6. $26.95.
Basic counting, addition, and subtraction are taught in both English and Spanish in this interactive version of Barbara Knox's book (A+ Books, 2007) that allows readers to progress at their own pace and to listen to the text in English or Spanish. (Rev: SLJ 3/08)

5 🖱 **Clever Island** (K–3).
www.cleverisland.com
A self-paced, interactive program of activities for K–3 children to use at home to reinforce reading, math, and art. (Rev: SLJ 7/07; CTR 11/01)

6 ⦿ **Curious Buddies: Let's Build!** (K). 2005. 30 min. Series: Curious Buddies. Paramount Home Entertainment. Closed captioned. ISBN 978-1-4157-0559-9. $14.99.
The buddies — five adorable animal puppets — learn about construction and shapes in this segment from the Nick Jr. series. (Rev: VL 7–8/05)

7 🖳 **Disney Princess Enchanted Learning** (K). 2005. Leapfrog. Leapster. Players: 1. $24.99.
Leapster handheld users learn early reading and math concepts as they play five games featuring Cinderella and Ariel. (Rev: CTR 5/05)

8 🖱 **Enchanted Learning** (K–3).
www.enchantedlearning.com
Provides students, teachers, and parents with an array of online worksheets, games, activities, and arts and crafts on subjects such as math, science, reading, foreign language, and geography/history. This low-cost site is actually free if users accept advertising; a subscription brings ad-free access and printer-friendly pages. (Rev: SLJ 8/07)

9 ✪ **Lots to Learn, Vol. 2: In My House**
(K). 2004. 30 min. Series: Lots to Learn. Lots
to Learn (dist. by Big Kids Productions).
PPR. $19.95.
Counting, spelling, singing, and playing, children explore the different rooms in their
houses and discover sizes, shapes, colors, and
other concepts. Also use *Lots to Learn:
Nature* (2004). (Rev: SLJ 5/05; VL 5–6/05)

10 💻 **Math Baseball** (1–3). 2005. Leapfrog.
Leapster. Players: 1. $19.99.
Leapster handheld users can practice math
skills — addition, subtraction, multiplication
and division — as they hone their baseball
knowledge. (Rev: CTR 7/05)

11 💻 **Math Missions** (1–3). 2005. Scholastic.
Leapster. $24.99.
Children learn addition, multiplication, and
other basic math skills as they earn money
participating in four activities at a shopping
mall — filling orders in a candy store, for
example. They can then spend their cash on a
choice of exciting (and addicting) arcade
games. (Rev: CTR Summer 05)

12 💻 **Mole's Huge Nose** (K–1). 2005. Series:
Leapster Reading with Phonics. LeapFrog.
Leapster. $19.99.
This controlled-vocabulary 28-page electronic book about a mole with a huge nose is
enlivened by simple games that appear every
few pages. This program allows children to
hear single words or full sentences, and
teaches reading and comprehension as well as
long and short vowels. (Rev: CTR Spring 05)

13 ✪ **Money and Making Change** (K–3).
2006. 57 min. Rock 'n Learn (dist. by Big
Kids Productions). ISBN 978-1-878489-28-9.
$19.95.
Animated characters — a coin called Penny
and a dollar called Bill — entertain with
music and dance as they explain the various
parts of money. (Rev: SLJ 11/06)

14 ✪ **The Mr. Ray Show: Songs from the
Stickered Guitar** (K). 2006. 21 min. Mr.
Ray KidWonders (dist. by AV Café). $19.95.
Mr. Ray sings original tunes as well as old
favorites. Animated segments featuring Ellie
Elephant and George the Groovy Giraffe add

to the entertainment value of this kid-friendly
presentation that teaches essentials such numbers, letters, and days of the week. (Rev: SLJ
11/07)

15 ✪ **Preschool Prep Presents Meet the Letters** (K). 2005. 30 min. Preschool Prep. ISBN
978-0-9767008-4-5. $14.95.
An appealing introduction to letters and their
sounds, using animation and alliteration to
good effect. (Rev: BL 9/15/05)

16 ✪ **Ready for Beginning Math** (K). 2007.
55 min. Quality Time Education. $45.
Twenty-five basic math concepts are introduced in viewer-friendly fashion using animation and live-action footage; counting
(forward and backward), telling time, and
measuring are among the topics covered.
(Rev: BL 7/07; SLJ 8/07)

17 🎮 **Smart Boy's Gameroom** (K–1). 2007.
UFO Interactive Games. Nintendo DS. Players: 1. ESRB: E.
Twelve mini-games specifically intended for
boys offer a variety of activities that introduce basic concepts; playing a keyboard and
matching sounds are just two examples. A
companion product is *Smart Girl's Playhouse*. (Rev: CTR 10/07)

18 🎮 **Spelling 1-2** (1–3). 2006. School Zone.
Windows, Macintosh. ISBN 978-1-58947-
827-5. $15.99.
Students will enjoy this CD-ROM featuring
three underwater-themed games that teach
spelling. As the player's spelling improves,
more difficult words are introduced; there are
more than 1,700 words in all. Teachers can
add words. A workbook is included. (Rev:
SLJ 4/07)

19 ✪ **Two Alphabet Stories by June Sobel**
(K). 2007. 12 min. Nutmeg Media. PPR.
ISBN 978-1-933938-35-6. $69.95.
Iconographic presentations of Sobel's *Shiver
Me Letters* and *B Is for Bulldozer*. The first is
a pirate-themed alphabet, and the second features construction vehicles for each letter of
the alphabet. Young children will enjoy
learning their letters and watching an interview with the author. Study guide included.
(Rev: BL 1/1–15/08)

20 📖 **Vamos a ordenar por colores/Sorting by Color** (K–1). 2007. Capstone. Windows, Macintosh. ISBN 978-1-4296-1130-5. $26.95.
This bilingual interactive version of Jennifer Marks's book (Capstone, 2007) about colors allows young users to hear the words read and to absorb basic information on diagrams. (Rev: SLJ 3/08)

21 💿 **Vroom, Chugga, Vroom-Vroom** (K–1). 2004. 8 min. Nutmeg Media. ISBN 978-0-9772338-8-5. $49.95.
Learn to count while watching 20 race cars compete for a golden cup. (Rev: BL 5/1/04)

22 📖 **Wonder Words Combo: Beginning Sight Words and Picture Words** (K–2). 2006. School Zone. Windows, Macintosh. ISBN 978-1-60159-112-8. $15.99.
With Flash Action software, this easy-to-use CD-ROM allows children to practice sight and picture words, alphabetical order, and other basic skills, all cheered on by an enthusiastic audience. Five correct answers are rewarded with access to a game. Workbook included. (Rev: SLJ 3/08)

Art, Music, and Poetry

23 🔊 **The Biscuit Brothers: Go Make Music! Volume 1** (K–3). 2006. 84 min. Big Kids Productions. PPR. $14.95.
This entertaining production, set on Old Mac-Donald's farm EIEIO ("Environmental Institute for Every Instrument in the Orchestra"), introduces rhythm and pitch and features many well-known songs. (Rev: VL 9–10/06)

24 🔊 **The Dot** (K–3). 2004. 9 min. Weston Woods. ISBN 978-0-439-73456-1. $59.95.
Vashti's inspiring transformation into an artist is retained in this animated adaptation of Peter H. Reynolds's book. (Rev: BL 3/1/05; SLJ 12/04)
🏆 ALA ALSC Notable Children's Videos 2005; Andrew Carnegie Medal for Excellence in Children's Video 2005

25 🔊 **Everybody's in the Band** (K–3). 2004. 43 min. Ivy Video. $14.99.
Billy Jonas inspires young students to enjoy music in a lively performance at a North Carolina elementary school. (Rev: BL 11/15/04; SLJ 1/05)

26 🔊 **Flower Child: Beautiful Poetry for Beautiful Children** (K–3). 2007. 30 min. Wonderworld. $18.95.
Classic and contemporary works — by poets ranging from Langston Hughes and Emily Dickinson to Karla Kuskin — are read by children and adults and accompanied by joyful still and live-action shots of children playing and dancing and by the sounds of nature. (Rev: BL 5/1/07; SLJ 7/07)

27 🔊 **The Great Race** (K–3). 2007. Series: Draw Me a Story. Televisio de Catalunya (dist. by Film Ideas). ISBN 978-1-57557-919-1. $99.
In this creative series, viewers not only hear a story but also watch as an artist draws illustrations to accompany it. *The Great Race* is the story of the tortoise and the hare, illustrated in watercolor and crayon. Also in this set: *Draw Me a Story: The Violin's Ghost*. There are thirty DVDs in the series. (Rev: SLJ 9/07)

28 🔊 **He's Got the Whole World in His Hands** (K–2). 2006. 6 min. Weston Woods. ISBN 978-0-439-90568-8. $59.95.
The familiar song comes to life in this iconographic version of the book by Kadir Nelson. An African American boy displays cheerful drawings of his family and "the whole world" safely in God's hands. (Rev: BL 2/1/07; LMC 10/07; SLJ 3/07)

29 🔊 **Imagination Movers: Stir It Up** (K–3). 2004. 40 min. Imagination Movers (dist. by Big Kids Productions). $15.
Rich, Scott, Dave, and Smitty sing catchy Wiggles-style tunes that will have viewers dancing. Fifteen original songs in various styles along with entertaining action. (Rev: BL 5/15/05; SLJ 6/05; VL 5–6/05)

30 🔊 **Inspiring Figures: Duke Ellington and Ella Fitzgerald** (K–3). 2005. 34 min. Weston Woods. ISBN 978-0-439-79931-7. $59.95.
This DVD contains two award-winning video adaptations of books by Andrea Davis Pinkney and Brian Pinkney: *Duke Ellington*, a vivid introduction to the jazz great, and *Ella*

Fitzgerald: The Tale of a Vocal Virtuosa, in which a cool cat recounts the life of the singer and the excitement of seeing her perform.

🎖 *Duke Ellington*: ALA ALSC Notable Children's Videos 2001; *Ella Fitzgerald*: ALA ALSC Notable Children's Videos 2004

31 **Ish** (K–3). 2005. 8 min. Weston Woods. PPR. ISBN 978-0-439-80427-1. $59.95.
An animated version of Peter Reynolds's popular 2004 picture book about young Ramon's artistic efforts. Study guide included. (Rev: BL 3/1/06; SLJ 5/06; VL 5–6/06)

32 **Kweezletown: Let's Work Together** (K–2). 2006. 56 min. Rainbows Within Reach. ISBN 978-0-9705987-5-2. $24.95.
Entertaining songs and stories presented in voice and sign language illustrate the benefits of cooperation and the joys of nature. Puppets assist the human singer/signer. (Rev: BL 1/1–1507; SLJ 1/07)

33 **Little Einsteins: Our Huge Adventure** (K–1). 2005. 61 min. Walt Disney Home Entertainment. Closed captioned. ISBN 978-0-7888-5999-1. $19.99.
Leo, June, Quincy, and Annie are in search of the Musical Tree of Many Colors in this episode of the animated series designed to integrate classical music and art into children's entertainment. The Little Einsteins travel through landscapes by Monet, Van Gogh, and others, accompanied by Beethoven tunes. (Rev: VL 11–12/05)

34 **The Little Musician! Vol. 1: Do Re Mi in the Key of C** (K). 2006. 35 min. The Little Musician. $21.95.
An appealing introduction to basic musical concepts for very young children, with live-action footage and animation. (Rev: SLJ 12/06)

35 **Magical Music Express: It's Fun to Learn About Music!** (K–3). 2006. 60 min. Big Vision Entertainment (dist. by Instructional Video). $14.95.
Viewers learn about the basics of music — rhythm, timing, clefs, and so forth — in two half-hour animated segments titled "What Is Music?" and "The Language of Music." A bonus sing-along CD is included. (Rev: VL 7/06)

36 **Mr. Stinky Feet's Road Trip Live** (K–1). 2006. 33 min. Hiccup Productions. Closed captioned. $12.99.
A concert by Mr. Stinky Feet and the Hiccups in Overland Park, Kansas, is just as much fun for the viewer of this DVD as for the concertgoers. Favorites such as "Slug Bug," "Little Red Wagon," and "Fancy Pants Dance" will entertain little ones and their families. (Rev: SLJ 3/07)

37 **She'll Be Coming 'Round the Mountain** (K–3). 2005. 10 min. Nutmeg Media. ISBN 978-0-9772338-7-8. $49.95.
The classic song is reimagined as a host of animals prepare for the arrival of a bookmobile-driving pig librarian; this iconographic production is based on the 2004 picture book by Philemon Sturges, illustrated by Ashley Wolff. (Rev: BL 5/05; SLJ 6/05; VL 1–2/06)

38 **Toddler Toons** (K). 2006. 25 min. ThingamaKid. $9.95.
Familiar children's songs along with animation, in English and Spanish. Sing-along versions display the lyrics. An accompanying CD adds to the fun. (Rev: SLJ 2/07)

39 **A Treasure in My Garden** (K). 2007. 50 min. Ryko. ISBN 978-2-9231631-4-7. $16.95.
Thirteen animated music segments feature imaginative lyrics about everyday topics such as food, toys, and feelings; the melodies represent a variety of musical styles. (Rev: BL 8/07*; SLJ 8/07)

40 **Welcome to the Workshop** (K–3). 2007. 35 min. Deep Rooted Music. ISBN 978-0-9791575-0-9. $15.95.
Musician Eric Ode visits the library, the zoo, an amusment park, and other settings, singing all the while and accompanied by a huge orange cat named Scratch. (Rev: BL 4/1/07; SLJ 4/07)

41 **The Wheels on the Bus** (K–2). 2004. 6 min. Weston Woods. ISBN 978-0-439-79938-6. $59.95.
Paul Zelinsky's eye-catching adaptation of the children's song is animated here and accompanied by toe-tapping music from the Bacon Brothers. (Rev: BL 8/04; LMC 1/05; SLJ 7/04; VL 11–12/04)

🎖 ALA ALSC Notable Children's Videos 2005

42 ● **Zakland** (K–2). 2007. 51 min. Tiodnaci. $24.99.

Zak Morgan sings and plays the guitar in an original mix of songs that address such issues as sibling rivalry, chicken pox, and late bloomers, with additional live-action segments and puppetry to entertain young viewers. (Rev: BL 11/1/07)

Bedtime and Nursery Rhymes

43 ❁ **Nursery Tap, Hip to Toe** (K–2). 2005. 33 min. Nursery Tap. $21.95.

Toe-tapping nursery rhymes accompanied by views of costumed legs dancing against a suitably decorated black background will get young children moving and chanting. A second volume of these tap, ballet, and hip-hop steps, *Nursery Tap, Hip to Toe, Vol. 2*, was released in 2006. (Rev: BL 10/1/05; SLJ 11-12/05)

44 ❁ **This Is the House That Jack Built** (K–2). 2004. 7 min. Weston Woods. Closed captioned. ISBN 978-0-439-79936-2. $59.95.

An animated adaptation of Simms Taback's hilarious version of the cumulative rhyme about the series of events that start when Jack builds a house. Teacher's guide included. (Rev: BL 9/15/04; SLJ 4/05)

🏆 ALA ALSC Notable Children's Videos 2005

Story Collections, Literacy, and Reading

45 🖰 **BookFlix** (K–3). Scholastic.
http://teacher.scholastic.com/products/
bookflixfreetrial/
Scholastic's BookFlix pairs fiction videos from Weston Woods with nonfiction Scholastic e-titles to give young readers the opportunity to explore beyond the original story (*Click, Clack, Moo*, for example, is paired with *Let's Visit a Dairy Farm*.) A read-along feature allows children to see each word as it is narrated. (Rev: LMC 11–12/07; SLJ 10/07)

46 🖰 **One More Story** (K–3). One More Story, Inc.
www.onemorestory.com
A growing collection of classic and contemporary books that students can listen to, following along with the highlighted words. In the I Can Read It mode, beginning readers can mute the narration and read for themselves, clicking on words they would like to hear pronounced. (Rev: LMC 11–12/06; PL 11–12/07)

Imaginative Stories — Fantasies

47 ● **Arnie the Doughnut** (K–3). 2005. 19 min. Weston Woods. PPR. Closed captioned. $59.95.

Arnie the doughnut and the man who buys him at the bakery discuss what else Arnie could be (other than breakfast) in this adaptation of the 2003 picture book. (Rev: VL 11–12/05)

48 ● **Backyardigans: It's Great to Be a Ghost** (K–2). 2005. 98 min. Paramount Home Entertainment. Closed captioned. ISBN 978-1-4157-0981-8. $16.99.

Animated characters Pablo, Tyrone, Tasha, Uniqua, and Austin visit a haunted house, play soccer, and pretend to be pirates in this collection of stories from the lively and musical Nickelodeon series. (Rev: VL 11–12/05)

49 ● **Barbie in the 12 Dancing Princesses** (3–6). 2006. 81 min. Universal Studios Home Entertainment. Closed captioned. ISBN 978-1-4170-1631-0. $19.98.

CGI animation adds to the appeal of a story of Princess Genevieve (Barbie) and her 11 boisterous sisters, who resist their father's admonitions to behave and find a magical world in which to dance the night away. (Rev: VL 11–12/06)

50 ● **Brum: Soccer Hero and Other Stories** (K). 2004. 70 min. Koch Vision. ISBN 978-1-4172-2671-9. $14.98.

An antique car called Brum has many adventures and ends up the hero in all of them in this appealing series made by the creators of *The Teletubbies*. The seven episodes compiled here feature Brum in escapades involv-

ing a soccer team, a missing birthday cake, and a dog in need of help. (Rev: BL 12/15/04; SLJ 11/04)

51 ● **Company's Coming** (K–3). 2003. 9 min. Spoken Arts. $50.

An iconographic adaptation of the classic picture book by Arthur Yorinks, illustrated by David Small, about meatball-loving aliens who come to visit an elderly couple on Earth.
♟ ALA ALSC Notable Children's Videos 2003

52 ● **Corneil and Bernie: Season 1, Vol. 1** (K–3). 2006. 88 min. First National Pictures. ISBN 978-1-933656-13-7. $16.98.

Corneil, a talking dog with a very high IQ, meets his match when Bernie becomes his dog-sitter; the series (produced in France and dubbed in Britain, and consisting of 11-minute episodes) can be seen on Nicktoons. Volumes 2 and 3 also available. (Rev: VL 9–10/06)

53 ● **The Girl Who Hated Books** (K–3). 2005. 7 min. Series: Talespinners 2. National Film Board of Canada. PPR. $129.

An accident that leaves many literary characters stranded in her house causes Meena to revise her dislike of books in this enjoyable adaptation of the book by Manjusha Pawagi. (Rev: LMC 4/07; SLJ 1/07; VL 1–2/07)

54 ● **Harold and the Purple Crayon: The Complete Series** (K–1). 2002. 2 discs. 289 min. Columbia TriStar Home Entertainment.

11

Closed captioned. ISBN 978-0-7678-8922-3. $24.98.

Thirteen stories from the Emmy-award-winning HBO series based on the books by Crockett Johnson, in which Harold's imagination and purple crayon take viewers on great expeditions. (Rev: VL 1–2/05)

55 ● **The Journey of Oliver K. Woodman** (K–3). 2005. 14 min. Nutmeg Media. PPR. ISBN 978-0-9776262-1-2. $49.95.

Oliver is a little figure made of wood who meets interesting people as he travels across the country; his journey is documented in postcards sent by people who help him on his way. Based on the book by Darcy Pattison. (Rev: BL 5/1/06; SLJ 5/05; VL 11–12/05)

⚇ ALA ALSC Notable Children's Videos 2006

56 ● **LazyTown: New Superhero** (K). 2005. 60 min. Paramount Home Entertainment. Closed captioned. ISBN 978-1-4157-0998-6. $16.99.

Young viewers will have fun while being active and learning about healthy habits in this episode of the Nick Jr. series. Will the live actors and their puppet friends keep Robbie Rotten from running Sportacus out of LazyTown? (Rev: VL 11–12/05)

57 ● **Leonardo, the Terrible Monster** (K). 2007. 8 min. Weston Woods. Closed captioned. ISBN 978-0-439-02764-9. $59.95.

Leonardo the terrible monster's failures at scaring people lead him to decide it's better just to be his un-scary self and make a good friend; author Mo Willems narrates. (Rev: BL 10/15/07)

⚇ ALA ALSC Notable Children's Videos 2008

58 ● **Moongirl** (K–3). 2006. 8 min. Laika Films (dist. by Candlewick Books). ISBN 978-0-7636-3068-3. $22.99.

An animated fantasy in which Leon is transported to the moon by a fishing line and uses lightning bugs to help Moongirl relight the moon. Based on the book by Henry Selick. (Rev: SLJ 1/07)

59 ● **Punchinello and the Most Marvelous Gift** (K–3). 2004. 40 min. Tommy Nelson.

Closed captioned. ISBN 978-1-4003-0350-2. $14.99.

When the puppets of Wemmicksville try to honor their creator, Eli the carpenter, on Maker Day, Punchinello finds the perfect gift to give — a song from the heart. Based on a book by Christian author Max Lucado. (Rev: BL 11/15/04; SLJ 1/05; VL 11–12/04)

60 ● **Shape Masters** (K–3). 2003. 30 min. Series: Northpoint. Fort Fun Productions. $12.95.

Five computer-animated children spend time in the woods looking at the sky and the clouds. They create a story from what they see, involving samurai warriors, dragons, and royalty. Young children are urged to use their own imaginations creatively. (Rev: BL 1/1–15/04; LMC 1/04; SLJ 11/03)

61 ● **Sheerluck Holmes and the Golden Ruler: A Lesson in Friendship** (K–3). 2005. 52 min. Series: VeggieTales. Big Idea. ISBN 978-0-7389-3460-0. $14.98.

Sheerluck Holmes (Larry the Cucumber) and Dr. Watson (Bob the Tomato) clash when Sheerluck appears to be grabbing the limelight at Watson's expense as they investigate a mystery involving the monarch. Also in this installment in the Christian series is a story of friendship called "The Asparagus of La Mancha." (Rev: VL 5–6/06)

62 ● **Strawberry Shortcake: The Sweet Dreams Movie** (K–3). 2006. 83 min. Fox Home Entertainment. $19.98.

The beloved scented doll and her friends Ginger Snap, Raspberry Torte, and Lil' Lemon Meringue plant a berry patch — and dream of success — with the help of the Sandman in this animated movie. (Rev: VL 5–6/07)

63 ● **The Velveteen Rabbit** (1–4). 2003. 24 min. The Adelante Project. ISBN 978-1-56364-739-0. $17.95.

An excellent Claymation adaptation of the classic story about the beloved toy. (Rev: BL 5/1/04)

⚇ ALA ALSC Notable Children's Videos 2004

64 ● **Armadilly Chili** (K–2). 2007. 10 min. Nutmeg Media. PPR. ISBN 978-1-933938-27-1. $49.95.

Miss Billy, an armadillo, gets no help from her animal friends when it's time to make her famous chili, and, as a result, they don't get to enjoy it with her. Does this sound familiar? It's an adaptation of the 2004 picture book, a twist on the little red hen story. (Rev: VL 3–4/07)

65 ● **Arthur's Missing Pal** (K–3). 2006. 68 min. Lionsgate Entertainment. Closed captioned. $19.98.

Fed up with Arthur's neglect, his puppy Pal decamps; with the help of Buster, D.W., and others, Arthur manages to find the little pooch in this arresting CGI animated movie. (Rev: VL 11–12/06)

66 ● **Bear Snores On** (K–1). 2002. 9 min. Weston Woods. PPR. Closed captioned. ISBN 978-0-439-76657-9. $59.95.

An appealing animated version of Karma Wilson's charming story, illustrated by Jane Chapman, about a hibernating bear who sleeps through most of a party. (Rev: SLJ 10/05; VL 1–2/06)

67 ● **Bear Wants More** (K–2). 2006. 8 min. Weston Woods. Closed captioned. ISBN 978-0-439-90467-7. $59.95.

Bear eats and eats until he can't fit into his lair in this rhyming tale based on the 2003 story by Karma Wilson. The film consists of the charming illustrations from the book. (Rev: SLJ 2/07)

68 ● **Big Brown Bear Stories** (K–2). 2007. 24 min. Nutmeg Media. ISBN 978-1-933938-31-8. $69.95.

Gentle, humorous stories based on David McPhail's books *Big Brown Bear's Up and Down Day*, *Big Brown Bear Goes to Town*, and *Big Brown Bear's Birthday Surprise*. McPhail talks about his life and writing, and expresses his affection for these characters. (Rev: BL 1/1–15/08; SLJ 12/07)

ALA ALSC Notable Children's Videos 2008

69 ● **Binky Goes Nuts** (K–3). 2007. 52 min. WGBH Boston. ISBN 978-1-59375-727-4. $12.95.

Contains four stories from the animated series Arthur, featuring Arthur, Binky Barnes, and the rest of the crew as they deal with food allergies, healthy eating, exercise, and bullies. (Rev: BL 9/15/07; SLJ 7/07)

70 ● **Buster's Western Adventures** (K–2). 2007. 6 discs. 312 min. WGBH Boston. ISBN 978-1-59375-643-7. $59.95.

Join Arthur's friend Buster as he heads to the West Coast with his father and the Los Viajeros rock band, making videotapes of all the adventures he has on the way. Includes 14 *Postcards from Buster* episodes.

71 ● **Chato and the Party Animals** (K–3). 2004. 14 min. Weston Woods. ISBN 978-0-439-90429-2. $59.95.

A lively and compelling version of Gary Soto's book (Putnam, 2000) in which Chato the cat organizes a surprise party for Novio

Boy, a pound cat who doesn't know when he was born. (Rev: BL 8/04; SLJ 10/04)

72 ● **Chicken Little** (K–3). 2005. 81 min. Walt Disney. $29.99.
A charming, animated version of the Chicken Little story that adults will also enjoy for its social asides. Extras include a feature on the making of the movie, an interactive game, and a karaoke sing-along. (Rev: VL 3–4/06)

73 ● **The Cow Who Clucked** (K–1). 2007. 10 min. Spoken Arts. ISBN 978-0-8045-9720-3. $50.
This version of the 2006 story by Denise Fleming stars the beautiful artwork from the book, with some animation. It's the story of a cow who has lost her moo and goes around the barnyard in search of the animal who has it. (Rev: SLJ 10/07)

74 ● **Curious George: Rocket Ride and Other Adventures** (K). 2007. 108 min. Universal Studios Home Entertainment. $16.98.
Eight delightful stories from the popular PBS show are narrated by William H. Macy. George flies a kite, gets lost, roller-skates, befriends some beavers, and more. Viewers will be charmed by George and his curiosity. (Rev: SLJ 9/07)

75 ● **Dooby Dooby Moo** (K). 2007. 10 min. Weston Woods. $59.95.
An animated version of Doreen Cronin's 2006 book, illustrated by Betsy Lewin, in which Farmer Brown's animals compete in a local talent show in hopes of winning the first prize — a trampoline.
♫ ALA ALSC Notable Children's Videos 2008

76 ● **Ella the Elegant Elephant** (K–3). 2006. 11 min. Spoken Arts. $50.
An iconographic version of Carmela and Steven D'Amico's story about a shy elephant who finds a way to deal with a bully.
♫ ALA ALSC Notable Children's Videos 2006

77 ● **Giggle, Giggle, Quack** (K–3). 10 min. Weston Woods. ISBN 978-0-439-83957-0. $59.95.
Doreen Cronin's and Betsy Lewin's funny picture book about a bossy duck and a novice farmer lives on in this animated version. In English and Spanish. (Rev: VL 5–6/04)

♫ Andrew Carnegie Medal for Excellence in Children's Video 2004; ALA ALSC Notable Children's Videos 2004

78 ● **Giraffes Can't Dance** (K–3). 2007. 10 min. Weston Woods. Closed captioned. ISBN 978-0-439-02732-8. $59.95.
Gerald the giraffe is teased by the other animals when he trips over his own long legs at the Jungle Dance. An animated iconographic adaptation of the book by Giles Andreae and Guy Parker Rees. Narrated by Billy Dee Williams. Teacher's guide included. (Rev: BL 8/07; SLJ 8/07)

79 ● **The Great Fuzz Frenzy** (K–2). 2006. 14 min. Spoken Arts. ISBN 978-0-8045-9042-6. $50.
The lives of a community of prairie dogs change for the worse when a green tennis ball falls into their hole. Disputes arise as creativity with the green fuzz booms. The inventive illustrations of the book by Janet Stevens and Susan Stevens Crummel (Harcourt, 2005) are retained, and the authors appear in their own feature. (Rev: SLJ 12/06)

80 ● **Horace, Morris and Dolores** (K–2). 2007. 13 min. Nutmeg Media. ISBN 978-1-933938-18-9. $69.95.
An adaptation of two James Howe books — *Horace and Morris but Mostly Dolores* (1999) and *Horace and Morris Join the Chorus (but What About Dolores?)* (2002) — featuring the well-loved mouse characters Horace, Morris, and Dolores and their adventures with friends and at school. (Rev: BL 5/1/07; SLJ 5/07)

81 ● **How Do Dinosaurs Eat Their Food?** (K–2). 2007. 10 min. Weston Woods. Closed captioned. ISBN 978-0-439-02744-1. $59.95.
Dinosaurs are polite at the table, of course, and always eat all their peas. An animated version of the book by Jane Yolen and Mark Teague. Teacher's guide included. (Rev: SLJ 10/07)

82 ● **How Do Dinosaurs Get Well Soon?** (K–2). 2005. 8 min. Weston Woods. ISBN 978-0-439-76716-3. $59.95.
Young dinosaurs demonstrate appropriate behavior in the sick bay in this funny presentation narrated by Jane Yolen, author of the 2003 picture book by the same name, and illustrated by Mark Teague. (Rev: BL 10/1/05)

83 ❸ **How Do Dinosaurs Say Good Night?**
(K–3). 2003. 8 min. Weston Woods. ISBN
978-0-439-90428-5. $59.95.
An appealing animated adaptation of the picture book written by Jane Yolen and illustrated by Mark Teague that features all sorts of
baby dinosaurs behaving like human children
at bedtime. Narrated by the author.
☙ ALA ALSC Notable Children's Videos
2003

84 ❸ **Inch by Inch** (K–1). 2006. 7 min. Weston Woods. Closed captioned. ISBN 978-0-
439-90570-1. $59.95.
A charming animation of Leo Lionni's 1961
picture book in which a tiny captive inch-
worm measures his way to freedom. Teacher's
guide included. (Rev: SLJ 3/07)

85 ❸ **Jakers! Sheep on the Loose** (K). 2006.
92 min. Paramount Home Entertainment.
Closed captioned. ISBN 978-1-4157-2482-8.
$14.99.
In four episodes from the popular computer-
animated PBS series — "Sheep on the Loose,"
"Waking Thor," "Donkeys into Racehorses,"
and "Molly Had a Little Lamb" — Grandpig
Piggley teaches his grandchildren about the
importance of respect and responsibility.
(Rev: VL 1–2/07)

86 ❸ **Land Before Time: Invasion of the
Tinysauruses** (K–2). 2004. 81 min. Universal Home Video. Closed captioned. ISBN
978-1-4170-0361-7. $19.98.
Littlefoot learns a lesson about the importance of honesty in this latest installment in
the popular animated series about dinosaurs.
(Rev: VL 3–4/05)

87 ❸ **Look! Look! Look!** (K–3). 2006. 13
min. Nutmeg Media. ISBN 978-1-933938-20-
2. $59.95.
An iconographic film of the 2006 picture
book by the same name, in which a mouse
family has fun examining the artwork on a
postcard and making their own art. Additional features provide ideas for discussion and
activities. (Rev: BL 3/1/07; SLJ 2/07)

88 ❸ **Roberto the Insect Architect** (K–3).
2005. 12 min. Weston Woods. PPR. ISBN
978-0-439-80454-7. $59.95.
Full of puns, the story of Roberto the ter-
mite's architectural career (first seen in Nina
Laden's 2000 picture book) is rendered in
animated collages. Study guide included.
(Rev: BL 3/1/06; VL 5–6/06)

89 ❸ **Sophie's Masterpiece** (K–3). 2005. 7
min. Nutmeg Media. ISBN 978-0-9776262-8-
1. $49.95.
Music and deft use of the illustrations by Jane
Dyer make this an appealing adaptation of
Eileen Spinelli's 2001 book about an unap-
preciated spider named Sophie, who weaves a
beautiful baby blanket for a pregnant woman.
(Rev: BL 1/1–15/06)

90 ❸ **Stuart Little: The Animated Series:
Fun Around Every Curve!** (K–3). 2003. 67
min. Sony Pictures Home Entertainment.
Closed captioned. ISBN 978-1-4248-5240-6.
$14.95.
Three animated stories based on the Stuart
Little movie (which is in turn loosely based
on the E. B. White book). Stuart goes skateboarding, camps out with his family, and par-
ticipates in a school election. (Rev: VL
7–8/07)

91 ❸ **Wallace's Lists** (K–3). 2007. 15 min.
Weston Woods. Closed captioned. ISBN 978-
0-545-04271-0. $59.95.
An animated adaptation of Barbara Bottner
and Gerald Kruglik's entertaining story
(2004) about Wallace's obsession with lists.
A read-along script at the bottom of the
screen highlights words as they are being
read. (Rev: SLJ 5/08)
☙ ALA ALSC Notable Children's Videos
2008

92 ❸ **The Wheels on the Bus Video: Mango
and Papaya's Animal Adventure** (K–1).
2004. 33 min. Armstrong Moving Pictures.
ISBN 978-0-9746944-1-2. $16.99.
Mango the monkey and Papaya the toucan
(both puppets) get lots of help when they
can't remember their way home in this colorful production with Roger Daltrey singing the
part of the dragon/bus driver. (Rev: BL
11/1/04)

93 ❸ **Wild About Books** (K–2). 2005. 8 min.
Weston Woods. ISBN 978-0-439-80483-7.
$59.95.
Judy Sierra's 2004 picture book about the
librarian who inspires a love of books among
the animals at the zoo comes to life in this
bright and lively rendering. (Rev: BL 3/1/06*)
☙ ALA ALSC Notable Children's Videos
2006

94 ✪ **The Adventures of Teddy P. Brains: Journey into the Rain Forest** (K–3). 2006. 60 min. Clarendon Entertainment. $19.95.
Teddy, a young African American boy, is an explorer who must solve a mystery in the rainforest in this animated program full of music and information. (Rev: SLJ 10/07)

95 ▦ **Adventureville: The Cosmic Kitty Adventure** (K–2). 2006. 60 min. U-Pic Entertainment (dist. by Tapeworm). $10.95.
An interactive DVD in which Jenna and Jason have lost their cat. Viewers help the children make decisions about which avenues to take. The adventure can be played over and over again, making different choices throughout. (Rev: SLJ 12/06)

96 ✪ **My Bedbugs, Vol. 1** (K–1). 2006. 65 min. GreeneStuff. ISBN 978-0-9786124-2-9. $14.98.
Gooby, Joofy, and Woozy have fun and learn to cooperate in this video, in which the actors are costumed adults in pajamas. Children will enjoy singing along, dancing, and using their imagination while viewing the three stories: "The Lost Sock Adventure," "Pirates of the Bugabean," and "Rainy Day." (Rev: SLJ 4/07)

Community and Everyday Life

97 ☺ **The Adventures of Andy AppleButter** (K–2). 2006. 35 min. Spazzmania Entertainment (dist. by Library Video Company). $14.99.

Andy and his friends, who are all kitchen staples (Billy Bob Baking Soda, the Sisters of Spice, and so on), teach important lessons about getting along with others in this cartoon. At the end of each segment, there is a review of the moral of the story. Activity book online. (Rev: SLJ 8/07)

98 ☺ **Animal Yoga for Kids** (K–2). 2003. 45 min. Golden Treasures. ISBN 978-0-9654554-4-2. $22.95.

An instructional presentation for kids on basic yoga poses that mimic various animal movements. (Rev: BL 11/15/04; SLJ 7/04)

99 ☺ **Arthur: Sleepovers, Sports and More** (K–2). 2007. 5 discs. 270 min. Cookie Jar Entertainment and WGBH Boston (dist. by WGBH Boston). ISBN 978-1-59375-646-8. $49.95.

A collection of 18 episodes of "Arthur," the beloved cartoon featuring an aardvark and his family and friends that has been a mainstay of PBS's children's programming. The series is based on the books by Marc Brown. Teacher's materials are included. (Rev: SLJ 4/07)

100 ☺ **Auto-B-Good: A Road Less Traveled** (K–1). 2004. 60 min. Series: Auto-B-Good. Wet Cement Productions. Closed captioned. $14.99.

Six stories — "Friends in High Places," "Heavenly Event," "Sunny Side Up?" "Up from the Depths," "Cooler Heads Prevail," and "Digging for Gold" — teach character values (the accompanying teacher's guide adds a Christian element that is not present in the film) through the adventures of anthropomorphic animated cars. The other title in the series is *Auto-B-Good: Where the Rubber Meets the Road*. (Rev: SLJ 5/05; VL 1–2/05)

101 ☺ **Danger Rangers: Safe and Sound** (K–2). 2006. 40 min. Educational Adventures (dist. by Big Kids Productions). ISBN 978-1-933934-12-9. $14.95.

The dangers of loud noise, particularly music, are underlined in this program about a rock band called the Decibulls. (Rev: SLJ 12/06)

102 ☺ **Daydream** (K–1). 2005. 30 min. Wai Lana Productions. ISBN 978-1-932493-32-0. $12.95.

Yoga, soothing narration, and beautiful images combine to make an effectively relaxing cartoon for little ones. (Rev: SLJ 1/06)

103 ☺ **Dora the Explorer: Big Sister Dora** (K–1). 2005. 96 min. Paramount Home Entertainment. Closed captioned. ISBN 978-1-4157-0553-7. $16.99.

Beloved animated character Dora becomes a big sister and gets a workout on the way to a soccer game in these two episodes from the Nickelodeon show. (Rev: VL 5–6/05)

104 ☺ **Elmo's World: Food, Water and Exercise** (K). 2005. 46 min. Sony Wonder. ISBN 978-0-7389-2874-6. $12.98.

Three episodes of *Elmo's World*, a segment on PBS's "Sesame Street," featuring the lovable furry red monster talking about eating and living healthily. (Rev: VL 7–8/05)

105 ● **Gallop, Hop and Stomp!** (K). 2004. 23 min. Series: The Monkeydoos Movement and Learning. Thinkeroo (dist. by Big Kids Productions). PPR. ISBN 978-1-929944-60-6. $14.95.
Animated monkeys Flip, Tumble, and Twist pretend to be all sorts of animals, singing songs and encouraging young viewers to imitate every move. (Rev: SLJ 3/05; VL 3–4/05)

106 ● **Get Fit Kids: Hustle Bustle Move Your Muscles!** (K). 2004. 30 min. Get Fit Kids (dist. by AV Café). PPR. $19.99.
A human trainer and her animated bear friend JoJo lead a group of children through fun exercises and talk about healthy eating. (Rev: SLJ 1/05; VL 3–4/05)

107 ● **Happy Healthy Monsters** (K–1). 2005. 45 min. $14.98. Sony Wonder. ISBN 978-0-7389-2839-5. $14.98.
Elmo, Zoe, and their friends enjoy watching the Happy Healthy Monsters Network, which features Grover's exercise program. Short segments and "commercials" with other "Sesame Street" characters will keep children interested. (Rev: VL 5–6/05)

108 ● **The Honest-to-Goodness Truth** (K–2). 2007. 14 min. Nutmeg Media. PPR. ISBN 978-1-933938-17-2. $49.95.
Libby learns the difference between telling the truth and being unkind in this iconographic adaptation of the picture book by the same name. (Rev: VL 3–4/07)

109 ● **Jojo's Circus: Take a Bow!** (K). 2005. 50 min. Walt Disney Home Entertainment. Closed captioned. ISBN 978-0-7888-5811-6. $19.99.
Jojo learns all about being a circus clown — and a fair bit about life — in these episodes of Playhouse Disney's animated series. (Rev: VL 7–8/05)

110 ● **Kideosyncrasy, Vol. 1** (K–3). 2003. 30 min. Kideosyncrasy (dist. by Big Kids Productions). PPR. $19.99.
Dance along with this energetic video featuring a group of children performing Western line dance and hip-hop moves along with the twist and the jitterbug. (Rev: SLJ 10/04; VL 3–4/05)

111 ● **Knuffle Bunny** (K–1). 2006. 10 min. Weston Woods. Closed captioned. ISBN 978-0-439-90571-8. $59.95.
This animated version of Mo Willems's book is narrated by the author and his daughter Trixie, whose beloved bunny was accidentally tossed in the wash and became the subject of this Caldecott Honor book. Includes teacher's guide. (Rev: BL 1/1–15/07*; LMC 8–9/07; SLJ 2/07)
☟ Andrew Carnegie Medal for Excellence in Children's Video 2007

112 ● **Magic Backyard** (K–2). 2004. 30 min. Mosley Productions. ISBN 978-0-9760795-0-7. $14.97.
A collection of children's dreams in one bright and musical package — a puppet show, a train ride, magic tricks, circus acrobats, a farm, an aquarium, and a zoo. (Rev: BL 8/05)

113 ● **Mister Rogers' Neighborhood: Adventures in Friendship** (K–1). 2005. 58 min. Anchor Bay Entertainment. $16.99.
Two episodes of the gentle, reassuring show that ran for years on PBS. Puppet characters Henrietta Pussycat and X the Owl make an appearance, as does human Lady Aberlin. Parents who remember Mr. Rogers will be thrilled to introduce their children to him. (Rev: VL 7–8/05)

114 ● **Mister Rogers' Neighborhood: What Do You Do with the Mad That You Feel?** (K). 2005. 57 min. Anchor Bay Entertainment. $14.98.
Anger management is the focus here as Mr. Rogers looks at ways to deal with jealousy and other unpleasant emotions; includes a tour of a construction paper factory. (Rev: VL 5–6/06)

115 ● **The Money Mammals: Saving Money Is Fun** (K–3). 2006. 30 min. Snigglezoo Entertainment. PPR. Closed captioned. $19.99.
Puppets Joe the Monkey and Piggs the Bank must choose between spending their allowance on a trading card or saving for a birthday present for Clara J. Camel. (Rev: VL 9–10/06)

116 ● **Mr. George Baker** (1–6). 2004. 29 min. GPN. PPR. Closed captioned. $39.95.
This episode of the PBS series "Reading Rainbow," hosted by LeVar Burton, is about

the elderly and what they can teach others, featuring the picture book written by Amy Hest and illustrated by Jon J Muth. (Rev: VL 3–4/05)

117 ● **Mustard Pancakes: See How the Garden Grows** (K–3). 2005. 107 min. Arrow Distributing. $19.98.
Three entertaining and informative episodes from the PBS program feature singer/storyteller Courtney Campbell and her puppet pets — "See How the Garden Grows," "Oogleberry Ink Dog," and "Tongue Twister"; the original pilot is also included. (Rev: VL 5–6/06)

118 ● **Open Wide: Tooth School Inside** (K–3). 2006. 20 min. Weston Woods. PPR. Closed captioned. ISBN 978-0-439-84916-6. $59.95.
Molars, incisors, and their friends learn all about teeth in this animated adaptation of the 2000 picture book by Laurie Keller. Songs, funny tidbits, and lots of information about caring for teeth will entertain and educate young students. Study guide included. (Rev: VL 5–6/07)

119 ● **Post Office** (K–3). 2006. 15 min. Series: My Community. Schlessinger Media (dist. by Library Video Company). Closed captioned. ISBN 978-1-4171-0480-2. $29.95.
An entertaining look at the American mail service and its history. Other titles in the series include *What Is a Community?*, *Fire Station*, and *Hospital*. Teacher's guide included. (Rev: VL 7/06)

120 ● **Rainy Day Stories** (K–3). 2006. 43 min. Weston Woods. ISBN 978-0-439-90440-7. $59.95.
This DVD offers video adaptations of two popular stories: Karen Hesse's *Come On, Rain!* (Scholastic, 1999), illustrated by Jon J Muth, about a group of children who enjoy a cloudburst during a sweltering day in the big city; and Jerry Pinkney's inventive *Noah's Ark* (North-South, 2002).
♫ *Come On, Rain*: ALA ALSC Notable Children's Videos 2004

121 ● **Recycling Coordinator** (K–3). 2006. 10 min. New Dimension Media. PPR. ISBN 978-1-59522-478-1. $49 (single site), $99 (multi-site).
Recycling plastics, metals, and paper is covered along with various ways in which to use the resulting products. Teacher's guide included. (Rev: VL 1–2/07)

122 ● **Table Time** (K). 2005. 30 min. Time for Manners. $16.95.
Puppets help to communicate the basics of good table manners. (Rev: BL 11/15/05)

123 ● **ToddWorld: Hi! I'm Todd** (K). 2005. 40 min. Series: ToddWorld. HIT Entertainment. Closed captioned. ISBN 978-1-58668-369-6. $12.99.
Four episodes from the series on Discovery Kids encourage teamwork, tolerance, and togetherness using colorful animation and creative story lines. (Rev: VL 7–8/05)

124 ● **Tot-a-Doodle-Do!** (K–2). 2006. 30 min. Creative Programming. $19.95.
Lively episodes with music and short segments focus on kid-friendly themes such as crafts, snacks, and behavior. (Rev: SLJ 9/06)

125 🖥 **Una visita a la estacion de bomberos/ A Visit to the Fire Station** (K–2). 2007. Capstone. Windows, Macintosh. ISBN 978-0-7368-7912-5. $14.95.
English text appears above Spanish text in this facsimile version of the book about the fun of a visit to the fire station. Viewers can choose whether to keep the audio on or off, and can click on highlighted words to see a definition. (Rev: LMC 9/07; SLJ 6/07)

126 ● **Winter Fun** (K–2). 2006. 30 min. Series: This Is Daniel Cook Series 2. Marblemedia/Sinking Ship Productions (dist. by Bullfrog Films). ISBN 978-1-59458-548-7. $195.
Seven-year-old Daniel — frequently seen on children's TV — is an inquisitive boy who likes to learn things directly from adults. Here he visits a winter festival, gets to participate in sports like skiing and curling, and learns all about dog sledding. (Rev: SLJ 6/07)

Family Stories

127 ❂ **Because Your Daddy Loves You** (K–2). 2006. 9 min. Nutmeg Media. ISBN 978-1-933938-14-1. $49.95.
An iconographic film of the book by Andrew Clements in which a patient daddy helps out whenever his child needs him. Includes teacher's guide and a conversation with the author. (Rev: BL 1/1–15/07; SLJ 3/07)

128 ❂ **Charlie and Lola, Vol. One** (K–2). 2005. 84 min. BBC Video. Closed captioned. ISBN 978-1-4198-3470-7. $14.98.
Charlie and younger sister Lola deal inventively with everyday trials such as detested foods, spiders, and homesickness in this British animated production based on the books by Lauren Child. (Rev: VL 7/06)

129 ❂ **Harriet, You'll Drive Me Wild!** (K–1). 2005. 7 min. Nutmeg Media. PPR. ISBN 978-0-9747118-8-1. $49.95.
Harriet's antics drive her patient mother "wild" in this iconographic representation of the picture book by Mem Fox. (Rev: SLJ 5/05; VL 11–12/05)

130 ❂ **I Love You the Purplest** (K–3). 2005. 7 min. Nutmeg Media. ISBN 978-0-9761981-6-1. $49.95.
A gentle story, from the picture book written by Barbara Joosse and illustrated by Mary Whyte (Chronicle, 1996), in which a mother proves that she loves her two young sons equally. (Rev: SLJ 1/06)

131 ❂ **Jaime Lo, Small and Shy** (K–3). 2007. 8 min. Series: Talespinner's II. National Film Board of Canada. $59.95.
In this charming animated short film, Jaime is disappointed that her father must work in China while her family waits for his return to Canada. She helps to ease her frustration by drawing her family on the photographs her father sends from overseas.

132 ❂ **Max's Words** (K–3). 2007. 10 min. Weston Woods. ISBN 978-0-545-04285-7. $59.95.
When Max's older brothers refuse to share their stamp and coin collections with him, the young boy starts a very special collection of his own. The DVD combines animation and iconographic elements from the book written by Kate Banks and illustrated by Boris Kulikov (Farrar, 2006). (Rev: VL 7–8/08)
⚱ ALA ALSC Notable Children's Videos 2008

133 ❂ **A Picnic in October** (K–3). 2005. 12 min. Nutmeg Media. PPR. ISBN 978-0-9772338-6-1. $49.95.
Tony and his Italian American family enjoy a picnic by the Statue of Liberty in this iconographic adaptation of the Eve Bunting picture book. (Rev: SLJ 5/05; VL 9–10/05)

134 ❂ **The Seven Silly Eaters** (K–3). 2005. 13 min. Nutmeg Media. PPR. ISBN 978-0-97746-809-6. $49.95.
An animated version of Mary Ann Hoberman's story (illustrated by Marla Frazee) about Mrs. Peters's seven picky children and their nutritional preferences. (Rev: BL 1/1–15/06; SLJ 1/06; VL 5–6/06)

Folklore, Fairy Tales, and Storytelling

135 ⊙ **American Tall Tales** (K–3). 2005. 50 min. Center for Puppetry Arts (dist. by Quality Books, Inc.). PPR. $19.95.
The stories of Paul Bunyan, John Henry, Pecos Bill, and Hekeke are presented by Dr. Bigelow's Wild West Puppet Show, a collaboration of humans and puppets. This is footage of a live performance at the Center for Puppetry Arts. Study guide included. (Rev: VL 9–10/05)

136 ⊙ **The Elves and the Shoemaker** (K). 2004. 10 min. Weston Woods. PPR. Closed captioned. ISBN 978-0-7882-0533-0. $59.95.
Based on the beautiful 2003 picture book by Jim LaMarche, this brief film tells the classic story iconographically with a touch of animation. Study guide included. (Rev: LMC 8–9/05; SLJ 2/05; VL 3–4/05)

137 ⊙ **Fairy Tales, Fantasy, and Storytellin' Fun!** (K–3). 2007. 36 min. Storytellin' Time. ISBN 978-0-9722213-5-1. $19.95.
Storyteller Mary Jo Huff and her puppet friends tell ten stories to a group of young children. (Rev: SLJ 8/07)

138 ⊙ **Hansel and Gretel** (K–2). 2005. 14 min. Weston Woods. ISBN 978-0-439-80417-2. $59.95.
An animated adaptation of James Marshall's innovative and often humorous treatment of the classic story. (Rev: BL 4/15/06)

139 ⊙ **The Hunterman and the Crocodile** (K–3). 2006. 10 min. Nutmeg Media. $49.95.
A striking animated version of Baba Wague Diakite's retelling of a West African tale about a hunter who rescues a crocodile only to find it is threatening to eat him. (Rev: SLJ 1/06; VL 7/06)

140 ⊙ **James Marshall's Cinderella** (K–3). 2006. 13 min. Weston Woods. PPR. Closed captioned. ISBN 978-0-439-84876-3. $59.95.
Marshall's illustrations grace this faithful retelling of the classic story. Study guide included. (Rev: VL 9–10/06)

141 ⊙ **Keys to Imagination: StoryWatchers Club Adventures in Storytelling** (K–3). 2005. 45 min. StoryWatchers Club. ISBN 978-0-9770343-0-7. $19.95.
A collection of short performances by six storytellers, all with a theme of imagination. (Rev: BL 2/1/06)

142 ⊙ **La Cucaracha Martina** (K–2). 2003. 16 min. Nutmeg Media. ISBN 978-0-9772338-1-6. $59.95.
An iconographic presentation of Daniel Moreton's retelling of the Caribbean folktale about a cockroach on a quest to find the source of a beautiful sound. (Rev: BL 4/1/04; SLJ 10/04)

143 ⊙ **Lon Po Po** (K–3). 2006. 14 min. Weston Woods. PPR. Closed captioned. ISBN 978-0-439-87371-0. $59.95.
An animated version of the Caldecott-winning 1989 variation on Red Riding Hood by Ed Young, in which Mother goes to visit Grandmother ("Po Po"), leaving the children alone. (Rev: LMC 2/07; VL 9–10/06)

144 ✪ **Seven Blind Mice** (K–3). 2007. 7 min. Weston Woods. ISBN 978-0-439-02781-6. $59.95.

An animated version of Ed Young's picture book about a group of blind mice (each a different color) trying to figure out what the object is in front of them and finally putting the evidence together to reveal it's an elephant. The story is based on an Indian fable. (Rev: BL 9/15/07; SLJ 8/07)

♟ ALA ALSC Notable Children's Videos 2008

145 ✪ **Stories from Around the World** (K–3). 2007. 30 min. Series: BookBox. Master Communications. ISBN 978-1-60480-005-0. $14.95.

Five animated, folktale-like stories about themes such as friendship, the environment, and work ethics each have a different narrator. Same Language Subtitling gives the text on the screen as the story is read aloud, and viewers can select between a number of English and Spanish combinations. (Rev: SLJ 12/07)

146 ✪ **The Three Wishes** (K–3). 2006. 4 min. National Film Board of Canada. PPR. $89.

Koppel the peasant and his wife foolishly waste the three wishes they have been granted in this retelling of an old folktale. An animated story set to klezmer music. Study guide included.

147 ✪ **Two Chinese Tales** (K–3). 2007. 18 min. Nutmeg Media. PPR. ISBN 978-1-933938-25-7. $69.95.

An iconographic adaptation of two picture books: *The Seven Chinese Sisters* by Kathy Tucker, a new take on *The Seven Chinese Brothers* about seven sisters who have their own special (decidedly modern) talents; and *Two of Everything* by Lilly Toy Hong, about a poor Chinese farmer who finds a magical pot and learns to be careful what he wishes for. Study guide included. (Rev: BL 4/15/07; SLJ 8/07)

Foreign Languages and ESL

148 ❂ **Aprendamos Ingles/Let's Learn English** (1–6). 2007. 54 min. Rock 'n' Learn (dist. by Big Kids Productions). ISBN 978-1-934312-03-2. $19.95.

An introduction to English for Spanish-speaking children, with lessons on basic conversation, parts of the body, foods, colors, numbers, time, and so on. The rhythmic presentation in live-action and animation will help students remember the terms. (Rev: SLJ 12/07)

149 ❂ **Early Start Mandarin Chinese with Bao Bei the Panda: Colors and Animals** (K–2). 2006. 30 min. Victory. ISBN 978-0-9779512-0-8. $19.95.

Bao Bei, a panda hand puppet, and Chu Chu, an animated cricket, introduce simple Chinese words, phrases, and tones relating to colors and animals. (Rev: BL 1/1–15/07)

150 ❂ **I Like Animals!/¡Me Gustan los Animales!** (K). 2006. 30 min. Boca Beth (dist. by Victory Multimedia). $19.99.

Playful animals help little ones learn Spanish. Puppets, children, and animal footage combine for an entertaining presentation of more than 200 words. (Rev: SLJ 2/07)

151 ❂ **Kids Love Spanish: Volume 1; Basic Words** (K). 2007. 30 min. Big Kids. ISBN 978-0-9785757-0-0. $17.99.

A simple and colorful tutorial that introduces Spanish words (with their English translations); the words are then repeated several times and used in sentences to reinforce the lesson. (Rev: BL 9/15/07)

152 ❂ **Let's Play/Vamos a jugar** (K–1). 2007. 23 min. Series: Spanish for Beginners. Whistlefritz. $19.99.

Children and their teacher play and sing in Spanish, making unfamiliar words clear through actions rather than translations. A colorful and fun introduction to beginning words in Spanish. (Rev: SLJ 12/07)

Holidays, Holy Days, and Religion

General and Miscellaneous

153 ⊚ **Action Bible Toons** (K). 2006. 25 min. ThingamaKid. $9.99.
Well-loved Sunday school songs (such as "Joshua Fought the Battle of Jericho," "Jesus Loves the Little Children," and "Rise and Shine") with animated action and a CD. (Rev: SLJ 1/07)

154 ⊚ **April Foolishness** (K–2). 2006. 10 min. Nutmeg Media. ISBN 978-1-933938-13-4. $49.95.
An adaptation, narrated by the author, of Teresa Bateman's funny picture book about two children who try to fool their grandfather on the day before April Fool's Day. (Rev: VL 11–12/06)

155 ⊚ **From Aardvark to Zucchini: My Very Own Alphabet of Prayers** (K). 2004. 30 min. Creative Communications for the Parish (dist. by Vision Video). $14.99.
A lively introduction to prayers and Bible verses, conducted by a jolly purple aardvark. (Rev: VL 1–2/07)

156 ⊚ **Kids' Ten Commandments** (K–3). 2003. 5 discs. 150 min. Lionsgate. Closed captioned. $24.98.
Each animated disc contains songs and stories relating to two commandments and featuring an 11-year-old boy named Seth. (Rev: VL 7/06)

157 ⊚ **Our Wonderful World** (K–3). 2003. 80 min. SISU Home Entertainment. ISBN 978-1-56086-170-6. $24.95.
In English or Hebrew with English subtitles, Israeli TV host Dalik, puppet Stam, and a group of children explore the creation of the world (as told in the book of Genesis) along with some of the basic beliefs of Judaism; 12 songs and a parent/teacher guide are included. (Rev: VL 1–2/07)

Birthdays

158 ⊚ **Blue's Room: Fred's Birthday** (K). 2006. 100 min. Paramount Home Entertainment. Closed captioned. ISBN 978-1-4157-1651-9. $14.99.
A lively, imaginative episode in the computer-animated series that is a companion to *Blue's Clues* (also seen on Nick Jr.); Blue, the non-speaking dog who turns into a talking puppet when she goes into her room, celebrates a friend's party. (Rev: VL 5–6/06)

159 ⊞ **Disney Winnie the Pooh's Rumbly Tumbly Adventure** (K–3). 2005. Ubisoft. PlayStation 2, GameCube, Game Boy Advance. Players: 1–2. ESRB: E.
Winnie, Eeyore, Piglet, and Tigger enjoy five adventures involving birthdays. (Rev: SLJ 2/07; CTR Summer 05)

Christmas

160 ◈ **Christmas: StoryWatchers Club; Adventures in Storytelling** (K–3). 2006. 45 min. StoryWatchers Club. ISBN 978-0-9770343-4-5. $19.95.
Storytellers present a group of diverse Christmas tales, with multicultural puppets providing smooth transitions. (Rev: VL 11–12/06)

161 ◈ **Eloise: Little Miss Christmas** (K–3). 2006. 66 min. Anchor Bay Entertainment. Closed captioned. $14.98.
Eloise and her diverse friends living at the Plaza Hotel decide to stage a holiday show incorporating many cultures. This animated program is based on the character created by author Kay Thompson and illustrator Hilary Knight. (Rev: VL 11–12/06)

162 ◈ **Enchanting Christmas Stories** (K–3). 2007. 30 min. Series: BookBox. Master Communications. ISBN 978-1-60480-025-8.
Five animated Christmas tales are accompanied by narration and subtitles so that young viewers can follow along (in English or Spanish) to improve their reading skills. (Rev: BL 11/1/07; LMC 4–5/08; SLJ 1/08)

163 ◈ **William Wegman's Fay's Twelve Days of Christmas** (K–2). 2006. 30 min. William Wegman (dist. by Microcinema International). $19.99.
Wegman's Weimaraners get ready for Christmas — choosing a tree, cleaning the house, making decorations, and so forth. (Rev: VL 11–12/06)

164 ◈ **Ziggy's Gift** (K–3). 2005. 24 min. Ziggy & Friends (dist. by B.F.S. Entertainment & Multimedia). ISBN 978-0-7792-5721-8. $12.95.
In this animated feature, cartoon character Ziggy dresses as Santa and takes to the streets with his dog Fuzz to collect money for the poor. (Rev: SLJ 2/06)

Halloween

165 ◈ **Maggie and the Ferocious Beast: Trick or Treat** (K). 2007. 90 min. Series: Maggie and the Ferocious Beast. Shout! Factory. $14.99.
Four episodes featuring red-headed heroine Maggie and her stuffed animal friends, Beast and Hamilton, as they go trick-or-treating, play dress up, get along with friends, and handle being scared. (Rev: BL 11/15/07)

166 ◈ **A Very Brave Witch** (K–2). 2007. 7 min. Weston Woods. ISBN 978-0-545-04263-5. $59.95.
Alison McGhee's 2006 book (Simon & Schuster), illustrated by Harry Bliss, comes to life in this animated adaptation featuring the young witch brave enough to encounter scary trick-or-treaters.
☡ ALA ALSC Notable Children's Videos 2008

Thanksgiving

167 ◈ **Thank You, Sarah: The Woman Who Saved Thanksgiving** (K–3). 2004. 11 min. Spoken Arts. $50.
An iconographic treatment of Laurie Halse Anderson's book, illustrated by Matt Faulkner (Simon & Schuster, 2002), about a woman who campaigned for almost four decades to make Thanksgiving a national holiday.
☡ ALA ALSC Notable Children's Videos 2005

Humorous Stories

168 🔊 **Bark, George** (K–2). 2004. 7 min. Weston Woods. ISBN 978-0-439-90426-1. $59.95.
George the puppy who cannot "arf" but instead moos, oinks, and meows stars in this animated version of Jules Feiffer's 1999 book.
🏅 ALA ALSC Notable Children's Videos 2004

169 🔊 **Don't Be Silly, Mrs. Millie!** (K–2). 2005. 9 min. Nutmeg Media. ISBN 978-0-9772338-3-0. $49.95.
A bouncy adaptation of Judy Cox's entertaining picture book about a teacher who mixes up simple words much to the amusement of her class.

170 🔊 **Duck for President** (K–3). 2004. 16 min. Weston Woods. PPR. Closed captioned. ISBN 978-0-7882-0532-3. $59.95.
An animated adaptation of the clever 2003 picture book by Doreen Cronin in which Duck runs for president of the farm and then the nation. Study guide included. (Rev: BL 2/1/05; LMC 8–9/05; SLJ 2/05; VL 3–4/05)
🏅 ALA ALSC Notable Children's Videos 2005

171 🔊 **Eloise in Hollywood** (K–2). 2007. 45 min. Starz Media. $14.98.
Eloise of the beloved books by Kay Thompson visits Hollywood and ends up starring in a movie before she decides to return to the Plaza. Stars including Tim Curry and Lynn Redgrave provide voices. (Rev: SLJ 6/07)

172 🔊 **Here Comes the Clown** (K–2). 2005. 31 min. Headliner Productions. $19.95.
Former Ringling Brothers clown Boswick has a habit of focusing on the task immediately in front of him, but even then often gets things wrong in this funny and suspenseful account of a day full of silliness. (Rev: SLJ 3/06)

173 🔊 **Let George Do It!** (K–2). 2006. 6 min. Nutmeg Media. ISBN 978-1-933938-19-6. $49.95.
George Foreman narrates this funny tale about a family of five sons who are all named after their father George; confusion is inevitable when they try to work together to plan a party. (Rev: VL 11–12/06)

174 🔊 **The Librarian from the Black Lagoon** (K–2). 2007. 9 min. Weston Woods. Closed captioned. ISBN 978-0-439-02772-4. $59.95.
Is the library the lair of the Librarian from the Black Lagoon? Or is it a friendly place to learn and explore? Viewers will find out in this animated adaptation of the humorous Mike Thaler book. Includes teacher's guide. (Rev: SLJ 8/07)

175 🔊 **Lizard Man of Crabtree County** (K–3). 2005. 9 min. Nutmeg Media. PPR. ISBN 978-0-9772338-5-4. $49.95.
Young James Arthur creates a stir in sleepy Crabtree County when he is mistaken for a lizard man. Based on the 1999 picture book by Lucy Nolan with illustrations by Jill Kastner. Study guide included. (Rev: SLJ 3/05; VL 5–6/05)

176 ● **Mark Teague Favorites: The Secret Shortcut/The Lost and Found** (K–3). 2006. 17 min. Nutmeg Media. PPR. $49.95.
Animated adaptations of two Teague picture books featuring Wendell and Floyd, best friends subject to wild flights of imagination and a tendency to get into trouble. (Rev: SLJ 1/06; VL 9–10/06)

177 ● **Noisy Nora . . . and More Stories About Mischief** (K–3). 2007. 45 min. Scholastic. ISBN 978-0-545-00114-4. $14.95.
Making trouble is the theme of three short iconographic stories (*Noisy Nora,* about a middle child seeking attention; *T Is for Terrible,* about a naughty T. rex; and *Goggles,* about an exciting chase) and the longer *Cannonball Simp,* which features a runaway dog who joins the circus. Jules Feiffer's *Munro* with its 4-year-old draftee ends the entertaining program. (Rev: SLJ 6/07)

178 ● **Serious Farm** (K–3). 2005. 9 min. Nutmeg Media. PPR. ISBN 978-0-9774680-0-3. $49.95.
The animals try everything to make Farmer Fred laugh, and he finally sees the funny side of farming in this brief iconographic adaptation of Tim Egan's 2003 picture book. Study guide included. (Rev: SLJ 5/05; VL 7–8/05)

179 ● **While Mama Had a Quick Little Chat** (K–3). 2006. 9 min. Nutmeg Media. PPR. Closed captioned. $49.95.
An effective soundtrack adds to the energy of this story of the hapless Rose, whose mother remains on the phone even though spectacular events are taking place in their house; based on the award-winning book (Atheneum, 2005) written by Amy Reichert and illustrated by Alexandra Bolger. (Rev: VL 1–2/07)

180 ● **Woodhead Saves the Farm** (K–3). 2006. 30 min. It's a Fine Mess Productions (dist. by AV Café). ISBN 978-0-9664968-3-3. $12.95.
The senator is on his way, and the farm is a mess! Woodhead and his young friends sing and dance while they clean up just in time for his arrival. Great songs in different styles add to the fun. (Rev: SLJ 8/07)

Nature and Science

181 🜚 **Best of Nature: Silver 25th Anniversary Collection** (K–12). 2007 86 min. Questar. ISBN 978-1-59464-282-1. $24.99.
Featuring highlights of 25 years of the PBS series "Nature," this DVD has many moving and fascinating moments. Footage of animals hunting, mating, eating, playing, and interacting (with humans and with one another) will interest viewers of all ages. (Rev: VL 9–10/07)

182 🜚 **Dem Bones** (K–3). 2003. 10 min. Weston Woods. ISBN 978-0-439-90427-8. $59.95.
Animation and the addition of lively music bring a new dimension to Bob Barner's entertaining book (Chronicle, 1996) introducing the bones of the body to the spiritual "Dem Dry Bones." (Rev: VL 5–6/04)
🜚 ALA ALSC Notable Children's Videos 2004

183 🜚 **It's a Big Big World: Investigate Your World** (K–2). 2007. 73 min. Sony Pictures Home Entertainment. Closed captioned. ISBN 978-1-4248-4347-3. $14.95.
Four episodes of the green-themed PBS Kids' program "It's a Big Big World" feature Snook, a sloth, and his animal friends learning more about the world and how to get along in it. (Rev: VL 3–4/07)

184 🜚 **My Fantastic Field Trip to the Planets** (2–4). 2005. 29 min. Wonderscape. ISBN 978-0-9770520-0-4. $14.98.
Young Jake takes a trip around the solar system in his toy rocket ship, learning about the planets' respective positions and their feelings about their distance from the sun. (Rev: BL 12/1/05)

185 🜚 **One Tiny Turtle** (K–3). 2005. 9 min. Nutmeg Media. PPR. ISBN 978-0-9776262-6-7. $49.95.
This appealing introduction to the loggerhead sea turtle and its long migration, introduced by the story of one turtle's life from hatching to laying her own eggs on the beach of her birth, is based on the 2001 picture book written by Nicola Davies and illustrated by Jane Chapman. (Rev: SLJ 2/06; VL 9–10/06)

186 🜚 **Peep and the Big Wide World** (K). 2005. 3 discs. 180 min. WGBH Boston. ISBN 978-1-59375-351-1. $29.95.
Eighteen animated segments illustrate basic scientific concepts as bird friends Peep, Chirp, and Quack explore the world around them. The three titles included here are *Peep Finds*, *Peep Floats*, and *Peep's New Friends*. (Rev: BL 12/1/05)

187 🜚 **The Solar System: A First Look** (K–3). 2007. 16 min. SchoolMedia (dist. by 100% Educational Videos). ISBN 978-1-58541-930-2. $39.95.
An introduction to the solar system with an up-to-date treatment of Pluto, now considered a dwarf planet. Photographs, video, and graphics help to present the information. Teacher's guide included. (Rev: SLJ 9/07)

188 ● **SpaceTrekkers** (K–3). 2004. 30 min. Series: Way Cool Science for Curious Kids! . Thinkeroo. ISBN 978-1-929944-92-7. $14.95.
Using satellite footage, photographs, and computer animation, this entertaining program introduces the solar system, and its planets, moons, and other cosmic bodies. (Rev: BL 12/1/04; LMC 3/05)

189 ● **Thinking Like a Scientist: Scientific Method No. 1** (K–2). 2007. 17 min. School-Media (dist. by 100% Educational Videos). ISBN 978-1-58541-925-8. $39.95.
Students Megan, Brandon, and Zoey perform experiments while following the scientific method to predict and record their results. Teacher's guide included. (Rev: SLJ 10/07)

190 ● **White Owl, Barn Owl** (K–3). 2007. 9 min. Nutmeg Media. PPR. ISBN 978-1-933938-26-4. $49.95.
A girl and her grandfather watch an owl family make themselves a home in a box in this iconographic presentation of the 2007 book by Nicola Davies, illustrated by Michael Foreman. Study guide included. (Rev: BL 1/1–15/08; LMC 11–12/07; SLJ 4/08)

191 ● **Whose Garden Is It?** (K–3). 2006. 6 min. Nutmeg Media. ISBN 978-1-933938-29-5. $49.95.
Does this beautiful garden belong to the gardener, the rabbit, or even the tiny seed that grows within it? Rhyming text, watercolor illustrations, and gentle music combine for a lovely program. Teacher's guide available. (Rev: SLJ 5/07)

192 ● **Why Dragonfly? What's Up with the Moon?** (K–3). 2005. 30 min. Why Dragonfly? ISBN 978-0-9778518-0-5. $19.95.
Live-action footage and effective fantasy sequences tell the story of a magical dragonfly called Archimedes who shrinks two curious children and whisks them off to learn about the earth, the sun, and the moon. (Rev: SLJ 1/07; VL 7/06)

193 ● **Wild Animal Baby: A Tall Tail and Other Stories** (K–3). 2006. 45 min. Series: Wild Animal Baby. Topics Entertainment. ISBN 978-1-60077-044-9. $9.99.
Izzy Owl, Skip the Rabbit, Sandy Salamander, and Rosie the River Otter are featured in three stories about animals. Animation is interspersed with live-action footage of animals. The other titles in the series are *Flying Whales and Other Stories*, *Sandy's Bored Game and Other Stories,* and *Wow! Wetland! and Other Stories*. (Rev: VL 3–4/07)

194 🔊 **The Adventures of Dave and Augie, Episode Three: Theodore Roosevelt** (K–3). 2005. 30 min. Freggie Productions (dist. by Library Video Company). ISBN 978-0-9758786-4-4. $21.95.
Sock puppets Dave and Augie take young Hillary on a tour of Theodore Roosevelt's New York residence in this introduction to the president's life and accomplishments. (Rev: BL 1/1–15/06)

195 🔊 **Boxes for Katje** (K–3). 2006. 19 min. Spoken Arts. $50.
An adaptation, with some animation, of Candace Fleming's book based on actual events about an Indiana town's efforts to help Dutch people suffering from severe postwar shortages in 1945.
🔔 ALA ALSC Notable Children's Videos 2006

196 🔊 **Finding Daddy: A Story of the Great Depression** (K–3). 2007. 17 min. Nutmeg Media. ISBN 978-1-933938-16-5. $59.95.
An iconographic film of Jo Harper and Josephine Harper's picture book about a girl searching for her father during the Great Depression. (Rev: BL 6/1–15/07; SLJ 4/07)

197 🔊 **The Firekeeper's Son** (K–3). 2006. 11 min. Nutmeg Media. ISBN 978-1-933938-27-1. $49.95.
Linda Sue Park narrates this presentation of her picture book set in early 19th-century Korea about a young boy named Sang-Hee who carries on the family tradition of lighting the nightly fire even though he longs for excitement.

198 🔊 **John, Paul, George, and Ben** (K–3). 2007. 9 min. Weston Woods. ISBN 978-0-439-02752-6. $59.95.
The Founding Fathers (John Hancock, Paul Revere, George Washington, Ben Franklin — and Thomas Jefferson) demonstrate behaviors that may serve them well as adults but are exasperating when they are children in this animated adaptation of Lane Smith's book that blends fact, fiction, and humor. (Rev: BL 10/15/07; LMC 8–9/06; SLJ 10/07)
🔔 ALA ALSC Notable Children's Videos 2008

199 🔊 **Johnny Appleseed** (1–3). 2005. 52 min. Series: Tall Tales and Legends. Koch Vision. ISBN 978-1-4172-2768-6. $14.98.
Martin Short, Rob Reiner, Molly Ringwald, and other stars of the 1980s act out the story of the famous nature-lover. Originally produced in VHS format in 1985. (Rev: VL 3–4/05)

200 🔊 **One Wee World Celebrates Mexico** (K). 2006. 30 min. One Wee World. $19.95.
For the youngest viewers, this colorful celebration of Mexican culture with music, live action, dance, animation, and Spanish narration is fun and exciting. Subtitles in English. (Rev: BL 3/15/07; SLJ 2/07)

201 🔊 **Ruby's Wish** (K–3). 2005. 10 min. Nutmeg Media. PPR. ISBN 978-0-9776262-7-4. $49.95.
Based on the 2002 book written by Shirin Yim Bridges and illustrated by Sophie Blackall, this is the story of Ruby, an intelligent girl from a wealthy Chinese family who aspires to go to university at a time when few girls were educated and, to her surprise, gets her wish. (Rev: VL 5–6/06)

202 ◉ **Adventures with Wink and Blink: A Day in the Life of a Zoo!** (K–2). 2005. 30 min. Laurel Hill. ISBN 978-0-9753885-3-2. $12.98.

Hosts Wink and Blink introduce zoos, their animals, and the work of zookeepers using short films presented in their "magic theater." Also in this series: *Adventures with Wink and Blink: A Day in the Life of a Firefighter!* (2005) and *Adventures with Wink and Blink: A Day in the Life of a Garbage Truck!* (2004). (Rev: BL 10/1/05)

203 ◉ **Animals in Action** (K–2). 2006. Discovery School. ISBN 978-1-59527-496-0. $69.95.

How do animals get around? Some crawl, some gallop, some slither. Children will enjoy the footage in this presentation of many animals in motion. Humans copy the motions to help viewers understand how the animals move. (Rev: SLJ 3/07)

204 ◉ **Antarctic Antics . . . and More Hilarious Animal Stories** (K–3). 2007. 60 min. Series: Scholastic Storybook Treasures. New Video Group. $14.95.

In addition to the award-winning *Antarctic Antics* (2000), based on Judy Sierra's 1998 book of poems about an emperor penguin, this DVD includes *In the Small, Small Pond; Bear Snores On; Bark, George;* and three additional stories. (Rev: BL *Antarctic Antics:* BL 4/1/03; VL *Antarctic Antics:* VL 3–4/01)

⚱ *Antarctic Antics:* Andrew Carnegie Medal for Excellence in Children's Video 2001

205 ◉ **Billy Blue Hair: Why Do Giraffes Have Long Necks?** (K–3). 2006. 30 min. Kayo. $14.95.

Billy (of the blue hair) finds himself transported into a strange live-action world where he finds a variety of animals and asks questions about them. (Rev: BL 2/15/06)

206 ◉ **Boomer's Great Adventures** (K). 2006. 15 min. Nutmeg Media. ISBN 978-0-9776262-0-5. $49.95.

Boomer the golden retriever has a series of adventures — going to school for a day, moving house, and a new puppy to tolerate. This animated production is based on stories by Constance W. McGeorge, illustrated by Mary Whyte. (Rev: SLJ 2/06; VL 7/06)

207 ◉ **Chameleons Are Cool** (K–3). 2007. 8 min. Nutmeg Media. ISBN 978-1-933938-15-8. $49.95.

This iconographic presentation of the 1997 book by Martin Jenkins will fascinate viewers who already love chameleons as well as those who have yet to discover them. Teacher's guide available. (Rev: SLJ 4/07)

208 ◉ **Dance with the Animals** (K). 2006. 45 min. Rock 'n Learn. ISBN 978-1-878489-02-9. $19.99.

Zoo animals, farm animals, wild animals, and pets are presented by Katie Cat, Rex Rooster, and Freddie Fox in this romp set to music. (Rev: SLJ 2/07)

209 ◉ **Diary of a Spider** (K–3). 2006. 9 min. Weston Woods. Closed captioned. ISBN 978-0-439-90566-4. $59.95.

Flies, webs, and vacuum cleaners are all part of a spider's day in this animation of Harry

Bliss's illustrations for the 2005 book by Doreen Cronin. (Rev: SLJ 2/07)

210 ● **Diary of a Worm** (K–2). 2004. 10 min. Weston Woods. PPR. Closed captioned. ISBN 978-0-7882-0522-4. $59.95.
Based on the book by Doreen Cronin, this brief but charming film about a day in the life of a worm will entertain young viewers. Study guide included. (Rev: SLJ 6/05; VL 3–4/05)
ᵭ ALA ALSC Notable Children's Videos 2005

211 ● **Dinosaur Bones** (K–2). 2006. 10 min. Weston Woods. Closed captioned. ISBN 978-0-439-90567-1. $60.
An animated version of the book by Bob Barner, this film identifies dinosaur parts and offers plenty of other interesting facts for younger students. (Rev: SLJ 2/07)

212 ● **The Emperor's Egg** (K–3). 2006. 10 min. Nutmeg Media. ISBN 978-0-9774680-8-9. $49.95.
Based on the 1999 picture book by Martin Jenkins, this is a lighthearted tale about emperor penguins with factual information included throughout. (Rev: VL 3–4/06)

213 ● **Harry the Dirty Dog** (K–2). 2006. 9 min. Weston Woods. Closed captioned. ISBN 978-0-439-90589-3. $59.95.
The classic illustrations of the 1956 picture book are updated and animated in this film about the white dog with black spots who runs away and returns home so dirty that his family does not recognize him. In English and Spanish with subtitles. (Rev: SLJ 6/07)

214 ● **Hondo and Fabian** (K–2). 2006. 6 min. Weston Woods. ISBN 978-0-439-84910-4. $59.95.
Peter McCarty's beloved 2002 picture book about Hondo the dog, Fabian the cat, and their special friendship is brought to life in this iconographic adaptation. (Rev: VL 11–12/06)

215 ● **I Want a Dog** (K–3). 2004. 10 min. National Film Board of Canada. $129.
This animated adaptation of Dayal Kaur Khalsa's 1987 book retains all the humor of the story of young May's determination to get a dog. (Rev: BL 3/1/04; SLJ 2/04)
ᵭ ALA ALSC Notable Children's Videos 2004

216 ● **Lost in the Woods: The Movie** (K–2). 2006. 29 min. Carl R. Sams II Photography. PPR. ISBN 978-0-9770108-1-3. $19.95.
In a beautiful woodland area, animals with well-chosen, original voices help each other to find lost relatives. (Rev: BL 4/15/06; VL 5–6/06)

217 ● **Our Feathered Friends: Adventures on a Chicken Farm** (K–3). 2007. 28 min. Choices. ISBN 978-1-9337241-5-7. $24.95.
This informative and appealing live-action introduction to chickens is narrated by a young boy visiting his grandmother's farm. (Rev: BL BL 12/1/07; LMC 3/08; SLJ 12/07)

218 ● **Puppytown** (K–2). 2007. 35 min. Victory. $19.99.
An educational and engaging look at puppies and the care they require, for young viewers. There is a quiz and an interactive look at the puppy's body. (Rev: SLJ 6/07)

219 ● **Stanley's Party and Stanley's Wild Ride** (K–2). 2006. 17 min. Nutmeg Media. ISBN 978-1-933938-23-3. $69.95.
Bad dog Stanley has lots of fun in these two adventures first seen in the picture books (Kids Can Press; 2003, 2006, respectively) written by Linda Bailey and illustrated by Bill Slavin. (Rev: SLJ 12/06)

220 ● **A Tale of Two Dogs** (K–3). 2004. 8 min. Nutmeg Media. PPR. ISBN 978-0-9774680-6-5. $49.95.
A family trades in their new dog for a beagle, but find they miss the old one. Based on the 2004 picture book by Steven Kroll. Study guide included. (Rev: SLJ 2/05; VL 3–4/05)

221 ● **That New Animal** (K–2). 2006. 9 min. Weston Woods. PPR. Closed captioned. ISBN 978-0-439-84923-4. $59.95.
Narrated by Emily Jenkins, author of the 2004 award-winning picture book illustrated by Pierre Pratt, this is an entertaining tale about two dogs learning to cope with the arrival of a baby in the family. (Rev: BL 9/15/06; VL 9–10/06)

School Stories

222 🔊 **Eloise Goes to School** (K–2). 2007. 45 min. Starz Media. $14.98.

The much-loved Eloise, who has been tutored at home, decides to try attending prep school and makes quite an impression on her teachers and fellow students in this animated film based on the books by Kay Thompson. (Rev: SLJ 10/07)

223 🔊 **Emily's First 100 Days of School** (K–3). 2006. 35 min. Weston Woods. ISBN 978-0-439-84896-1. $59.95.

An adaptation of Rosemary Wells's counting book featuring Miss Cribbage and her class as they count and learn a number each day until day 100, and then celebrate with a party. (Rev: BL 1/1–15/07; SLJ 8/06)

224 🔊 **Hooway for Wodney Wat** (K–3). 2005. 9 min. Nutmeg Media. PPR. ISBN 978-0-9771510-4-2. $49.95.

Poor Rodney is teased for mispronouncing the letter R — until he unwittingly drives away a class bully. Study guide included. (Rev: BL 5/15/05; SLJ 6/05; VL 7–8/05)

225 🔊 **I Hate English** (K–3). 2006. 15 min. Nutmeg Media. ISBN 978-1-933938-22-6. $49.95.

The difficulties of a young Chinese girl in an American school are overcome by a sympathetic teacher. This is an iconographic adaptation of the 1989 book by Ellen Levine. An interview with the author is included. (Rev: BL 4/15/07; SLJ 4/07)

226 🔊 **Miss Nelson Has a Field Day . . . and Miss Nelson Is Back** (K–3). 2003. 56 min.

Series: Scholastic Video Collection. New Video Group. $14.95.

Animated adaptations of two hilarious Harry Allard stories about the resourceful Miss Nelson. (Rev: *Miss Nelson Has a Field Day:* BL 3/15/00; VL 6/6/00 Web review)

🏆 *Miss Nelson Has a Field Day:* Andrew Carnegie Medal for Excellence in Children's Video 2000

227 🔊 **Miss Smith's Incredible Storybook** (1–3). 2007. 8 min. Spoken Arts. ISBN 978-0-8045-8047-2. $50.

When Miss Smith reads from her storybook, the characters come alive! One day when Miss Smith isn't at school, things go awry. Author Michael Garland introduces this iconographic adaptation of his book. (Rev: LMC 10/07; SLJ 5/07)

228 🔊 **Mr. Ouchy's First Day** (K–3). 2007. 12 min. Spoken Arts. ISBN 978-0-8045-8048-9. $50.

New teacher Mr. Ouchy is nervous about the first day of school. Brief episodes capture the excitement and worries of the big day. Based on the 2006 picture book by B. G. Hennessy. (Rev: SLJ 5/07)

229 🔊 **Wormhead** (K–2). 2007. 13 min. Kool-Kidz. $15.

With help from her parents and teacher, Jesse finds a way to show her classmates that her new friend Nia shouldn't be disliked just because she has dreadlocks. (Rev: BL 7/07; SLJ 7/07)

Transportation and Machines

230 🔊 **All About John Deere for Kids** (K–3). 2004. 40 min. TM Books & Video (dist. by Big Kids Productions). ISBN 978-1-932291-27-8. $14.95.

John Deere makes tractors, lawn mowers, and construction equipment — all objects of fascination for many children. John Deere toys are also popular, so this bright, live-action production, featuring the real things in action, will appeal to young children everywhere. (Rev: SLJ 9/05; VL 5–6/05)

231 🔊 **All About Trains for Kids** (K–2). 2007. 55 min. TM Books & Video (dist. by Big Kids Productions). PPR. ISBN 978-1-932291-80-3. $14.95.

Young train fans will adore this presentation of all kinds of trains, including steam, diesel, toy, and even animated (an iconographic adaptation of the book *A Lucky Dog: Owney, U.S. Rail Mail Mascot*). Train-themed music adds to the fun. (Rev: VL 708/07)

232 🔊 **Baby Einstein: On the Go — Riding, Sailing and Soaring** (K). 2003. 40 min. The Baby Einstein Company. ISBN 978-0-7888-6248-9. $19.99.

From strollers to trains, rowboats to steamboats, and hot air balloons to helicopters, this colorful and music-filled presentation introduces forms of transport. (Rev: VL 1–2/06)

233 🔊 **The Busy Little Engine (and His Friend, Pig)** (K). 2005. 34 min. Squirrel Tracks Wooden Trains. PPR. $15.95.

A toy train with a lively imagination sets out with his friend Pig to make cookies in this entertaining and educational production featuring live action, computer animation, and original songs by Jimmy Magoo. (Rev: BL 11/15/06; VL 5–6/06)

234 🔊 **Fireboat: The Heroic Adventures of the John J. Harvey** (K–3). 2004. 13 min. Spoken Arts. $49.95.

The story of the *John J. Harvey* fireboat, from its launch in 1931 through its restoration in the 1990s and its role in fighting fires in New York City on September 11, 2001, is shown in this iconographic adaptation of Maira Kalman's 2002 picture book.

⚱ ALA ALSC Notable Children's Videos 2005

235 🔊 **Firefighter George and Amazing Airplanes** (K–3). 2004. 45 min. Start Smarter (dist. by Big Kids Productions). PPR. $14.95.

Viewers meet Pilot Sean, Lt. Ray, Pilot Bambi, Flight Attendant Tonja, and Major Lisa, pilots and aircraft workers who demonstrate the fun of flying and the importance of safety. (Rev: SLJ 11/05; VL 11–12/05)

236 🔊 **Firefighter George and Fire Engines, Vol. 2** (K–3). 2005. 42 min. Start Smarter (dist. by Big Kids Productions). $14.95.

Firefighter George introduces a fire engine and fire house, complete with Fire Dog Maggie, and looks carefully at a fire truck's components. (Rev: SLJ 3/06)

237 🔊 **I Stink!** (K–2). 2004. 9 min. Weston Woods. ISBN 978-0-439-79937-9. $59.95.

The stinky garbage truck of Kate and Jim McMullan's 2002 book comes to life in this animated version with great narration by

Andy Richter and accompanying jazz by Joel Goodman. (Rev: VL 9–10/04)

🏆 ALA ALSC Notable Children's Videos 2005

238 🌐 **Kids Love Fire Engines** (K–3). 2006. 30 min. Big Kids Productions. $14.95.

Real firefighters from the Los Angeles Fire Department show off the equipment they use, including a fireboat and a rescue helicopter. (Rev: SLJ 4/07)

239 🌐 **Lots and Lots of Fire Trucks: Brave Heroes and Big Rigs!** (K–3). 2007. 30 min. Marshall. ISBN 978-0-9789286-0-5. $14.95.

An intriguing look at what a firefighter's job is like, exploring fire stations, the trucks they use, everyday chores, battling real fires, and rescues. (Rev: BL 4/15/07)

240 🌐 **Percy Saves the Day and Other Adventures** (K–2). 2005. 35 min. Series: Thomas and Friends. HIT Entertainment (dist. by Anchor Bay). $17.98.

Thomas the Tank Engine's friend Percy (the No. 6 green train) has six adventures that convey a moral. (Rev: SLJ 1/06)

241 🌐 **Thomas and Friends: On Site with Thomas and Other Adventures** (K). 2006. 35 min. HIT Entertainment (dist. by Anchor Bay). $17.98.

Six stories about the beloved engine will entertain young children. Bonus features include a matching game, a trivia game, a read-along story, and two sing-along songs. (Rev: SLJ 1/07)

242 🌐 **Thomas and Friends: Songs from the Station** (K). 2005. 40 min. Anchor Bay Entertainment. ISBN 978-1-57132-979-0. $16.98.

The beloved engine and his coworkers appear in eight compelling sing-along songs as well as two stories: "Thomas and the Tuba" and "Thomas and the Firework Display." (Rev: VL 7–8/05)

MATERIALS FOR
OLDER CHILDREN
(GRADES 4–12)

Literary Forms

Fiction

Adventure and Survival Stories

243 ◎ **Area 88** (6–12). 2007. 2 discs. 105 min. ADV Films. ISBN 978-1-4139-1431-3. $29.98. First released more than 20 years ago, this is one of the classics of manga animation. Against his will, a young pilot ends up flying for the Asran Mercenary Air Force and sees nonstop action and bloodshed. Choose between a dubbed version and a subtitled Japanese version. Includes an interview with the creator, Kaoru Shintani. (Rev: SLJ 9/07; VL 9–10/06)

244 ◎ **The Boy Who Wanted to Be a Bear** (4–8). 2002. 76 min. Central Park Media. ISBN 978-1-58664-449-9. $19.95. An animated story, based on an Inuit legend, of a boy brought up by polar bears who must choose between his two families when his father eventually finds him. Available in French with subtitles or dubbed in English. Note that there is brief nudity. (Rev: VL 3–4/05)

245 ◎ **Choose Your Own Adventure: The Abominable Snowman** (2–6). 2006. 80 min. Goldhil Entertainment. PPR. ISBN 978-1-59443-673-4. $19.98. Viewers select between options at a number of points as three children travel to the Himalayas in this animated adventure that also offers information on life in Nepal, maps, and a glossary. (Rev: VL 9–10/06)

246 ▦ **Fable** (11–12). Microsoft Game Studios. Windows, Xbox. Players: 1. ESRB: M (blood, strong language, violence). An action-packed adventure in which the hero sets out to avenge his village and his family after the destruction of both by an unknown enemy. The player faces many choices between good and evil and his decisions determine the path of his life. ⚵ YALSA Top 50 Core Recommended Collection Titles

247 ◎ **Kim Possible: So the Drama** (4–8). 2005. 71 min. Walt Disney Home Entertainment. Closed captioned. ISBN 978-0-7888-5837-6. $19.99. Can Kim save the world from Dr. Drakken's evil plot — and get a date for the prom? Kim is a favorite on the Disney Channel, and this animated program will be a hit with her fans. (Rev: VL 7–8/05)

248 ▦ **Lara Croft Tomb Raider: Anniversary** (8–12). Eidos Interactive. Windows, PlayStation 2, Xbox, Xbox 360, Wii. Players: 1. ESRB: T (mild suggestive themes, violence). A collection of all the Tomb Raider games and expansions. Lara Croft encounters countless enemies and traps while trying to complete numerous puzzles as she searches for important historical artifacts. ⚵ YALSA Top 50 Core Recommended Collection Titles

249 ▦ **LEGO Indiana Jones: The Original Adventures** (1–12). 2008. LucasArts. Windows, Nintendo DS, PlayStation 2, Xbox 360,

Wii. Players: 1–2. ESRB: E10+ (cartoon violence).

Raiders of the Lost Ark, Temple of Doom, and *The Last Crusade* are featured in this game that offers six jungle adventures and more than 60 playable characters, whose body parts can be mixed and matched. Cooperative gameplay and creative puzzles add to the fun. (Rev: CTR 6/08)

250 ▓ **Pirate Poppers** (2–10). 2006. Brighter Minds Media. Windows, Macintosh. $19.95.
Players work their way up through increasingly difficult levels, collecting prizes as they identify pieces of a treasure map. The main Adventure mode is accompanied by a Puzzle mode and an Arcade mode.
ಠ ALA Notable Children's Software 2007

251 ▓ **Prince of Persia: The Sands of Time** (9–12). Ubisoft. Windows, PlayStation 2, Game Boy Advance, Xbox. Players: 1. ESRB: T (blood, violence).
Players must use logical thinking skills to control the powers of the Sands of Time — allowing time to stop, slow, and accelerate; in the course of the adventure, they encounter many enemies and obstacles as they swing, climb, and jump their way to victory.
ಠ YALSA Top 50 Core Recommended Collection Titles

252 ◉ **Princess Natasha: Season One** (9–12). 2006. 72 min. Anchor Bay Entertainment. $14.98.
Seen on AOL and then the Cartoon Network, the animated exploits of Princess Natasha of Zoravia, who must juggle her royal roles with those of secret agent and exchange student in Illinois, are still engaging. (Rev: VL 9–10/06)

253 ▓ **Tomb Raider Legend** (8–12). 2006. Eidos Interactive. Windows, PlayStation 2, GameCube, Nintendo DS, Xbox, Xbox 360. Players: 1. ESRB: T (blood, language, suggestive themes, violence).
The intrepid Lara Croft accomplishes a number of missions in locations around the world as part of her quest to find a missing artifact. This well-constructed game is full of action and puzzles.

Classics

Europe

GREAT BRITAIN AND IRELAND

254 ◉ **Jane Eyre** (10–12). 2006. 2 discs. 228 min. Series: Masterpiece Theatre. BBC and WGBH Boston (dist. by WGBH Boston). ISBN 978-1-59375-705-2. $29.95.
A beautiful and engaging version of the Charlotte Brontë novel, with Ruth Wilson as Jane and Toby Stephens as Rochester. (Rev: BL 5/1/07*; LMC 11–12/07; SLJ 6/07)

255 ◉ **Kidnapped** (8–11). 2005. 180 min. WGBH Boston. ISBN 978-1-59375-309-2. $19.95.
An excellent "Masterpiece Theatre" production of the classic Robert Louis Stevenson tale set in Scotland. (Rev: BL 2/1/06*; SLJ 5/06; VL 3–4/06)
ಠ ALA ALSC Notable Children's Videos 2006

256 ◉ **Pride and Prejudice** (8–12). 2006. 129 min. Focus. $29.99.
An excellent adaptation of Jane Austen's classic romance. (Rev: VL 3–4/06)

257 ◉ **Pride and Prejudice: A DVD Study Guide** (9–12). 2007. 76 min. Rocketbook. ISBN 978-0-9770790-3-2. $14.95.
Readers tackling *Pride and Prejudice* will benefit from the additional insight offered by this DVD. Each chapter is reviewed and brief quizzes help the viewer keep up. (Rev: SLJ 10/07)

United States

258 ◉ **Pollyanna** (4–7). 2004. 100 min. WGBH Boston. $19.95.
A "Masterpiece Theatre" presentation of the classic novel by Eleanor H. Porter, moving the setting from Vermont to England. (Rev: VL 1–2/05)
ಠ ALA ALSC Notable Children's Videos 2005

259 ◉ **To Kill a Mockingbird: Exploring the Text** (9–12). 2007. 32 min. VEA. $89.95.
Two adult experts discuss the novel's historical context, significance, and meaning between segments that present a reading of the text accompanied by period photographs. (Rev: SLJ 7/07; VL 11–12/07)

Contemporary Life and Problems

Family Life and Problems

260 ● **Grandfather's Birthday** (6–10). 2007. 18 min. Tundra Films. $49.95.
Grandfather is looking forward to a visit from his family on his 79th birthday, and is disappointed when they call to say they are just too busy to come. A touching look at old age and the loneliness that sometimes accompanies it. (Rev: SLJ 10/07)

261 ● **My Louisiana Sky** (6–9). 2002. 98 min. Showtime. $14.98.
This award-winning movie is based on the book by Kimberley Willis Holt (Holt, 1998), set in 1950s Louisiana, about preteen Tiger Ann's efforts to cope with her mentally disabled parents. (Rev: VL 7–8/02)
♙ Andrew Carnegie Medal for Excellence in Children's Video 2002

262 ● **Under the Biltmore Clock** (9–12). 2006. 79 min. Rubison Productions (dist. by Monterey Home Video). ISBN 978-1-56994-267-3. $19.95.
An adaptation of F. Scott Fitzgerald's short story "Myra Meets His Family." This live-action film set in the 1920s features engaging actors in the roles of Myra and her fiancé Knowlton as Myra meets her in-laws-to-be for the first time. (Rev: SLJ 7/07)

263 ● **Visiting Day** (1–6). 2004. 29 min. GPN. PPR. Closed captioned. $29.95.
This episode of PBS's "Reading Rainbow" features the book *Visiting Day* by Jacqueline Woodson in which a little girl goes to visit her father in prison. The story is followed by a trip by a real-life family to visit their loved one in prison. The difficulties of having an incarcerated family member are shown in a compassionate and child-friendly way. (Rev: VL 5–6/05)

Personal Problems and Growing into Maturity

264 ● **Fishbowl** (8–12). 2005. 28 min. Center for Asian American Media. $175.
In 1970s Hawaii, 13-year-old Lovey is an outsider with a bad perm and large glasses who longs to make an impression. Based on Lois-Ann Yamanaka's novel *Wild Meat and the Bully Burgers* (Farrar, 1996). (Rev: VL 3–4/07)
♙ YALSA 2008 Selected DVDs and Videos

265 ● **From an Objective Point of View** (7–12). 2002. 10 min. Scenarios USA. $50.
Two girls make a pact not to have sex without consulting the other first. (Rev: BL 3/15/04)
♙ YALSA 2004 Selected Videos and DVDs

266 ● **Holes** (4–8). 2003. 114 min. Disney. $29.99.
This excellent movie version of Louis Sachar's Newbery-winning YA novel about Stanley Yelnats (played by Shia LaBeouf) — who is wrongly accused of stealing and sent to an isolated youth detention camp, where he's forced to dig holes for the cruel warden (Sigourney Weaver) and her henchman (Jon Voigt) — also features a discussion and activity guide and a commentary by Sachar. (Rev: BL 1/1–15/04; VL 9–10/03)

267 ● **Lipstick** (10–12). 2002. 10 min. Scenarios USA. $55.
A young woman braves coming out to her high school friends.
♙ YALSA 2004 Selected Videos and DVDs

268 ● **Nicole's Choice** (7–12). 2003. 14 min. Select Media. $80.
Nicole contracts gonorrhea during a one-night stand — a fact she doesn't discover until seeking birth control for a new relationship — and must make difficult decisions. (Rev: BL 3/15/04; VL 7–8/04)
♙ YALSA 2004 Selected Videos and DVDs

269 ● **Nightmare at School** (3–9). 2007. 9 min. National Film Board of Canada. $99.
A young student's anxiety distorts his world in this clever animated film. (Rev: VL 1–2/08)
♙ ALA ALSC Notable Children's Videos 2008

270 ● **On the Outs** (10–12). 2005. 83 min. Polychrome Pictures. $19.98.
This award-winning drama portrays the lives of three Jersey City girls coping with challenges including poverty, pregnancy, and drug addiction. (Rev: VL 8/8/06 Web review)
♙ YALSA 2007 Selected Videos and DVDs

World Affairs and Contemporary Problems

271 ● **Invasion of the Space Lobsters** (5–12). 2006. 7 min. National Film Board of Canada. $99 (Rental: $40).

Can you read the instructions that accompany most appliances? A father driven mad by his new barbecue is further confused when a flying saucer delivers two large lobsters plus a supposed translation machine. All turns out well in the end, however, when plain English is restored as the way to communicate. (Rev: SLJ 12/06)

⚇ YALSA 2006 Selected Videos and DVDs

Fantasy

272 🎲 **Ape Escape 3** (3–6). 2006. Sony Computer Entertainment. PlayStation 2. Players: 1. ESRB: E10+ (cartoon violence, crude humor). Evil monkeys led by Specter intend to ruin the world with their mind-numbing TV shows, and the player must stop them. The levels increase in complexity, and players — who can choose between a male and a female character — will enjoy using the monkey net, monkey cam, and monkey radar. (Rev: SLJ 7/06)

273 ● **At Home with Mrs. Hen** (3–5). 2006. 8 min. National Film Board of Canada. $99. Mrs. Hen's unappreciative eldest chick learns a lesson when she leaves him alone all day to care for his younger sibling; a wordless film with animated images and background music. (Rev: BL 1/1–15/07; LMC 2/07; SLJ 12/06)

274 🎲 **Avatar: The Last Airbender** (6–9). 2006. THQ. PlayStation 2, GameCube, Xbox, Wii. Players: 1. ESRB: E10+ (cartoon violence).

An action/role-playing game in which the player seeks to bring peace to the four nations — Air, Earth, Fire, and Water — that make up the world. Based on the Nickelodeon cartoon series. (Rev: SLJ 12/06)

275 ● **Avatar: The Last Airbender — Book 1: Water, Vol. 1** (7–12). 2006. 95 min. Paramount Home Entertainment. Closed captioned. ISBN 978-1-4157-1896-4. $16.99. Twelve-year-old Aang, a reincarnation of an ancient being, uses his powers over wind and

air to defeat evil in this anime production; includes the first four episodes of the series shown on Nickelodeon. Also available: Volumes 2 through 5. (Rev: VL 5–6/06)

276 🎲 **Batman: Justice Unbalanced** (2–5). 2003. Riverdeep. Windows, Macintosh. Players: 1. ESRB: E (mild cartoon violence). Challenging activities — which stimulate problem solving, pattern recognition, and logical thinking — are a major component of this adventure in which Batman and Robin seek treasures stolen by Penguin and Two Face. (Rev: CTR 11/03)

277 💻 **Blast to the Past** (2–5). 2007. Stone Arch Books. Windows, Macintosh. ISBN 978-1-59889-294-9. $23.95.

An interactive version of the book by Scott Nickel (Stone Arch, 2007), illustrated by Steve Harpster, that relates in graphic-novel format the adventure of two boys who travel back through time in an effort to pass a test. The audio can be turned on and off and there are sound effects and some animation, plus extras such as a glossary, facts, discussion topics, and information on the author and illustrator. (Rev: SLJ 3/08)

278 ● **The Chronicles of Narnia: The Lion, the Witch and the Wardrobe** (4–8). 2006. 132 min. Buena Vista. $29.99.

An excellent adaptation of C. S. Lewis's classic fantasy. (Rev: VL 3–4/06)

279 🎲 **DragonBall Z Sagas** (7–12). 2006. Atari. PlayStation 2, GameCube, Xbox. Players: 1–2. ESRB: T (animated blood, violence).

In this anime style game, players can choose among six heroes and then fight alien creatures and a final villain. Playing together, the two heroes cooperate to fight evil. (Rev: SLJ 6/06; CTR Spring 05)

280 🎲 **The Elder Scrolls IV: Oblivion** (11–12). Bethesda Softworks. Windows, PlayStation 3, PSP, Xbox 360. Players: 1. ESRB: M (language, sexual themes, use of alcohol, violence, blood and gore).

After the emperor of Tamriel dies, the player must join forces with other characters to find the heir to the kingdom.

⚇ YALSA Top 50 Core Recommended Collection Titles

281 🎲 **Enchanted Arms** (8–12). 2006. UBI Soft. PlayStation 3, Xbox 360. Players: 1.

ESRB: T (alcohol reference, mild fantasy violence, mild language, simulated gambling, suggestive themes).

Battle against the golems is joined by Atsuma and his friends from Yokohama Enchanter's University. As the characters become more experienced, they earn better weapons and magical abilities. Anime-style, with good graphics. (Rev: SLJ 11/06)

282 ⚙ **Flushed Away** (6–12). 2006. D3P. PlayStation 2, GameCube, Xbox. Players: 1–2. ESRB: E.

Pet mouse Roddy and sewer rat Sid star in this animated multilevel movie tie-in game played out in London's sewer system. Good for beginners who need to develop basic skills. (Rev: SLJ 1/07)

283 ⚙ **Fullmetal Alchemist: Dual Sympathy** (7–12). 2006. Destineer Studios. Nintendo DS. Players: 1. ESRB: T (blood, fantasy violence, mild language).

Play as Edward Elric the alchemist as you seek to capture the Philosopher's Stone in this single-player game based on the Cartoon Network show. (Rev: CTR 1/07)

284 ⚙ **Halo 3** (11–12). Microsoft Game Studios. Xbox 360. Players: 1–16. ESRB: M (blood and gore, mild language, violence).

Choose humans or aliens and battle it out to the end. This very popular first-person shooter is set in the future and includes many high-powered and exciting vehicles and weapons that are needed to eliminate the enemy. The last installment in the Halo trilogy.

⚇ YALSA Top 50 Core Recommended Collection Titles

285 ⚙ **Harry Potter and the Goblet of Fire** (5–12). Electronic Arts. Windows, PlayStation 2, PSP, GameCube, Nintendo DS, Game Boy Advance, Xbox. Players: 1–3. ESRB: E10+ (comic mischief, fantasy violence).

Choose to be Harry, Ron, or Hermione as they prepare to compete in the TriWizard Tournament. Players solve puzzles and use spells to gain power as they tackle challenges and progress to higher levels. (Rev: CTR 4/06)

⚇ YALSA Top 50 Core Recommended Collection Titles

286 ⚙ **Harry Potter and the Order of Phoenix** (3–12). 2007. Electronic Arts. Windows, Macintosh, PlayStation 2, PlayStation 3, PSP,

Game Boy Advance, Nintendo DS, Xbox 360, Wii. Players: 1. ESRB: E10+.

Relive the events of the book and movie as you follow clues and solve puzzles, meanwhile casting spells and exploring Hogwarts. (Rev: CTR 8/07)

287 🎬 **Howl's Moving Castle** (5–12). 2006. 119 min. Walt Disney. $29.99.

Hayao Miyazaki made this amusing and appealing animated version of Diana Wynne Jones's book about a fearful young girl who is changed into an old woman and in that disguise moves into the castle of Wizard Howl. (Rev: VL 3–4/06)

288 🎬 **Jinki: Extend, Vol. 1** (6–12). 2006. 126 min. ADV Films. ISBN 978-1-4139-1449-8. $29.98.

A 13-year-old girl is the star of this animated manga adventure set in several time periods. Aoba, a "cognate," is captured by a group that uses giant robots to fight off aliens. (Rev: SLJ 5/07)

289 ⚙ **Katamari Damacy** (3–12). Namco-Homotek. PlayStation 2. Players: 1–2. ESRB: E.

Repair the problems in the galaxy wrought by your father, the king, by rolling a *katamari* around and picking up all kinds of objects — from lawn mowers to cows to cruise ships. Compete with your fellow player to create the biggest ball.

⚇ YALSA Top 50 Core Recommended Collection Titles

290 ⚙ **Kingdom Hearts** (3–12). Square Enix, USA Inc. PlayStation 2. Players: 1. ESRB: E.

Mickey Mouse, Donald Duck, and all your favorite Disney characters are used in this role-playing game. Team up your characters and defeat villains — the Heartless and the Nobodies — with spells and weapons. There are three levels of play.

⚇ YALSA Top 50 Core Recommended Collection Titles

291 ⚙ **Kingdom Hearts II** (4–12). 2006. BVG/Square Enix. PlayStation 2. Players: 1. ESRB: E10+ (mild blood, use of alcohol, violence).

A single-player battle/exploration game in which the player guides Sora and his Final Fantasy and Disney partners through many adventures on the way to conquering the Heartless and the Nobodies. Excellent graphics and a good story line are matched by a good soundtrack. (Rev: CTR 10/06)

292 🎮 **Legend of Zelda: Collectors Edition** (3–12). Nintendo. GameCube. Players: 1. ESRB: E (fantasy violence).
A collection of classic Zelda games — *Ocarina of Time, The Legend of Zelda, The Adventure of Link,* and *Majora's Mask.* Play as Link as you battle through many different levels of great action and many foes.
☻ YALSA Top 50 Core Recommended Collection Titles

293 🎮 **Legend of Zelda: Phantom Hourglass** (3–12). 2007. Nintendo. Nintendo DS. Players: 1–2. ESRB: E.
Great visual effects and good moves with the stylus are features of this addition to the popular series, in which Link seeks to rescue Tetra. (Rev: CTR 11/07)

294 🎮 **Legend of Zelda: The Wind Waker** (3–12). Nintendo. GameCube. Players: 1–2. ESRB: E.
In this sequel to the classic Zelda series, Link defeats villains of all kinds as he explores numerous islands looking for Ganondorf, his nemesis. (Rev: CTR 5/03)
☻ YALSA Top 50 Core Recommended Collection Titles

295 🎮 **Legend of Zelda: Twilight Princess** (5–12). Nintendo. GameCube, Wii. Players: 1. ESRB: T (animated blood, fantasy violence).
Follow Link, our hero, as he sets off to avenge his fellow villagers and transforms into a wolf. Link faces many challenges in this multilayered story. (Rev: CTR 1/07)
☻ YALSA Top 50 Core Recommended Collection Titles

296 🎮 **Lord of the Rings: Battle for Middle-Earth II** (9–12). 2006. Electronic Arts. Xbox 360. Players: 1. ESRB: T (fantasy violence).
In Middle Earth, players must choose to play on the side of good or evil, and then gear up for battle, creating armies and building fortresses. (Rev: SLJ 11/06)

297 🎮 **Marvel Nemesis: Rise of the Imperfects** (7–12). 2005. Electronic Arts. PlayStation 2, GameCube, Xbox. Players: 1–2. ESRB: T (violence, blood, suggestive themes).
Spider Man, Wolverine, and the Thing are only three of the Marvel characters featured in this game that offers two modes, one a fighting game. (Rev: SLJ 10/06)

298 🎮 **Marvel Ultimate Alliance** (6–12). 2006. Activision. PlayStation 2, PlayStation 3, Xbox, Xbox 360, Wii. Players: 1–4. ESRB: T (mild language, violence).
Choose four members for your team. You can select any of the Marvel characters you've ever known. Battle your way to save the Marvel universe in this game that combines action and role playing. (Rev: SLJ 1/07; CTR 6/07)

299 🎮 **Neverwinter Nights 2** (9–12). Atari, Inc. Windows. Players: 1+. ESRB: T (alcohol reference, blood, mild language, sexual themes, violence).
Players team up to defeat the evil King of Shadows in this online role-playing game.
☻ YALSA Top 50 Core Recommended Collection Titles

300 ⬤ **Painted Tales, Volume 1: In Winter Still/Almond Blossoms** (2–6). 2006. 22 min. Auryn. PPR. $12.99.
Two imaginative stories are animated with art based on the work of Claude Monet and Vincent Van Gogh. "In Winter Still" — about Claude Monet and a mean gardener who keeps children out of the garden — is an adaptation of Oscar Wilde's "The Selfish Giant"; "Almond Blossoms" — about Vincent van Gogh and his friendship with a young girl whose mother is ill — is based on O. Henry's "The Last Leaf." (Rev: BL 4/07; SLJ 7/07)

301 🎮 **Paper Mario: The Thousand-Year Door** (3–8). Nintendo. GameCube. Players: 1. ESRB: E.
A role-playing game full of humor, in which Mario — who can use his paper form to great advantage — searches for Princess Peach and valuable treasure.
☻ YALSA Top 50 Core Recommended Collection Titles

302 🎮 **Pokémon Colosseum** (1–8). Nintendo. GameCube. Players: 1–4. ESRB: E.
Build your Pokémon team and defeat the criminals of the Orre region in this program that features both story and battle modes.
☻ YALSA Top 50 Core Recommended Collection Titles

303 ♦ **Pokémon Diamond** (2–12). 2007. Nintendo. Nintendo DS. Players: 1+. ESRB: E.
In the region of Sinnoh, the player — boy or girl — aims to capture and train Pokémon while defeating the evil Team Galactic. The player solves clues and wins battles to become a Pokémon champion. This companion to *Pokémon Pearl* allows play against others in the room or online, as well as the import of Pokémon from previous games. (Rev: CTR 5/07)

304 ● **Sister Princess, Episodes 1–26** (5–8). 2006. 5 discs. 90 min. ADV Films. ISBN 978-1-4139-1363-7. $49.98.
Wataru Minakami, a talented middle-school student in Tokyo, suddenly finds himself attending Stargazer's Hill School on a remote island. And here, it turns out, reside his 12 princess sisters! (Rev: SLJ 12/06)

305 ♦ **Soul Calibur III** (9–12). 2005. Namco. PlayStation 2. Players: 1–2. ESRB: T (violence, suggestive themes).
Players can customize their characters to search a mythical world for two swords — a holy one, Soul Calibur, and an evil one, Soul Edge. Single players can enjoy the "Tales of Souls," which presents characters' stories with action game play sequences. "Chronicles of the Sword" offers progression through 20 levels, and "World Competition" and "Soul Arena" allow the player to battle against the computer. *Soul Calibur IV*, for PlayStation 3 and Xbox 360, was released in July 2008. (Rev: SLJ 10/06)

306 ♦ **SpongeBob SquarePants: Lights, Camera, Pants!** (3–8). 2005. THQ. PlayStation 2, GameCube, Xbox. Players: 1–4. ESRB: E (mild cartoon violence).
SpongeBob, Patrick, Sandy, Mr. Krabs, and Squidward compete for a part in "New Adventures of Mermaid Man and Barnacle Bob," playing 30 mini-games. This game is best for multiple players. (Rev: SLJ 2/07; CTR Winter 05)

307 ♦ **Suikoden V** (9–12). 2006. Konami. PlayStation 2. Players: 1. ESRB: T (violence, mild language, partial nudity, use of alcohol).
There has been a rebellion in the town of Lordlake and the queen of Falena is behaving oddly. Characters including the prince (the player) and the queen's sister set out to inves-

tigate, using magic and their skills in battle. (Rev: SLJ 12/06)

308 ♦ **Super Princess Peach** (1–6). 2006. Nintendo. Nintendo DS. Players: 1. ESRB: E (comic mischief).
This time the Princess has to fight through colorful and magical worlds to save Mario from the evil Bowser. (Rev: CTR 2/06)

309 ♦ **Tales of Symphonia** (8–12). Namco Hometek. Windows, PlayStation 2, GameCube, Xbox. Players: 1–4. ESRB: T (fantasy violence, language, suggestive themes).
Save the planet of Sylvarant by combining powers with other characters and defeating enemies; a role-playing game with good graphics and narrative. (Rev: SLJ 12/06)
♟ YALSA Top 50 Core Recommended Collection Titles

310 ● **Time Warp Trio: Passport to Adventure** (4–6). 2005. 75 min. Series: Time Warp Trio. WGBH Boston. ISBN 978-1-4210-1344-2. $14.98.
The Time Warp Trio (three 10-year-old boys from Brooklyn created by author Jon Scieszka and illustrator Lane Smith) open their magical book and travel to the past to have educational adventures with Blackbeard ("The Not-So-Jolly Roger"), with explorer Leif Erikson ("Viking It and Liking It"), and with a queen in Colonial Africa ("Jinga All the Way"); viewers learn a lot in the process. (Rev: VL 11–12/06)

311 ● **The Toy Castle: Twinkle Twinkle** (K–2). 2006. 90 min. Questar. ISBN 978-1-59464-226-5. $14.99.
Dancers from the Royal Winnipeg Ballet play toy characters come to life in 12 child-friendly stories created by Neil and Katherine Jeans. Also available: *The Toy Castle: Beautiful Ballerina* and *The Toy Castle: Birthday Bash*. (Rev: SLJ 9/06; VL 9–10/06)

312 ♦ **Transformers: The Game** (8–12). 2007. Activision. Windows, PlayStation 2, PlayStation 3, Xbox 360, Wii. Players: 1. ESRB: T (fantasy violence).
Based on the Dreamworks film, this fairly violent game allows the player to choose between saving Earth (as an Autobot) or destroying it (as a Decepticon). The robots can choose between a number of weapons, as well as buildings and vehicles, and there are

some racing elements. A Nintendo DS version is also available. (Rev: CTR 9/07)

313 ⬦ **Valkyrie Profile 2: Silmeria** (9–12). 2006. Square Inix. PlayStation 2. Players: 1. ESRB: T (fantasy violence, suggestive themes, use of alcohol, language).

In a medieval kingdom, a Valkyrie named Silmeria has been imprisoned in the body of a princess named Alicia, threatening the princess's survival. (Rev: SLJ 12/06)

Historical Fiction and Foreign Lands

Asia and the Pacific

314 ● **Cromartie High School, Episodes 1–26** (9–12). 2006. 330 min. ADV Films. ISBN 978-1-4139-1402-3. $44.98.

An animé-style spoof of life in a Japanese high school. Viewers will be fascinated by the inside look at Japanese culture. (Rev: LMC 8–9/07; SLJ 1/07)

315 ● **Ping Pong** (7–12). 2007. 105 min. VIZ Media. $29.95.

An animated manga in which two Japanese boys, both on their school's table-tennis team, make important choices about their lives. Viewers will enjoy the story and the insight into this aspect of Japanese culture. (Rev: SLJ 9/07)

United States

POST WORLD WAR II UNITED STATES (1945–)

316 ● **Summer's End** (4–6). 2005. 33 min. Luminous. ISBN 978-0-9773287-2-7. $14.98. Produced in 1986, this drama newly available on DVD is set in 1948 Arkansas. It focuses on Kathy, an independent tomboy whose mother pushes her to conform. (Rev: BL 5/06)

Twentieth-Century Wars

WORLD WAR II AND THE HOLOCAUST

317 ● **Carrie's War** (4–9). 2006. 90 min. WGBH Boston. Closed captioned. ISBN 978-1-59375-586-7. $19.95.

A live-action adaptation of Nina Bawden's classic story about 14-year-old Carrie's evac-

uation to Wales during World War II. (Rev: BL 10/1/06*; LMC 2/07; VL 9–10/06)

� ALA ALSC Notable Children's Videos 2007

318 ● **Mr. Christmas** (3–5). 2005. 56 min. Luminous Films. ISBN 978-0-9773287-0-3. $14.98.

In small-town Arkansas in the early 1940s, a father does his best to give his children the presents they want. (Rev: BL 2/15/06; SLJ 6/06)

319 ● **Showa Shinzan** (6–9). 2004. 13 min. National Film Board of Canada. $129.

Archival film and drawings with elements of traditional puppetry are blended with computer animation in this beautiful film about a young Japanese girl's experiences during World War II. (Rev: BL 3/15/04; SLJ 8/03; VL 9–10/03)

� ALA ALSC Notable Children's Videos 2004

Humor

320 ● **The Danish Poet** (9–12). 2006. 15 min. National Film Board of Canada. $129.

Narrated by Liv Ullmann, this brief animated feature is a humorous, philosophical love story about a Danish poet, Kasper, who is searching for meaning in life. (Rev: VL 5–6/07)

� YALSA 2007 Selected Videos and DVDs

321 ● **The Hungry Squid** (2–8). 2003. 14 min. National Film Board of Canada. $129.

A clever, humorous tale about Dorothy Sue Ann's family and homework tribulations, enhanced by great visual effects. (Rev: VL 11–12/02; VOYA 4/03)

322 ● **Wallace and Gromit: The Curse of the Were-Rabbit** (K–12). 2006. 85 min. DreamWorks. $29.99.

Claymation characters Wallace and dog Gromit are having great success with their humane pest-control company "Anti-Pesto" when a monster rabbit threatens the entries for the Giant Vegetable Competition. (Rev: VL 3–4/06)

Mysteries, Thrillers, and Horror Stories

323 ☖ **Castlevania: Portrait of Ruin** (8–12). 2006. Konami. Nintendo DS. Players: 1–2. ESRB: T (blood and gore, mild language, suggestive themes, violence).
In World War II, battle a plan to resurrect Dracula.

324 ☖ **Eternal Darkness: Sanity's Requiem** (11–12). Nintendo. GameCube. Players: 1. ESRB: M (blood and gore, violence).
Investigate your grandfather's death and crack a mystery while playing the roles of many different historical people.
☗ YALSA Top 50 Core Recommended Collection Titles

325 ☗ **Laundry Blues: The Case of the Missing Necklace** (7–10). 2006. 17 min. Learning Learning ZoneXpress. PPR. Closed captioned. ISBN 978-1-57175-228-4. $49.95.
Viewers learn the ins and outs of doing laundry while watching an entertaining mystery about a missing necklace. Teacher's guide included. (Rev: SLJ 5/07; VL 1–2/07)

326 ☗ **Monster** (10–12). 2005. 10 min. Flickerfest. A$78.
This short and scary Australian film portrays a mother and son struggling against a sinister presence.
☗ YALSA 2007 Selected Videos and DVDs

327 ☖ **Monster House** (6–12). 2006. THQ. PlayStation 2, GameCube, Game Boy Advance, Nintendo DS. Players: 1. ESRB: E10+ (comic mischief, fantasy violence).
In this mild movie tie-in, players work to save trick-or-treaters from a haunted house. (Rev: SLJ 11/06; CTR 8/06)

328 ☖ **Nancy Drew: Curse of Blackmoor Manor** (5–10). 2007. Brighter Minds. Windows. Players: 1–2. ESRB: E.
Nancy must find out what is ailing her friend Linda, now living in an ancient house in England. Players seek clues and solve puzzles, choosing between two levels of play. (Rev: SLJ 11/07; CTR 9/07)

329 ☖ **Nancy Drew: Secret of the Old Clock** (5–12). 2005. Her Interactive. Windows. Players: 1. ESRB: E.

Puzzles and challenges abound as the player and Nancy try to help friend Emily hold onto her inn in this well-designed adventure set in a 1930 farming town. (Rev: CTR 2/05)

330 ☖ **Nancy Drew: The Creature of Kapu Cave** (5–12). 2006. Series: Nancy Drew. Her Interactive. Windows. Players: 1. ESRB: E (mild violence). $19.99.
Nancy and the Hardy Boys solve two interlocking mysteries in this adventure-filled program set in Hawaii. Players interact with the characters, solve puzzles, design necklaces, snorkel for shells, and learn a little about entomology. (Rev: CTR 11/06)
☗ ALA Great Interactive Software for Kids Fall 2007

331 ☖ **Psychonauts** (8–12). 2006. Budcat. PlayStation 2, Xbox. Players: 1. ESRB: T (crude humor, cartoon violence, language).
Raz is at summer camp and his bunkmates are disappearing. Raz sets out to unravel this mystery and must solve a number of puzzles along the way, earning merit badges as he goes. (Rev: SLJ 6/06)

332 ☗ **The Ruby in the Smoke** (7–12). 2007. 90 min. WGBH Boston. Closed captioned. ISBN 978-1-59375-725-0. $19.95.
Sally Lockhart must solve the mystery of her father's disappearance and the meaning of the "seven blessings" in this "Masterpiece Theatre" film set in Victorian England. (Rev: BL 8/07; VL 7–8/07)

333 ☖ **The Secrets of Da Vinci: The Forbidden Manuscript** (5–10). 2006. Tri Synergy/Nobilis. Windows. Players: 1–5. ESRB: E10+.
Players dive into a world of Renaissance mystery as apprentice Valdo searches for a valuable da Vinci notebook; key features are the historical accuracy, graphics, sophisticated puzzles, and ethical debates.
☗ ALA Notable Children's Software 2007

334 ☖ **Snapshot Adventures: Secret of Bird Island** (3–12). 2007. Large Animal Games. Windows. $19.95.
Your naturalist grandfather is missing and you set off to find him, armed with his camera. Along the way you photograph different birds to add to your journal and can earn various tools, such as a zoom lens, to help with this task.

⚇ ALA Great Interactive Software for Kids Fall 2007

Science Fiction

---

335 ⚅ **Beyond Good and Evil** (8–12). Ubisoft. Windows, PlayStation 2, GameCube, Xbox. Players: 1. ESRB: T13+ (comic mischief, violence).

Hillys, a planet in the distant future, is under attack. A reporter, Jade, seeks answers to the secrets of her past while defeating many enemies; players journey through high-tech cities and fantastic landscapes while seeking clues.
⚇ YALSA Top 50 Core Recommended Collection Titles

336 ⚅ **Final Fantasy VII** (8–12). Sony Computer Entertainment. PlayStation. Players: 1. ESRB: T (comic mischief, mild animated violence, mild language).

A well-produced sequel to the classic sci-fi favorite, *Final Fantasy VII* is a spell-filled, weapon-thrashing adventure. Build and control your team of heroes as you fight the opposition. Also recommended: *Final Fantasy XII*.
⚇ YALSA Top 50 Core Recommended Collection Titles

337 ⚅ **LEGO Star Wars: The Complete Saga** (K–12). 2007. Lucas Arts. PlayStation 3, Nintendo DS, Xbox 360, Wii. Players: 1–2. ESRB: E10+ (cartoon violence).

Players work together to solve problems as they save the universe from the evil empire in this game, which can be played by a single player, that features 160 LEGO Star Wars characters and scenes from all the movies. (Rev: CTR 12/07)

338 ⚅ **LEGO Star Wars II: The Original Trilogy** (5–12). LucasArts. Windows, PlayStation 2, PSP, GameCube, Xbox, Xbox 360. Players: 1–2. ESRB: E10+ (cartoon violence and crude humor).

Players can choose between LEGO characters with different skills in this 24-level humorous game based on the Star Wars trilogy, in which players work to stop Darth Vader's threat to the universe. One player can play alone; two players can play collaboratively. (Rev: SLJ 11/06; CTR 6/06)

⚇ YALSA Top 50 Core Recommended Collection Titles; ALA ALSC Notable Children's Software 2007

339 ⚅ **Metroid Prime 3: Corruption** (8–12). Nintendo. Wii. Players: 1. ESRB: T (animated blood, violence).

Samus, equipped with many new weapons, must defeat Space Pirates in this space adventure sequel.
⚇ YALSA Top 50 Core Recommended Collection Titles

340 ⚅ **Star Wars: Battlefront II** (6–12). 2006. Lucas Arts. PlayStation 2, Xbox. Players: 1–4; online play available. ESRB: T (violence, mild language).

Players progress through increasingly complex characters as they become more skillful in getting rid of their opponents in many scenarios that will be familiar to *Star Wars* fans. There is space combat, and players can become Jedi warriors and fight with lightsabers. (Rev: SLJ 6/06; CTR 6/06)

341 ⚅ **Super Mario Galaxy** (3–8). Nintendo. Wii. Players: 1–2. ESRB: E.

An outer space often-gravity-defying adventure in which Mario must again save Princess Peach.
⚇ YALSA Top 50 Core Recommended Collection Titles

Sports

---

342 ◕ **Jump In** (5–8). 2007. 85 min. Buena Vista Home Entertainment. $26.99.

A Disney Channel original movie about amateur teen boxer Izzy Daniels (played by Corbin Bleu), who reluctantly joins his friend Mary's double Dutch team and finds that he has a passion for competitive jump roping. (Rev: BL 5/1/07; VL 7–8/07)
⚇ Andrew Carnegie Medal for Excellence in Children's Video 2008

343 ◕ **The Prince of Tennis, Vol 1: Episodes 1–13** (5–12). 2007. 3 discs. 300 min. Viz Media. ISBN 978-1-4215-1416-1. $39.98.

An animated manga-like series about a talented young Japanese tennis player who takes on toughs and big kids and comes out on top every time. (Rev: SLJ 7/07)

Poetry

Geographical Regions

Europe

GREAT BRITAIN AND IRELAND

344 ⊗ **Beowulf** (9–12). 2006. 98 min. Koch Vision. ISBN 978-1-4172-2969-7. $29.99.
Benjamin Bagby, the director of medieval-music ensemble Sequentia, sings the first 1,062 lines of the epic poem in Old English, accompanied by a re-creation of a 7th-century instrument. Perfect for high-school English literature classes studying the poem, this presentation includes optional English subtitles. (Rev: VL 5–6/07)

United States

345 ⊗ **Ellington Was Not a Street** (3–5). 2005. 12 min. Weston Woods. ISBN 978-0-439-77573-1. $59.95.
In this adaptation of Ntozake Shange's 2004 picture book, the author — as a young girl — absorbs the atmosphere of her home, a haven for African American legends including Paul Robeson, W. E. B. Du Bois, and Dizzy Gillespie; Ellington's music, Phylicia Rashad's reading, and Kadir Nelson's illustrations make this a rich offering. (Rev: BL 11/1/05; SLJ 11/05; VL 1–2/06)
⚜ ALA ALSC Notable Children's Videos 2006

Folklore and Fairy Tales

General and Miscellaneous

346 🌐 **The Bully Billy Goat and Other Stories** (K–3). 2006. 40 min. Storyteller. $15.

Children gathered in a library enjoy hearing folktales from around the world: "The Bully Billy Goat," "The Pancake," "The Bellybutton Bird," "Drakestail," "The Village of No Cats," and "The Poor Little Bug on the Wall." Storyteller Priscilla Howe uses puppets to add to the presentation, which incorporates interactive elements. (Rev: SLJ 5/07)

347 🖰 **Tales Online** (K–12). Tales Unlimited, Inc.

www.talesunlimited.com/

An easily searchable database of hundreds of folktales, fairy tales, myths, legends, sagas, and fables from cultures around the world. Sources include journal articles and archival materials as well as published volumes of tales.

Geographical Regions

Africa

348 🌐 **Mabela the Clever** (K–5). 2006. 9 min. Nutmeg Media. ISBN 978-1-933938-21-9. $49.95.

An award-winning adaptation of Margaret Read MacDonald's 2000 book, set in West Africa, in which a clever mouse outwits a crafty cat. Teacher's guide included. (Rev: SLJ 10/06)

🏆 ALA ALSC Notable Children's Videos 2007

Asia and the Middle East

349 🌐 **Eyes of the Wise** (1–6). 2006. 59 min. Eth-Noh-Tec (dist. by AV Café). $20.

Storytellers present seven Asian folktales: "Heaven and Hell," "The Man Who Planted Onions," "Willow Tree," "The Bluebird and the Magic Pond," "Bird of Happiness," "The Original Goldfinger," and "Monkey Moon." (Rev: SLJ 2/07)

350 🌐 **Fools, Frogs and Folktales** (1–6). 2006. 64 min. Eth-Noh-Tec (dist. by AV Café). $20.

Six Asian folktales — "The New Ghost," "The Big Liar," "The Terrible Leak," "Pilandok's Magic," "Mr. and Mrs. Miser," and "Seven Silly Fellows" — are told through movement and voice by two performers. (Rev: SLJ 4/07)

North America

UNITED STATES

351 🌐 **John Henry** (2–5). 2006. 23 min. Series: Greatest American Tall Tales and Legends. Schlessinger Media (dist. by Library Video

Company). PPR. Closed captioned. ISBN 978-1-4171-0213-6. $29.95.

John Henry's legendary feats are placed in historical context; the animated production includes discussion questions and activities. Part of a 10-volume series that also covers Davy Crockett, Paul Bunyan, and Pecos Bill. Teacher's guide included. (Rev: BL 3/15/06; VL 5–6/06)

South and Central America

352 Mind Me Good Now! (K–3). 2005. 9 min. National Film Board of Canada. PPR. $129.

Tina and Dalby foil the evil plans of Mama Zee in this animated Caribbean take on the Hansel and Gretel tale based on Lynette Comissiong's 1997 picture book. Study guide included. (Rev: BL 3/15/06; VL 5–6/06)

Language and Communication

Signs and Symbols

353 ❖ **Sign-A-Lot: The Big Surprise** (K–3). 2005. 30 min. Sign-A-Lot. Closed captioned. $19.95.

Viewers learn some 80 signs as the See Me Sign Kids demonstrate how useful sign language is in all sorts of situations. (Rev: VL 7/06)

354 ❖ **Signs and Stories with Mr. C, Vol. 1** (K–4). 2004. 60 min. RainRunner. ISBN 978-0-9758544-0-2. $24.95.

A sign-language tutorial presented by Randall Clarkson, a sign-language teacher and storyteller, covering numbers and the alphabet; includes three stories and a review game. (Rev: BL 12/15/04)

Words and Languages

355 ⊛ **After School Chinese: Level 1** (4–8). 2002. 8 discs. 120 min. Asia for Kids (dist. by Master Communications). ISBN 978-1-888194-73-9. $199.95.

This comprehensive introduction to Mandarin Chinese features an American host and Chinese children in everyday activities; viewers can select among vocabulary, dialogue, and sentence pattern options. Includes two audio CDs and a student book. (Rev: BL 5/15/06; VL 7/06)

356 ⊛ **Find Your Voice** (9–12). 2006. 30 min. In the Mix. PPR. ISBN 978-1-931843-99-7. $69.95.

A group of students learn how to present themselves and their opinions through a theater program presented by communication coach Gail Noppe-Brandon. (Rev: VL 1–2/07)

357 ⊛ **Word Town: Basic English Vocabulary** (3–10). 2005. 35 min. Vocalis (dist. by MidWest Tape). ISBN 978-1-932653-55-7. $29.95.

More than 400 commonly used English nouns are introduced for ESL students in this simple tour of a typical town; also available in a Spanish version, *Word Town: Las Palabras del Pueblo*. (Rev: SLJ 1/06)

Writing and the Media

General and Miscellaneous

358 📀 **Becoming the Author of Your Life** (3–8). 2006. 78 min. Ben Mikaelsen. $24.99. Author Ben Mikaelsen describes his youth in Bolivia, his family's move to Minnesota, and his problems with bullies before going on to talk about his books and to urge young people to view their lives as stories that they can control. (Rev: SLJ 10/06)

359 📀 **Plagiarism: What Do You Value?** (9–12). 2007. 27 min. VEA. $89.95. This film from Australia discusses why students plagiarize and why it is wrong. Viewers will learn what constitutes plagiarism and how to avoid it using research skills and techniques. (Rev: SLJ 7/07; VL 9–10/07)

360 💻 **Stationery Studio** (K–5). 2006. FableVision. Windows, Macintosh. $69.95. An updated version of the award-winning program that offers many inventive stationery choices and encourages children to write and create.
🎖 ALA Notable Children's Software 2007

361 💻 **Storybook Creator: Charlotte's Web** (2–6). 2006. Planet Wide Media (dist. by AV Café). Windows. $29.99. Students will enjoy writing stories based on *Charlotte's Web* and illustrating them using clip art and other graphics; unfortunately, the multi-step installation limits this software's usefulness in schools. (Rev: SLJ 7/07)

Books and Publishing

362 💻 **Books by You: Create and Publish Your Own Books!** (4–8). 2006. Knowledge Adventure. Windows, Macintosh. $19.99. Students can produce professional-looking books with this software that guides them through the writing and publishing experience using customizable plots. Users can select from four stories and design the setting, characters, and other details. Then they can add their own illustrations or choose from a menu. Prompts and questions from the narrator help "authors" along. (Rev: LMC 8–9/07; SLJ 7/07)
🎖 Children's Technology Review Editor's Choice for Excellence in Design 2006

363 💻 **Comic Book Creator** (6–12). 2007. Planetwide Games (dist. by AV Café). Windows. $29.99. A lot of fun for students with artistic abilities as well as those who can't draw at all. Using templates, they can add art (from online sources, the CD's collection, or their computer) and embellish their stories with speech balloons, graphics, and so on. (Rev: SLJ 9/07)

Biography, Memoirs, Etc.

Adventurers and Explorers

364 ⊗ **Wings of Their Own** (10–12). 2006. 83 min. Make Believe TV. ISBN 978-0-9770218-0-2. $24.95.

An inspiring overview of women flyers, from Amelia Earhart and Bessie Coleman on through World War II pilots and today's astronauts, with interviews, archival footage, and in-flight film. (Rev: BL 8-06; SLJ 1/06)

Individual

COLUMBUS, CHRISTOPHER

365 ⊗ **Christopher Columbus** (6–12). 2000. 23 min. Series: Explorers of the World. Schlessinger Media. PPR. Closed captioned. $39.95.

Columbus tells two teen interviewers about his voyages and their successes and failures, defending some of the mistakes he made. Part of an extensive series that also includes *The American Frontier, Cortés and Pizarro, English Explorers, Ferdinand Magellan, French Explorers, Henry Hudson, History of Exploration, Lewis and Clark, Marco Polo, Portuguese Explorers, Spanish Explorers,* and *The Vikings.* (Rev: BL 12/1/00; VL 9–10/06)

MCAULIFFE, CHRISTA

366 ⊗ **Christa McAuliffe: Reach for the Stars** (7–12). 2005. 75 min. Traipsing Thru Films. $100 (public libraries w/PPR); $200 (schools).

The story of the teacher who died in the *Challenger* disaster is movingly told using home movie and documentary footage, personal photographs, and interviews with family, friends, and colleagues. (Rev: BL 6/1–15/06; SLJ 7/06; VL 7/06)

Artists, Authors, Composers, and Entertainers

Collective

367 ⌨ **Authors4Teens** (8–12). Greenwood Publishing.
www.authors4teens.com
Lengthy interviews with authors who write for young adults explore their lives, interests, and so forth, and are accompanied by bibliographies and reviews. Excellent material for reports.
🏅 ALA Notable Computer Software for Children 2004

Artists and Architects

BENTLEY, SNOWFLAKE

368 💿 **Snowflake Bentley** (1–5). 2004. 16 min. Weston Woods. ISBN 978-0-439-73458-5. $29.95.
An excellent adaptation of Jacqueline Briggs Martin's Caldecott-winning book (Houghton, 1998) about the nature photographer who greatly admired snowflakes. (Rev: BL 5/15/04; SLJ 10/04; VL 7–8/04)
🏅 ALA ALSC Notable Children's Videos 2004

DA VINCI, LEONARDO

369 💿 **Da Vinci and the Code He Lived By** (9–12). 2005. 91 min. The History Channel (dist. by A&E Home Video). PPR. Closed captioned. ISBN 978-0-7670-8787-2. $24.95.
This biography emphasizes da Vinci's struggle to overcome his illegitimacy and focuses on his strong work ethic, using reenactments, commentary by scholars, and narration. (Rev: BL 4/1/06)

DUCKWORTH, RUTH

370 💿 **Ruth Duckworth: A Life in Clay** (7–12). 2007. 30 min. Crystal Productions. ISBN 978-1-562905-52-1. $14.95.
A fascinating look at the life and work of an artist whose experiences have affected the art she produces. (Rev: SLJ 10/07)

MICHELANGELO

371 💿 **Getting to Know the World's Greatest Artists: Michelangelo** (K–8). 2005. 25 min. Getting to Know. $29.95.
Using animation and live footage, this production blends humor — Michelangelo is a larger-than-life cartoon character — and a serious look at the artist's sculptures, frescoes, and majestic ceilings. (Rev: SLJ 1/06)

QUEZADA, JUAN

372 💿 **The Pot That Juan Built** (1–5). 2004. 17 min. Weston Woods. ISBN 978-0-439-73457-8. $59.95.
This iconographic film of the 2004 book by Nancy Andrews-Goebel, illustrated by David Diaz, adds yet another dimension to the story

of Mexican potter Juan Quezada. (Rev: BL 3/1/05; SLJ 7/05)

☻ ALA ALSC Notable Children's Videos 2005

TABACK, SIMMS

373 ☻ **Getting to Know Simms Taback** (3–5). 2005. 15 min. Weston Woods. ISBN 978-0-439-82821-5. $59.95.

Children's book illustrator Taback talks about his well-known collages and cutouts, about his philosophy of catering both to children and the adult reader, and about his own childhood. (Rev: SLJ 4/06)

WARHOL, ANDY

374 ☻ **Andy Warhol** (4–6). 2007. 24 min. Series: Getting to Know the World's Greatest Artists. Getting to Know. $29.95.

An animated Andy Warhol describes his childhood, life, and career as a pop artist in New York City and shows reproductions of his work. (Rev: BL 11/1/07; SLJ 8/7)

☻ ALA ALSC Notable Children's Videos 2008

375 ☻ **Dropping In on Andy Warhol** (4–6). 2006. 18 min. Crystal $29.95.

An animated program featuring Puffin, a bird reporter, who visits Andy Warhol and gets a close-up look at the artist's work and an overview of his life. (Rev: BL 7/06; SLJ 7/06)

Authors

CUSHMAN, KAREN

376 ☻ **Good Conversation! A Talk with Karen Cushman** (4–8). 2006. 21 min. Tim Podell Productions. ISBN 978-1-58543-182-3. $59.98.

The author of *The Midwife's Apprentice* and *Catherine, Called Birdy* discusses her personal life, her interests and inspirations, and offers advice to viewers who enjoy writing. (Rev: SLJ 7/07)

DICKINSON, EMILY

377 ☻ **Emily Dickinson: "A Certain Slant of Light"** (7–12). 2006. 30 min. Rubicon Productions (dist. by Monterey Home Video). $19.95.

Originally released in 1977, this biography of the poet is hosted by Julie Harris. (Rev: SLJ 10/06)

FLEISCHMAN, SID

378 ☻ **Good Conversation! A Talk with Sid Fleischman** (3–8). 2005. 21 min. Tim Podell Productions. ISBN 978-1-58543-174-8. $59.98.

Fans of the Newbery Medal winner will enjoy this opportunity to meet him and hear his answers to many of their own questions. (Rev: SLJ 4/06)

SHAKESPEARE, WILLIAM

379 ☻ **Shakespeare Works!** (7–12). 2007. 46 min. KJ Films Ltd. (dist. by Landmark Media). $195.

Actors emphasize the down-to-earth aspects of Shakepeare's life and times in this light overview presented by wise-cracking Professor Avon Stratford and his female sidekick Dina. Students will find out why Shakespeare's plays have been popular through the ages and across cultures. Plays and scenes are compared to modern-day movies and TV shows to help students see the universal appeal. (Rev: SLJ 8/07)

Composers

MOZART, WOLFGANG AMADEUS

380 ☻ **Mozartballs** (11–12). 2007. 54 min. Prod. by Rhombus Media (dist. by Bullfrog Films). ISBN 978-1-59458-385-8. $250 (Rental: $85).

Mozart and his achievements are introduced through five contemporary Mozart enthusiasts: an astronaut, a teacher, a computer programmer, and a lesbian couple. The levels of obsession vary, but all of the Mozart aficionados seen here could be called eccentric. (Rev: BL 6/1–15/07)

Contemporary and Historical Americans

Collective

381 ❖ **So You Want to Be President?** (1–7). 2003. 27 min. Weston Woods. ISBN 978-1-55592-604-5. $59.95.
A delightful, lively compendium of facts about the presidency and the presidents covering such topics as favorite sports, appearance, pets, musical abilities, ages, and personalities. Narrated by Stockard Channing. (Rev: BL 3/15/03; LMC 1/03; SLJ 8/04; VL 9–10/02)
♟ ALA ALSC Notable Children's Videos 2003; Andrew Carnegie Medal for Excellence in Children's Video 2003

Civil and Human Rights Leaders

MORRIS, ESTHER

382 ❖ **I Could Do That! Esther Morris Gets Women the Vote** (2–4). 2006. 16 min. Weston Woods. Closed captioned. ISBN 978-0-439-90569-5. $59.95.
An adaptation of the 2005 book by Linda Arms White that emphasizes Morris's determination as she fought to win women the vote in Wyoming Territory and went on to become the first woman in the United States to hold a political office. (Rev: BL 3/1/07; LMC 8–9/07; SLJ 1/07)

PARKS, ROSA

383 ❖ **Rosa** (3–5). 2007. 14 min. Weston Woods. ISBN 978-0-545-04257-4. $59.95.
The award-winning picture book by Nikki Giovanni, illustrated by Bryan Collier (Holt, 2005), is carried over to the screen in this iconographic treatment. (Rev: BL 4/1/08*; SLJ 5/13/08; VL 7–8/08)
♟ ALA ALSC Notable Children's Videos 2008

Presidents and Their Families

ADAMS, JOHN AND ABIGAIL

384 ❖ **John and Abigail Adams** (9–12). 2005. 120 min. Series: The American Experience. PBS Video. Closed captioned. ISBN 978-1-4157-1690-8. $24.99 ($54.95 w/PPR).
With dramatic reenactments, commentary from experts, and on-location footage, this production draws on the Adamses' prolific writings to create a portrait of the couple and the era in which they lived. (Rev: BL 6/1–15/06)

LINCOLN, ABRAHAM

385 ❖ **Lincoln** (9–12). 2005. 140 min. The History Channel (dist. by A&E Home Video). PPR. Closed captioned. ISBN 978-0-7670-8801-5. $24.95.
Lincoln's character and struggles with depression are the focus of this two-part documentary that also covers his career and per-

sonal relationships. (Rev: BL 6/1/06; VL 5–6/06)

REAGAN, RONALD

386 ❸ **Ronald Reagan and the Cold War** (9–12). 2006. 33 min. Series: Decisions That Shook the World. Discovery School. ISBN 978-1-58380-557-2. $69.95.
Viewers will find out what the Cold War was, what happened during this time in history, and what ended the Cold War. Reagan's role in relations with the Soviet Union is covered, with much footage from the time period. Teacher's guide included. (Rev: SLJ 2/07)

ROOSEVELT, FRANKLIN D.

387 ❸ **Franklin Roosevelt and World War II** (7–12). 2006. 31 min. Discovery School. ISBN 978-1-59380-558-6. $69.95.
The emphasis here is on the prewar period from 1939 to the Japanese attack on Pearl Harbor. Viewers will come to understand what led the United States to enter World War II and why FDR is one of our country's most-admired presidents. (Rev: SLJ 1/07)

ROOSEVELT, THEODORE

388 ❸ **TR: The Story of Theodore Roosevelt** (9–12). 1996. 225 min. Series: The American Experience. PBS Home Video. Closed captioned. $24.99.
Narrated by Jason Robards, this life of Theodore Roosevelt — newly available on DVD — is a compelling and thorough profile and includes commentary by historians including David McCullough. (Rev: BL 6/1–15/97; SLJ 6/97; VL 3/97)

TRUMAN, HARRY S

389 ❸ **Truman** (10–12). 1997. 260 min. Series: The American Experience. PBS Paramount. Closed captioned. $29.95 ($79.95 w/PPR).
Narrated by *Truman* biographer David McCullough, this excellent profile of the former president is now available on DVD. (Rev: VL 3/98)

WASHINGTON, GEORGE

390 ❸ **George Washington** (1–4). 2007. 16 min. Getting to Know. $59.95.
This entertaining look at the life of George Washington, who is shown as an animated character, describes his role in many historic moments and how he became the first president. (Rev: BL 9/15/07; SLJ 10/07)

391 ❸ **Pursuit of Honor: The Rise of George Washington** (10–12). 2006. 85 min. Paladin. ISBN 978-0-9711685-6-5. $19.95.
This program goes beyond hagiography to reveal the humanity of our first president as he rose from soldier to commander of the Revolutionary Army. Reenactments at historic sites lend realism to the presentation. Includes teacher's guide. (Rev: SLJ 5/07)

Other Government and Public Figures

FRANKLIN, BENJAMIN

392 ❸ **Benjamin Franklin** (4–8). 2002. 23 min. Series: Inventors of the World. Schlessinger Media (dist. by Library Video Company). PPR. Closed captioned. ISBN 978-1-57225-457-2. $39.95.
Newly available on DVD, this biography focuses on Franklin's role as an inventor, using dramatic re-creations, archival films, photographs, and drawings. Teacher's guide included. (Rev: VL 7/06)

393 ❸ **Multimedia Classroom, American History, Vol. 1, Lesson 4: Benjamin Franklin** (9–12). 2006. 100 min. A&E Television Networks. ISBN 978-0-7670-9043-8. $24.95.
A frank and well-researched assessment of Franklin's life and accomplishments, with discussion of his relationships with his wife and with other women. (Rev: SLJ 11/06)

394 ❸ **Now and Ben: The Modern Inventions of Benjamin Franklin** (2–5). 2007. 13 min. Spoken Arts. ISBN 978-0-8045-8055-7. $50.
Did you know that Franklin came up with the idea for daylight savings time? That bifocals were his idea? He even invented a new musical instrument and a better rocking chair. This film of the book by Gene Barretta will give readers a new respect for an important figure in American history. (Rev: SLJ 10/07)

HENRY, PATRICK

395 ◕ **Patrick Henry: Quest for Freedom** (3–6). 2007. 35 min. Series: History's Heroes. American Animation Studios. ISBN 978-0-9796681-0-4. $39.95.

A friendly animated eagle named Boomer takes viewers through Henry's life and accomplishments, explaining the significance of his "Give me liberty or give me death" speech. (Rev: LMC 1/08; SLJ 11/07)

LILI'UOKALANI

396 ◕ **Hawaii's Last Queen** (9–12). 1997. 60 min. Series: The American Experience. PBS Home Video. $19.95.

This life of Lili'uokalani, which uses clear narrative and vintage footage and photographs, is newly available on DVD. (Rev: SLJ 1/98)

Miscellaneous Persons

HADDOCK, DORIS

397 ◕ **Granny D. Goes to Washington** (7–12). 2007. 27 min. Solday Productions (dist. by Bullfrog Films). Closed captioned. ISBN 978-1-59458-625-5. $195 (Rental: $45).

Viewers will meet a very determined woman who in 1999 walked across America in an effort to prompt changes in campaign financing. She was 89 at the time. At 94, she ran for the senate in New Hampshire. Students will be inspired by her actions and will see how slowly the wheels of government turn. (Rev: SLJ 9/07)

POCAHONTAS

398 ◕ **Pocahontas Revealed: Science Examines an American Legend** (7–12). 2007. 56 min. WGBH Boston. ISBN 978-1-59375-762-5. $19.95.

A "NOVA" presentation about what scholars know about Pocahontas and what is still unknown. Reenactments, graphics, interviews, and footage of the newly discovered site of Chief Powhatan's capital, Werowocomoco, combine to make this an interesting program. (Rev: BL 10/15/07; SLJ 11/07; VL 11–12/07)

Science, Medicine, Industry, and Business Figures

Collective

399 ❂ **Genius: The Science of Einstein, Newton, Darwin, and Galileo** (9–12). 2006. 4 discs. 420 min. WGBH Boston. ISBN 978-1-59375-574-4. $49.95.
Includes four well-received "NOVA" programs previously available only on videocassette: *Einstein's Big Idea, Darwin's Dangerous Idea, Galileo's Battle for the Heavens,* and *Newton's Dark Secrets.*

Individual

BOHR, NIELS

400 ❂ **Bohr's Model of the Atom** (9–12). 2006. 26 min. VEA. Closed captioned. $129.95.
Students who wonder just how we know what an atom looks like will enjoy this film about the Danish physicist who developed the model of the atom. Animation adds to the presentation. (Rev: SLJ 12/07)

EINSTEIN, ALBERT

401 ❂ **Einstein's Big Idea** (10–12). 2005. 112 min. WGBH Boston. PPR. Closed captioned. ISBN 978-1-59375-317-7. $19.95.
Effective reenactments, filmed on location in Europe and the United States, tell the story of Einstein's famous $E=mc^2$ equation and place it in historical context. (Rev: BL 12/1/05*; SLJ 6/06; VL 1–2/06)

GALILEO

402 ❂ **Galileo's Battle for the Heavens** (9–12). 2002. 120 min. WGBH Boston. PPR. Closed captioned. ISBN 978-1-59375-573-7. $19.95.
This "NOVA" dramatization — based on the 1999 biography *Galileo's Daughter* by Dava Sobel — of the astronomer's life covers his scientific accomplishments, his trial for heresy, and his relationship with his illegitimate daughter, a nun named Maria Celeste. (Rev: BL 3/1/03)

JULIAN, PERCY

403 ❂ **Percy Julian: Forgotten Genius** (9–12). 2007. 116 min. WGBH Boston. ISBN 978-1-59375-682-6. $19.95.
A "NOVA" program about the African American chemist who faced racism and even violence as he fought to advance in his career in the 1920s and 1930s. (Rev: BL 5/1/07*; SLJ 6/07)

PAYNE, ROGER

404 ❂ **A Life Among Whales** (9–12). 2005. 57 min. Uncommon Productions (dist. by Bullfrog Films). PPR. ISBN 978-1-59498-381-8. $250.
This is a biography of biologist Roger Payne, who discovered in the 1970s that whales sing and who has campaigned against whaling. Note that there are distressing whaling scenes. (Rev: VL 9–10/06)

World Figures

Collective

405 ⊗ **Richard the Lionheart and Saladin: Holy Warriors** (9–12). 2005.110 min. PBS Video. Closed captioned. ISBN 978-1-4157-1157-6. $24.99 ($54.95 w/PPR).
The conflict between the Muslim leader Saladin and the Catholic King Richard is described in thoughtful narrative and dramatic re-creations. (Rev: VL 1–2/06)

Asia and the Middle East

SUGIHARA, CHIUNE

406 ⊗ **Sugihara: Conspiracy of Kindness** (9–12). 2005. 82 min. WGBH Boston. PPR. Closed captioned. ISBN 978-1-59375-364-1. $19.95.
The Japanese diplomat Sugihara may have saved as many as 40,000 Eastern European Jews from the Nazis by providing them with visas to Japan, despite the dangers to himself and his family. With archival footage and interviews with his family, this is a thorough and compelling presentation. (Rev: SLJ 2/06; VL 12/27/05)

TERESA, MOTHER

407 ⊗ **Mother Teresa: Seeing the Face of Jesus** (2–5). 2006. 35 min. Morning Light Media (dist. by Vision Video). $14.99.
This animated biography covers Mother Teresa's childhood, work for the poor, activism on behalf of the suffering, and the strong religious beliefs that sustained her. (Rev: VL 1–2/07)

Europe

BLAIR, TONY

408 ⊗ **The Blair Decade** (10–12). 2007. 120 min. PBS Home Video. $24.99.
This documentary looks at the former British prime minister and what he accomplished during his time in office. Viewers will come away with a new understanding of the British government as well as Blair's decisions and their outcomes. (Rev: SLJ 10/07)

CHURCHILL, WINSTON

409 ⊗ **Greatest Speeches of the 20th Century: Winston Churchill** (9–12). 2006. 23 min. Series: Greatest Speeches of the 20th Century: Voices in Time. Schlessinger Media (dist. by Library Video Company). ISBN 978-1-4171-0760-5. $39.95.
Part of a 13-DVD series including speeches by Adolf Hitler, Ho Chi Minh, John F. Kennedy, Nelson Mandela, and Jawaharlal Nehru, this DVD provides a profile of Churchill, historical and social context, excerpts from key speeches, and analysis of their impact, all

accompanied by still and moving images. (Rev: LMC 10/07; SLJ 3/07)

JOHN PAUL II, POPE

410 ◉ **Pope John Paul II: Crusader for Human Dignity** (9–12). 2006. 56 min. Series: Great Souls. Aim International Television (dist. by Vision Video). $19.99.
Viewers will learn what led this pope to the priesthood and eventually the papacy. An admiring look at an important figure in the Catholic Church and in world politics. (Rev: SLJ 4/07)

SANTOS-DUMONT, ALBERTO

411 ◉ **Wings of Madness: The Daring Flights of Alberto Santos-Dumont** (7–12). 2007. 60 min. WGBH Boston. Closed captioned. ISBN 978-1-59375-656-7. $19.95.
Brazilian-born Santos-Dumont was fascinated by aviation and became the first person in Europe to fly an airplane. This "NOVA" program looks at his full life through photographs, reenactments, and graphics. Based on the 2003 biography by Paul Hoffman. (Rev: SLJ 10/07)

Miscellaneous Interesting Lives

Collective

412 ⬥ **Fly Girls** (9–12). 1999. 60 min. Series: The American Experience. PBS Video. Closed captioned. $19.95.

Although women pilots contributed to the war effort in World War II — testing planes, ferrying them across the country, and teaching male pilots — their role was not greeted with widespread appreciation. This is the story of the Women Air Force Service Pilots and the many obstacles they faced. Newly available on DVD. (Rev: BL 5/15/00; VL 7/06)

413 ⬥ **True Caribbean Pirates** (9–12). 2006. 94 min. The History Channel (dist. by A&E Home Video). PPR. ISBN 978-0-7670-8990-6. $19.95.

Pirates of the 17th and 18th centuries — both male and female — are profiled with dramatic reenactments. (Rev: VL 1–2/07)

Individual

PETIT, PHILIPPE

414 ⬥ **The Man Who Walked Between the Towers** (K–3). 2005. 10 min. Weston Woods. ISBN 978-0-439-76717-0. $59.95.

A successful adaptation of Mordicai Gerstein's Caldecott-winning book that captures French aerialist Philippe Petit's famous high-wire feat between the twin towers of New York's World Trade Center. (Rev: BL 11/15/05)

⚜ ALA ALSC Notable Children's Videos 2006; Andrew Carnegie Medal for Excellence in Children's Video 2006

REMPLE, HENRY D.

415 ⬥ **Henry D. Remple: Finding Hope in Troubled Times** (9–12). 2007. 35 min. Take Ten (dist. by National Film Network). ISBN 978-0-8026-0721-8. PPR. $249.95.

A now-elderly Mennonite man relates the fascinating story of his life. His family moved from Germany to Russia in the 1890s and found themselves in danger when they refused to fight in World War I. Now a resident of Kansas, Remple tells his story accompanied by photographs and film footage. (Rev: SLJ 12/07)

YEBOAH, EMMANUEL OFOSU

416 ⬥ **Emmanuel's Gift** (4–10). 2005. 80 min. First Look. Closed captioned. ISBN 978-1-59241-644-8. $26.99.

Oprah Winfrey narrates the inspiring story of a young Ghanaian called Emmanuel Ofosu Yeboah, who overcame a withered leg to become an internationally respected athlete. (Rev: SLJ 5/06; VL 3–4/06)

The Arts and Entertainment

General and Miscellaneous

417 ❸ **Arts Education A+** (9–12). 2004. 30 min. Series: In the Mix. Castle Works. $69.95.

This presentation explores innovative arts programs in the fields of music, visual arts, poetry, and dance and shows how arts education can benefit students in other areas including math, science, and written and verbal communication. (Rev: BL 3/15/04)

☒ YALSA 2004 Selected Videos and DVDs

Painting, Sculpture, and Photography

General and Miscellaneous

418 ◉ **Alchemy in Light: Making Art Glass** (9–12). 1995. 29 min. Roaring Rabbit Pictures. PPR. Closed captioned. $19.95.
Viewers learn how art glass is made in this beautifully shot documentary newly available on DVD. (Rev: VL 7/06)

History of Art

419 ◉ **The Art of the Northern Renaissance** (9–12). 2007. 6 discs. 1,080 min. The Teaching Company. PPR. ISBN 978-1-59803-333-5. $149.95.
Professor Catherine B. Scallen of Cleveland's Case Western Reserve University guides viewers through this time period and the art that was created in northern Europe (now Belgium and the Netherlands, northern France, Germany, and Switzerland). (Rev: VL 11–12/07)

420 ◉ **Dutch Masters: The Age of Rembrandt** (9–12). 2006. 6 discs. 1,080 min. The Teaching Company. PPR. ISBN 978-1-59803-256-7. $149.95.
Thirty-six segments hosted by Smithsonian art historian William Kloss look at the artwork of Frans Hals, Jan Steen, Pieter de Hooch, Johannes Vermeer, Van Goyen, Ruisdael, and Rembrandt. Social and political influences are discussed. (Rev: BL 3/1/07)

421 ◉ **A History of European Art** (9–12). 2005. 8 discs. 1,440 min. The Teaching Company. PPR. ISBN 978-1-59803-090-7. $199.95.
This thorough review of European art — from about 800 a.d. to the year 2000 — teaches viewers how to appreciate art as well as to recognize major works. (Rev: VL 11–12/06)

422 ◉ **Learn Art Styles with Lisa: Prehistoric Art to Medieval Art** (7–12). 2006. 20 min. Crystal Productions. PPR. $29.95.
A lively introduction to eight eras in art history — Prehistoric, Egyptian, Greek, Roman, Pre-Columbian, Byzantine, Early Chinese, and Medieval — that focuses on 24 works of art and their cultural context. (Rev: SLJ 2/07)

423 ◉ **Learn Art Styles with Lisa: Romanesque to Post-Impressionism** (8–11). 2005. 22 min. Crystal Productions. PPR. $29.95.
This brief overview focuses on three important works representing major art movements; also in the series are *Prehistoric Art to Medieval Art* (see above), *Fauvism to Nonfigurative*, and *Regionalism to Installation Art*. (Rev: BL 4/1/06)

424 ◉ **Magritte: An Attempt at the Impossible** (9–12). 2006. 55 min. Kultur International Films. ISBN 978-0-7697-8436-6. $19.99.
This film shows what the surrealist painter hoped to accomplish through his odd and remarkable work. Interesting camera work mimics his style and keeps viewers intrigued. Information about the artist's times is integrated into the presentation. (Rev: VL 3–4/07)

425 ⊘ **Masters of the Renaissance: Michelangelo, Leonardo da Vinci, and More** (4–7). 2006. 78 min. Greathall Productions. ISBN 978-1-882513-88-8. $13.95.
All about the major works of the Renaissance and the men behind them. Jim Weiss combines storytelling with facts for an interesting presentation on da Vinci, Michelangelo, Brunelleschi, Donatello, and Ghiberti. (Rev: BL 2/1/07; SLJ 4/07)

426 ⊘ **Museum Masterpieces: The Louvre** (10–12). 2006. 2 discs. 720 min. The Teaching Company. PPR. ISBN 978-1-59803-219-2. $59.95.
Art historian Richard Brettell guides viewers through the European paintings displayed in the Louvre; an introduction covers the history of the museum itself. (Rev: VL 1–2/07)

427 ⊘ **Sculptures of the Louvre** (9–12). 1996. 2 discs. 192 min. Koch Vision. ISBN 978-1-4172-2931-4. $39.98.
A look at some of the masterpieces found in the Louvre, from a depiction of an ancient Egyptian pharaoh to Michelangelo's bound slaves, providing historical context that will give students a new appreciation of sculpture and of the Louvre's vast collection. Recently released on DVD. (Rev: VL 1–2/07)

Regions

Africa

428 ⊘ **Modern African Art and Artisans** (6–8). 2006. 56 min. Discovery School. ISBN 978-1-59380-532-6. $69.95.
A sculptor, a potter, a leathermaker, a blacksmith, and a weaver explain (through an interpreter) how they produce their works. Viewers learn about the importance of these artisans to their communities. (Rev: SLJ 1/07)

Asia and the Middle East

429 ⊘ **The Ottomans and Their Capital, Istanbul** (11–12). 2007. 45 min. Series: The Glories of Islamic Art. Landmark Media. $195.
Part of a three-DVD series, this program covers the history of the Ottoman Empire and the art and architecture that was produced there and shows how it is inseparable from the religious beliefs and traditions practiced by the people of this part of the world. The two other titles in the series are *The Umayyads and Their Capital, Damascus*; and *Two Islamic Regimes in Cairo*. (Rev: SLJ 9/07)

Europe

430 ⊘ **Matryoshka Doll: A Symbol of Russian Folk Art** (K–8). 2006. 42 min. The Cultural Kaleidoscope. ISBN 978-0-9762013-1-1. $35.
A fascinating look at how these traditional nesting dolls are made, from the carving to the painting. It offers a peek into Russian culture as well. Filmed in Russia, with voice-overs in English translating interviews with artisans and craftspeople. Teacher's guide included. (Rev: SLJ 9/07)

North America

431 ⊘ **The Dancing Chickens of Ventura Fabian** (3–8). 2007. 10 min. Documentary Educational Resources. $29.95.
Viewers watch Mexican artist Ventura Fabian and his family prepare the wood for his bird sculptures, which are carved and painted. The DVD includes a version in Spanish with English subtitles and in Spanish with English voice-over. (Rev: SLJ 7/07)

Music

General and Miscellaneous

432 ⚃ **Elite Beat Agents** (5–12). 2006. Nintendo. Nintendo DS. Players: 1–4. ESRB: E10+ (suggestive themes, cartoon violence, crude humor, lyrics).
Rhythm and timing are the keys to this game in which the story line is dependent on the player's abilities. (Rev: CTR 12/06)

433 ⊘ **Music from the Inside Out** (10–12). 2005. 90 min. Emerging Pictures. Closed captioned. $24.95.
Members of the Philadelphia Orchestra reveal what music means to them, both inside and outside the concert hall. (Rev: VL 9–10/06)

Jazz and Popular Music (Country, Rap, Rock, etc.)

434 ⚃ **Guitar Hero II** (7–12). 2006. Red Octane. PlayStation 2. Players: 1–2 (2nd player requires additional guitar). ESRB: T (lyrics).
This game comes with one guitar controller. Players start off in a garage band and progress to rock star level by qualifying on a series of songs. Players can also compete against each other. (Rev: SLJ 1/07; CTR 12/06)

435 ⚃ **Guitar Hero III: Legends of Rock** (8–12). RedOctane. Windows, Macintosh, PlayStation 2, PlayStation 3, Xbox 360, Wii.

Players: 1–2. ESRB: T (lyrics, mild suggestive themes).
Create a virtual band using a guitar instead of a typical game controller. Strumming chords as the game instructs is the key to victory. Includes more than 70 well-known numbers.
♟ YALSA Top 50 Core Recommended Collection Titles

436 ⚃ **Karaoke Revolution** (6–12). 2003. Konami. PlayStation 2, PlayStation 3, GameCube, Xbox, Xbox 360, Wii. Players: 1–8. ESRB: E10+ (lyrics, suggestive themes).
Players are judged on pitch and rhythm, with a virtual audience to cheer them on or boo as necessary. This karaoke game, first released in North America in 2003, requires a microphone. There are many sequels to the first volume: two additional volumes of the original version — *Karaoke Revolution Party*, *Karaoke Revolution Country* — and most recently *Karaoke Revolution Presents: American Idol* (2006) and *Karaoke Revolution Presents: American Idol Encore* (2008). (Rev: SLJ 10/06; CTR 11/03)

437 ⊘ **Legends of Jazz, Season One, Volume 1** (6–12). 2006. 120 min. Legends of Jazz (dist. by LRS Media). $19.98.
Four half-hour episodes — "The Golden Horns," "The Jazz Singers," "Contemporary Jazz," and "The Altos" — from the TV series *Legends of Jazz*. Includes teacher's guide. (Rev: SLJ 12/06)

438 ⊘ **The Rhythm of My Soul: Kentucky Roots Music** (9–12). 2007. 60 min. Sektda-

Florentine Films (dist. by PBS Home Video). ISBN 978-0-7936-9361-0. $24.99.

The story of how music and southern culture come together in Kentucky's rolling hills. Performances by country music stars as well as everyday people make this a fascinating look at life and art in this part of the country. (Rev: SLJ 12/07)

439 🎲 **Rock Band** (8–12). MTV Games. PlayStation 2 and 3, XBox 360. Players: 1–4. ESRB: T (lyrics, mildly suggestive themes). Select one of four instruments and join with your friends to compete in band competitions. Includes hit songs from the 1960s through today.

♘ YALSA Top 50 Core Recommended Collection Titles

440 🎲 **SingStar Pop** (6–12). Sony Computer Entertainment America. PlayStation 2. Players: 1–2. ESRB: E10+ (alcohol reference, mild lyrics, mild violence, suggestive themes). Sing along with popular music videos. Singing on key (evaluated by the program itself) is the objective.

♘ YALSA Top 50 Core Recommended Collection Titles

Opera and Musicals

441 🎲 **High School Musical: Makin' the Cut** (2–12). 2007. Disney Interactive. Nintendo DS. ESRB: E.

Based on the popular TV show, this game takes the cast of characters on a journey to win an American Amateur Musical award. Includes rhythmic puzzles. (Rev: CTR 9/07)

442 💿 **Making Opera: The Creation of Verdi's La Forza del Destino** (9–12). 1988. 88 min. VIEW. $19.98.

Follows, over a 21-day period, the making of an opera and the myriad details involved;

extras on the newly released DVD include a biography of Giuseppe Verdi, a synopsis and history of the opera, and a history of the Canadian Opera Company. (Rev: BL 1/93; SLJ 8/93; VL 7/06)

Orchestra and Musical Instruments

443 💿 **How to Play Blues Guitar Lesson One** (7–12). 1991. 85 min. Stefan Grossman's Guitar Workshop. PPR. $29.95.

Now available on DVD, this is an excellent introduction to both the genre and playing techniques, starting with basics and progressing to improvisation. Also available: *How to Play Blues Guitar Lesson Two* and *How to Play Blues Guitar Lesson Three*. (Rev: VL 9–10/06)

Songs and Folk Songs

444 💿 **cELLAbration Live!** (K–5). 2007. 60 min. Smithsonian Folkways Recordings. $14.97.

A 2006 concert tribute to "First Lady of Children's Music" Ella Jenkins, with performances by notable folk singers and musicians such as Tom Paxton, Pete Seeger, and Bill Harley. (Rev: BL 10/15/07; SLJ 15/08)

445 💿 **My Best Day** (K–5). 2007. 53 min. Trout. $14.98.

Ezra Idlet and Keith Grimwood, also known as Trout Fishing in America, perform at a lively concert for families featuring their popular songs as well as new songs; all with silly titles accompanied by blues, jazz, rock, and folk style background music. (Rev: BL 4/1/07)

Theater, Dance, and Other Performing Arts

Dance (Ballet, Modern, etc.)

446 ⊗ **Ballroom Dancing Basics** (9–12). 2005. 57 min. Acorn Media. ISBN 978-1-56938-801-3. $24.99.

Viewers learn the basic dance moves — male and female — before seeing partners perform the waltz, foxtrot, samba, and other dances. Includes print booklet of steps and a CD of music for practice. (Rev: BL 12/15/05; VL 1–2/06)

447 ⊗ **Creating Ballet Dreams with Rochelle** (K–4). 2007. 35 min. Ballet Ovations (dist. by Victory Multimedia). ISBN 978-0-9773458-1-6. $19.99.

Young Rochelle choreographs ballets right in her own living room. A companion production is *Creating Ballet Fun with Rochelle* (2007). (Rev: SLJ 8/07)

448 ⊗ **Dance Dance Revolution SuperNOVA** (5–12). Konami. PlayStation 2. Players: 1–2. ESRB: E10+ (alcohol reference, mild lyrics, suggestive themes).

Dance against a friend or the computer to the tune of 303 different songs; this new version adds 64 new numbers. Dancers move on a special dance pad and follow the on-screen notifications to keep the beat; there are many skill levels.

⚇ YALSA Top 50 Core Recommended Collection Titles

449 ⊗ **Dance Praise 2: The Remix** (1–12). 2007. Digital Praise. Windows, Macintosh. Players: 1. ESRB: E.

The Christian rock equivalent of Dance Dance Revolution, this includes 50 songs, four custom-made steps, and 200 possible dances. Requires the Dance Praise pad. (Rev: CTR 11/07)

450 ⊗ **Getting Your Kicks** (8–12). 2006. 41 min. Meriwether Publishing. ISBN 978-1-56608-114-6. $34.95.

Viewers learn the terminology and techniques of choreography in eight separate sections followed by a dance routine that incorporates the steps learned. Teacher's guide included. (Rev: SLJ 10/06)

451 ⊗ **Making Ballet: Karen Kain and the National Ballet of Canada** (9–12). 1995. 86 min. VIEW. $24.98.

Starring prima ballerina Karen Kain, this is a behind-the-scenes look at the making of "The Actress," a ballet set to Chopin's Preludes; extras on this newly released DVD include a biography of the star and information about the ballet itself. (Rev: BL 11/1/95; VL 7/06)

452 ⊗ **Start Smarter: Girls Gotta Dance with Ballerina Jen** (K–5). 2006. 40 min. Marshall Fairman Productions (dist. by Big Kids Productions). $14.95.

A behind-the-scenes look at actual dance students preparing for a ballet performance. Viewers learn basic ballet positions and watch as the students make their own costumes. (Rev: SLJ 3/07)

Radio, Television, and Video

453 ● **Class Dismissed: How TV Frames the Working Class** (9–12). 2006. 62 min. Media Education Foundation. PPR. Closed captioned. ISBN 978-1-932869-03-3. $150.

Television's evolving use of ethnic and working-class characters is the focus of this thought-provoking documentary that includes many film clips. (Rev: VL 1–2/07)

History and Geography

Paleontology

454 ◉ **Bone Diggers: Australia's Lost Marsupials** (7–12). 2007. 53 min. WGBH Boston. ISBN 978-1-59375-754-0. $19.95.

Scientists travel to the Australian Outback in search of the remains of huge prehistoric creatures in this dramatic program. Viewers will be amazed by the animals that once lived there — including the Thylacoleo, a huge, lion-like marsupial. (Rev: SLJ 11/07)

455 ◉ **Dinosaur George Live!** (2–5). 2005. 60 min. Series: Dinosaur World Classroom. Dinosaur World (avail. from Big Kids Productions). PPR. $24.95.

Facts about dinosaurs are delivered with verve and humor. (Rev: SLJ 4/06; VL 5–6/06)

456 ◉ **Dinosaur George's Guide to Prehistoric Life** (4–8). 2004. 30 min. Dinosaur World (dist. by Instructional Video). PPR. $14.95.

Dinosaur George, a paleontologist, gives fascinating facts about dinosaurs, beginning with the origins of life and explaining all about fossils and what they tell us. The fast pace and interesting facts will keep students engaged. (Rev: SLJ 3/05; VL 3–4/05)

457 ◉ **Jewel of the Earth** (9–12). 2005. 56 min. WGBH Boston. PPR. Closed captioned. ISBN 978-1-59375-388-7. $19.95.

Sir David Attenborough hosts this "NOVA" program on amber and the many fossils that were preserved in this resin. (Rev: VL 11–12/06)

Anthropology and Evolution

458 🌐 **Ape to Man** (9–12). 2005. 100 min. The History Channel (dist. by A&E Home Video). PPR. ISBN 978-0-7670-8750-6. $24.95.
A look at the history — and evolution — of our knowledge of man's ancestors, starting with the discovery in 1856 of a 40,000-year-old bone; includes the story of the Piltdown Man hoax. (Rev: VL 1–2/06)

459 🌐 **Greatest Discoveries with Bill Nye: Evolution** (7–10). 2005. 45 min. WriteBrain. $69.95.
The Science Guy uses a number of famous scientific discoveries as jumping-off points for discussion of important evolutionary theories and key figures. Reenactments and interviews add interest. (Rev: BL 12/1/05)

460 🌐 **History of Life** (5–8). 2005. 80 min. Visual Learning. PPR. Closed captioned. ISBN 978-1-59234-123-8. $299.
"Early Life," "Life Through Time," "Evolution," and "Evidence of Change" are the four 20-minute programs in this thought-provoking overview of the origins of life and theories of evolution. Includes teacher's guide. (Rev: VL 1–2/06)

Archaeology

461 ✪ **Classical Archeology of Ancient Greece and Rome** (9–12). 2006. 6 discs. 1,080 min. The Teaching Company. PPR. ISBN 978-1-59803-213-0. $149.95.

Excavations at Delphi, Rome, and Bath are among the dozen featured in this collection of lectures about the practice and importance of archaeology. (Rev: VL 1–2/07)

462 ✪ **Egypt: Rediscovering a Lost World** (9–12). 2005. 2 discs. 360 min. BBC Video. Closed captioned. ISBN 978-1-4198-2917-8. $29.98.

The stories of three archaeologists — Howard Carter, Giovanni Belzoni, and Jean-Francois Champollion — are brought to life in creative re-enactments that interweave personal and historical details and introduce viewers to the wonders of Tutankhamun's tomb, the temple at Abu Simbel, and the Rosetta Stone hieroglyphs. (Rev: VL 7/06)

463 ✪ **The Perfect Corpse** (9–12). 2006. 56 min. WGBH Boston. Closed captioned. ISBN 978-1-59375-579-9. $19.95.

British scientists examine two "bog bodies" — corpses preserved more than 2,000 years in Ireland's peat marshes — and reveal that they were victims of violence. Is it a case of crime, politics, or perhaps religious ritual? (Rev: VL 7/06)

464 ✪ **Secrets of Archaeology** (9–12). 2006. 6 discs. 672 min. Koch Vision. ISBN 978-1-4172-2934-5. $89.98.

Twenty-seven episodes look at archaeological sites around the world — with a concentration on ancient Greece and Rome. Computer graphics, on-site footage, maps, and narration combine to give a feeling of the sites over time and how they look today. (Rev: BL 10/15/06; SLJ 5/03; VL 9–10/06)

World History and Geography

General

465 ● **Civilisation** (10–12). 1969. 4 discs. 670 min. BBC Video. $79.98.
First aired on the BBC in 1969, this acclaimed series — written and narrated by art historian Sir Kenneth Clark — is an ambitious and detailed review of the development of Western European culture. The newly available DVD includes Sir David Attenborough's account of the making of the series, which pioneered new documentary techniques. (Rev: VL 9–10/06)

466 ● **Seapower to Superpower** (9–12). 2006. 2 discs. 240 min. Robert Linnell Productions and Norflicks Productions for History Television Canada (dist. by Janson Media). ISBN 978-1-56839-229-5. $29.95.
From Britain's defeat of the Spanish Armada through the early 21st century, this is a review of the importance of military power in establishing economic strength. (Rev: SLJ 11/06)

Ancient History

General and Miscellaneous

467 ● **Alexander the Great and the Fall of the Persian Empire** (9–12). 2005. 50 min. Series: The Fall of Great Empires. ZDF Enterprises (dist. by Library Video Company). ISBN 978-1-4171-0656-1. $39.95.
The reasons for the fall of the Persian Empire (mainly, Alexander's armies) are discussed using computer animation, dramatic reenactments, and experts' comments. Also in this series: *Egypt: The End of the Pharaohs, The Fall of Rome,* and *Hannibal and the Fall of Carthage.* A teacher's guide is included. (Rev: BL 10/15/04; LMC 3/07; SLJ 1/07)

468 ● **Decisive Battles of the Ancient World** (9–12). 2006. 3 discs. 380 min. The History Channel. PPR. ISBN 978-0-7670-9159-6. $34.95.
Thirteen important land battles are covered in detail, with maps, footage of the sites, and CGI re-creations. (Rev: VL 1–2/07)

469 ● **Great Battles of the Ancient World** (9–12). 2005. 4 discs. 720 min. Series: Great Courses. The Teaching Company. PPR. ISBN 978-1-59803-050-1. $109.95.
In 24 lectures, Professor Garrett Fagan of Pennsylvania State University describes the most important conflicts from prehistory through the 4th century A.D., discusses their importance, profiles key characters, and explores such factors as weapons, armor, tactics, and training. (Rev: VL 1–2/06)

470 ● **Origins of Great Ancient Civilizations** (10–12). 2005. 4 discs. 720 min. The Teaching Company. PPR. ISBN 978-1-59803-107-2. $59.95.
Twelve well-illustrated lectures presented by Professor Kenneth W. Harl of Tulane University cover the history of the eastern Mediterranean — including Mesopotamia, Egypt,

and Persia — in the Bronze and Early Iron Ages. (Rev: VL 11–12/06)

471 ◐   **The Vikings** (9–12). 2000. 120 min. WGBH Boston. PPR. Closed captioned. ISBN 978-1-57807-479-2. $19.95.
The Vikings' positive attributes — their mercantile and shipbuilding skills and their artistic and inventive abilities — are emphasized in this "NOVA" presentation that is newly available on DVD. (Rev: VL 7/06)

472 ◐   **Vikings: Journey to New Worlds** (9–12). 2006. 62 min. Vista Point Entertainment. $14.95.
Re-enactments and digital graphics are a feature of this visually satisfying exploration of what Viking life must have been like. Viking achievements in exploration and arts and sciences are emphasized. (Rev: VL 11–12/06)

Egypt and Mesopotamia

473 ◐   **Culture and Math: The Egyptians** (10–12). 2006. 15 min. Discovery School. ISBN 978-1-59380-543-2. $69.95.
Students may be surprised to find out that the ancient Egyptians were quite advanced in their understanding and application of mathematics. The presentation explains how these ancient people used math in building the pyramids, studying the stars, and in commerce. (Rev: SLJ 3/07)

474 ◐   **Egypt: Engineering an Empire** (9–12). 2006. 92 min. The History Channel. PPR. ISBN 978-0-7670-9102-2. $24.95.
The ingenuity of the ancient Egyptians in building huge pyramids, obelisks, dams, and other structures will amaze viewers of this History Channel program. The classroom edition ($49.95) includes lesson plans and other extras. (Rev: VL 3–4/07)

Rome

475 ◐   **Roman Feats of Engineering** (8–12). 2007. 30 min. Series: Technology and Architecture in Ancient Civilizations . New Dimension Media. PPR. ISBN 978-1-59522-570-2. $49 (single site), $149 (multi-site).
The Circus Maximus, the Colosseum, and the Appian Way are some of the structures covered in this program that includes computer simulations, modern photography, reenact-

ments, interviews, and film footage. A teacher's guide is included. Other titles in the series include *Greek Designs of Beauty* and *Egyptian Monumental Structures*. (Rev: SLJ 6/07; VL 7–8/07)

Middle Ages Through the Renaissance (500–1700)

476 ◐   **Everyday Life in the Renaissance** (5–9). 2004. 23 min. Series: The Renaissance for Students. Library Video Company. $39.95.
A look at society and culture in the Renaissance, covering such topics as clothing and the rash of inventions and new foodstuffs that added spice to life. Part of a five-volume series that also contains *Renaissance Art, Music and Literature*. (Rev: BL 1/1–15/04)

477 ◐   **The Plague** (9–12). 2005. 100 min. The History Channel (dist. by A&E Home Video). PPR. ISBN 978-0-7670-8790-2. $24.95.
A detailed look at the bubonic plague that killed almost half of Europe's population in just three years in the mid-14th century, with discussion of the chances of a similar outbreak today. (Rev: VL 5–6/06)

Twentieth Century

World War I

478 ◐   **Blood and Oil: The Middle East in World War I** (9–12). 2006. 112 min. Inecom. PPR. ISBN 978-1-59218-042-4. $24.95.
With archival footage and commentary from experts, this is a thorough exploration of the decisions made about the Middle East at the end of World War I and the consequences that we are living with today. (Rev: SLJ 3/07; VL 1–2/07)

479 ◐   **World War I: American Legacy** (9–12). 2006. 112 min. Inecom. ISBN 978-1-59218-040-0. $24.95.
Discusses what led to the Great War, the people who fought in it, Americans' contributions, and the impact of the war in the United States and around the world. Newspaper articles, photographs, music, and other artifacts of the period add to the moving presentation. (Rev: BL 3/1/07; SLJ 3/07)

480 ● World War I: The "Great War" (9–12). 2006. 6 discs. 1,080 min. The Teaching Company. PPR. ISBN 978-1-59803-153-9. $129.95.

A comprehensive look at this long conflict that claimed so many lives, presented in 36 lectures by Dr. Vejas Gabriel Liulevicius of the University of Tennessee. (Rev: VL 11–12/06)

World War II and the Holocaust

481 ● Auschwitz: Inside the Nazi State (10–12). 2007. 60 min. KCET (dist. by Films Media Group). ISBN 978-1-4213-6085-0. $159.95.

An in-depth examination of what happened in Auschwitz, this program was produced by the BBC and PBS. Six segments use re-creations, interviews with survivors and former Nazis, film footage, and discussion sessions with Linda Ellerbee to enhance viewers' comprehension. Additional resources include maps and other teacher's aids. (Rev: SLJ 12/07)

482 ● The Blitz: London's Longest Night (9–12). 2006. 90 min. PBS Video. PPR. Closed captioned. ISBN 978-1-4157-1317-4. $24.99 ($54.95 w/PPR).

The story of the German attack on London on the night of December 29, 1940, is told in archival footage and first-person narratives with dramatic reenactments and special effects. (Rev: VL 5–6/06)

483 ● The History Channel Ultimate Collections: World War II (9–12). 2006. 10 discs. New Video. $59.95.

This newly available compilation of History Channel productions gives a comprehensive overview of the war and its key characters, looking also at the aviation industry, great blunders of the war, and the Nuremberg Trials.

484 ● Hitler's Sunken Secret (9–12). 2005. 56 min. WGBH Boston. PPR. Closed captioned. ISBN 978-1-59375-319-1. $19.95.

This "NOVA" episode tells the story of the 1944 sinking of a Norwegian ferry that was carrying "heavy water" for the Nazis' atomic bomb project; eyewitness accounts add to the drama. (Rev: BL 4/15/06)

485 ● Iwo Jima: Red Blood/Black Sand (9–12). 2007. 89 min. WGBH Boston. ISBN 978-1-59275-775-5. $19.99.

Twenty-three veterans remember the bloody assault on Iwo Jima in 1945. Live footage, photographs, and interviews will make history come to life for viewers. The account is at times disturbing and will not be soon forgotten. (Rev: SLJ 10/07)

486 ● Let Freedom Ring (10–12). 2007. 81 min. Outpost Pictures (www.letfreedomringforall.org). $29.

Four American high school teachers accompany three World War II veterans as they visit Belgian battlefields and relive their experiences during the conflict. Students will also hear from Belgian citizens who were involved in the war, some as prisoners. Stirring images from the war add to the program and will bring the meaning of the war home to today's students. (Rev: SLJ 6/07)

487 ● The Pacific War (9–12). 2005. 91 min. Koch Vision. ISBN 978-1-4172-2922-2. $19.98.

Placing the battles in the Pacific arena in the wider historical context of World War II, this compelling film features color footage. (Rev: VL 1–2/07)

488 ● Pearl Harbor Warriors: The Bugler, The Pilot, The Friendship (5–9). 2006. Woodson House. $19.95.

The moving story of a long friendship between two men — one American, one Japanese — despite the bombing of Pearl Harbor.

🏆 ALA ALSC Notable Children's Videos 2007

489 ● Profiles of Courage, Controversy, and Sacrifice (7–12). 2006. 119 min. OnDeck Video. $19.95 ($29.95 w/PPR).

Emphasizes the human element of World War II, explaining why the United States entered the war, the efforts on the home front, the contributions of minorities and women, and how the atomic bomb ended the war. (Rev: SLJ 2/07)

490 ● The Reckoning: Remembering the Dutch Resistance (9–12). 2007. 96 min. Vision Video. $24.99.

Six people who lived through the terrible days of the Nazi occupation of the Netherlands recount their disturbing memories. Historical footage and photographs add to their stories. (Rev: SLJ 10/07)

491 ◉ **Silent Wings: The American Glider Pilots of WWII** (9–12). 2006. 113 min. Series: The Minutes of History. Inecom. Closed captioned. ISBN 978-1-59218-041-7. $24.95.
This program focuses on a small group of brave World War II pilots who flew unpowered gliders into enemy territory. It includes interviews with veterans, film footage, and photographs. Narrated by Hal Holbrook. (Rev: BL 6/1–15/07*; SLJ 5/07)

Modern World History (1945–)

492 ◉ **Flag Day** (9–12). 2005. 7 min. National Film Network. ISBN 978-0-8026-0553-5. $19.95 ($99.95 w/PPR).
This brief documentary, featuring Tom Sadowski's planting of orange flags in his Maine front yard to honor each soldier killed in Iraq, underscores the loss of American life in this conflict. (Rev: VL 1–2/07)

Geographical Regions

Africa

Central and Eastern Africa

493 🔾 **God Sleeps in Rwanda** (10–12). 2004. 28 min. Women Make Movies. PPR. $89: public libraries; $195: colleges and universities.

A heartbreaking look at the aftermath of the 1994 Rwandan genocide. Women who must fend for themselves after the murder of their families recount experiences of torture and brutality, and describe how their country has changed since then. For older high school students. (Rev: VL 1–2/07)

494 🔾 **Mothers Courage, Thriving Survivors** (11–12). 2006. 52 min. Productions Via Le Monde (dist. by National Film Board of Canada). $195 (Rental: $70).

Women whose lives were changed by the Rwandan genocide tell their terrifying and inspirational stories. Viewers will come to admire the brave steps they have taken to move their people forward. In English and French. (Rev: SLJ 1/07)

495 🔾 **Refugees in Africa: Another Quiet Emergency** (9–12). 2006. 22 min. ABC News (dist. by Films Media Group). ISBN 978-1-4213-4110-1. $129.95.

The tragic story of Ugandan children who commute long distances from their villages to spend the night in cities where they are less likely to be kidnapped by the Lord's Resistance Army and forced to become soldiers. Violent scenes make this film, first seen on "Nightline," unsuitable for young viewers. (Rev: SLJ 11/06)

496 🔾 **Through My Eyes: A Film About Rwandan Youth** (10–12). 2006. 44 min. Choices, Inc. PPR. ISBN 978-1-933724-06-5. $99.95.

The plight of children caught up in the violence of the Rwandan genocide is revealed through the memories and future aspirations of young survivors; includes a photo gallery and an interview with a UNICEF representative. The presentation is in Rwandan with English subtitles. (Rev: SLJ 1/07; VL 1–2/07)

North Africa

497 🔾 **Adalil: The Mistress of Tents** (10–12). 2006. 45 min. National Film Network. PPR. ISBN 978-0-8026-0272-5. $139.95.

First released in 1991, this program explores the little-known world of the Tuareg nomads of North Africa. Using interviews, the focus is on the women of the group and how they live their lives. Viewers will find out about Tuareg traditions, diet, family relationships, and more. (Rev: SLJ 8/07)

Southern Africa

498 🔾 **Angola — Saudades from the One Who Loves You** (10–12). 2006. 60 min. Cinema Guild. ISBN 978-0-7815-1151-3. $99.95 (Rental: $65).

The tragic state of affairs in Angola, a former Portuguese colony in southern Africa, is devastatingly portrayed in this program. Viewers will get to know the people and problems of this country. (Rev: SLJ 12/07)

Asia

General and Miscellaneous

499 ● **Awakening: Empowering Women Through Microloans** (9–12). 2005. 48 min. Choices, Inc. PPR. ISBN 978-1-933724-05-8. $99.95.
Looks at the ability of small loans to make large differences to the lives of families throughout the less-developed countries, with a focus on efforts in India and Afghanistan. (Rev: VL 11–12/06)

China

500 ● **China Blue** (9–12). 2005. 88 min. Teddy Bear Films (dist. by Bullfrog Films). PPR. ISBN 978-1-59458-528-9. $295.
The story of young Jasmine, a girl from rural China who ends up working under harsh conditions in a Chinese sweatshop, will alert viewers to social problems in this fast-growing nation that supplies a significant percentage of America's clothes. (Rev: VL 1–2/07)

501 ● **A Song for China** (9–12). 2006. 55 min. National Film Network. ISBN 978-0-8026-0567-2. PPR. $139.95.
The story of a Missouri youth choir's trip to China in 2001, full of interesting commentary on what the teens see and learn. (Rev: SLJ 12/06)

502 ● **The Tank Man** (9–12). 2005. 90 min. PBS Video. Closed captioned. ISBN 978-0-7936-9239-2. $29.99 ($59.95 w/PPR).
The famous photograph of a lone unarmed man facing down a column of tanks has become a symbol of the 1989 Tiananmen Square protests in China. Who was that man? What was his fate? (Rev: VL 11–12/06)

India, Pakistan, and Bangladesh

503 ● **Going to School in India** (3–6). 2007. 76 min. Master Communications. Closed captioned. ISBN 978-1-88-819490-6. $29.95.
Takes viewers through an array of schools in India, showing their daily activities and cur-

riculum as well as the diversity in different areas of the country. (Rev: BL 8/07; SLJ 4/07)

504 ● **The Miseducation of Pakistan** (7–12). 2007. 30 min. Choices Inc. ISBN 978-1-933724-11-9. $59.95.
This disturbing look at the state of public education in Pakistan may cause American students to see their own schools with new eyes. (Rev: SLJ 6/07)

505 ● **Panihari: The Water Women of India** (10–12). 2006. 30 min. The Five Families (dist. by Choices Inc.). ISBN 978-1-933724-01-0. $59.95.
Paru lives in India's Rajasthan province and must walk up to 24 miles a day to get water for her family. When the family's animals die in a drought, Paru — despite her husband's opposition — borrows money from a women's cooperative to buy more. This film introduces young viewers to the customs and challenges of this remote region. (Rev: SLJ 11/06)

506 ● **Thin Ice** (7–12). 2007. 57 min. Cinema Guild. ISBN 978-0-7815-1207-7. $99.95 (Rental: $65).
Girls don't play ice hockey in India, yet teenaged Dolkar is determined to. It's up to her to organize a team, have a rink built, and even make the equipment by hand. Viewers will be impressed by Dolkar's spirit. (Rev: SLJ 10/07)

507 ● **Warrior Empire: The Mughals** (9–12). 2006. 91 min. The History Channel (dist. by A&E Home Video). PPR. ISBN 978-0-7670-9101-5. $24.95.
A fascinating and thorough introduction to the nomadic Indians known for their aggressiveness, innovation, and love of art and architecture. (Rev: VL 1–2/07)

Japan

508 ● **Chance Pop Session, Episodes 1–13** (6–12). 2006. 3 discs. 330 min. ADV Films. ISBN 978-1-4139-1446-7. $44.98.
Akari, Yuki, and Nozomi are three Japanese girls from different backgrounds who form a pop group called R3. Along with the good music, the relationships among the girls, and the gripping story of their success, there are mysteries about their pasts. (Rev: SLJ 12/06)

509 ● **Japanland** (10–12). 2005. 2 discs. 225 min. Firelight Productions (dist. by AV Café). $29.95.

Karin Muller, author of *Japanland: A Year in Search of Wa*, combines interesting cultural and historical information with details more typical of a traditional travelogue. (Rev: VL 1–2/07)

Other Asian Countries

510 ● **Dreaming of Tibet** (7–12). 2006. 58 min. Mill Valley Film Group (dist. by Bullfrog Films). Closed captioned. ISBN 978-1-59458-517-3. $250 (Rental: $85).

Tibetans who have fled their native land since the occupation of Communist China discuss their lives. Students will come away with a new understanding of what the takeover of Tibet has meant to people around the world. (Rev: SLJ 3/07)

511 ● **Tibet for Kids** (1–6). 2007. 30 min. Worlds Together. $29.95.

Children narrate this presentation of the culture, landscape, people, and traditions of Tibet. Students will be fascinated by the country's mix of ancient traditions and modern conveniences. (Rev: SLJ 6/07)

Australia and the Pacific Islands

512 ● **Families of Australia** (1–4). 2007. 30 min. Series: Families of the World. Master Communications. ISBN 978-1-88819-4-913. $29.95.

A look at everyday life for Australian children Phoebe, 8, and Joshua, 7— one who lives in the country and the other in the city. (Rev: BL 2/15/07; SLJ 4/07)

Europe

513 ● **A Conversation with Haris** (9–12). 2002. 6 min. Shelia Sofian Films. $50.

An animated documentary in which an 11-year-old Bosnian immigrant describes his experiences during the war in his homeland. (Rev: BL 3/15/04)

☒ YALSA 2004 Selected Videos and DVDs

Great Britain and Ireland

514 ● **Monarchy** (9–12). 2006. 2 discs. 317 min. Acorn Media. ISBN 978-1-56938-876-1. $39.99.

Dramatic re-creations and on-location footage add interest to this overview of England's monarchy up to the 1660s. Presented by British historian David Starkey. (Rev: VL 11–12/06)

515 ● **Windsor Castle: A Royal Year** (9–12). 2005. 2 discs. 297 min. Acorn Media. Closed captioned. ISBN 978-1-56938-851-8. $29.99.

A fascinating look at a year's events in the 900-room weekend home of the British queen, including details of a visit by the French president and footage of Prince Charles's wedding to Camilla. (Rev: BL 4/1/06)

Middle East

Israel and Palestine

516 ● **Hamas Victory** (9–12). 2006. 22 min. Australian Broadcasting Corp. (dist. by Landmark Media). $195.

This presentation uses interviews with experts and ordinary people to attempt to clarify the complex history, influence, and beliefs of this powerful Middle Eastern group. (Rev: SLJ 2/07)

517 ● **Middle East: Trauma and Hopes of the Young** (9–12). 2004. 65 min. National Film Network. ISBN 978-0-8026-0347-0. $29.95 ($179.95 w/PPR).

The first part of this documentary focuses on Israeli and Palestinian teenagers attending a "peace camp" in Austria; the second part looks at efforts to help children traumatized by terrorism. Includes many interviews with young people and with adult experts, with English subtitles as needed. (Rev: VL 5–6/06)

518 ● **A Team for Peace** (6–12). 2007. 45 min. Landmark Media. $195.

The story of a soccer team composed of Israeli and Palestinian boys, formed by Olympic speed skating champion Johann Olav Koss in the hopes of promoting peace between the two groups. (Rev: SLJ 12/07)

Other Middle East Countries

519 ● **Saudi Solutions** (9–12). 2006. 77 min. First Run/Icarus Films. $398.
An examination of the position of women in Saudi Arabia. Students may be surprised by the limitations women in Saudi Arabia face in their professional and everyday lives. Interviews with Saudi men and women show how slowly change comes about in this traditional society. A valuable but expensive presentation. (Rev: SLJ 4/07)

North and South America (excluding the United States)

North America

CANADA

520 ● **Carnaval de Québec: The Adventure with Sandy Fortier** (4–12). 2005. 26 min. Tralco-Lingo Fun. PPR. ISBN 978-1-55409-151-5. $39.95.
This tour of the famous Quebec winter fair, intended for French language courses, features both English and French language options plus an activity worksheet and curriculum notes. (Rev: VL 5–6/06)

521 ● **Families of Canada** (2–4). 2005. 30 min. Series: Families of the World. Master Communications. PPR. Closed captioned. ISBN 978-1-888194-12-8. $29.95.
Viewers see the contrasting lives of 7-year-old Hannah, who takes a ferry to her small school in Nova Scotia, and of 11-year-old John, who lives in a suburb of the large city of Toronto. (Rev: BL 3/1/06)

522 ● **Mohawk Girls** (6–12). 2006. 63 min. Women Make Movies. $89.
A look at the lives of three teen Mohawk girls who live on a Canadian Native reserve. (Rev: SLJ 12/06)

MEXICO

523 ● **Ancient Aztec Empire** (3–7). 1998. 30 min. Series: Ancient Civilizations for Children. Schlessinger Media (dist. by Library Video Company). PPR. Closed captioned. $29.95.
Historic re-creations, colorful 3-D illustrations, and archaeological sites and artifacts help viewers to understand the culture of the Aztec people and what life was like in this highly organized society. Part of an extensive series, newly available on DVD, that also covers ancient Greece, Rome, Egypt, Mesopotamia, as well as Africa, China, and the Incas and Maya. Study guide included. (Rev: LMC 2/07; SLJ 9/06; VL 7/06)

524 ● **Ancient Civilizations of Mexico: The Maya and the Aztec** (6–8). 2006. 20 min. Discovery School. ISBN 978-1-59380-553-1. $69.95.
The histories of the two cultures, including what we know about their ways of life and how they died out under Spanish rule. (Rev: SLJ 1/07)

PUERTO RICO, CUBA, AND OTHER CARIBBEAN ISLANDS

525 ● **Bloqueo: Looking at the U.S. Embargo Against Cuba** (9–12). 2006. 45 min. Cinema Guild. ISBN 978-0-7815-1162-9. $99.95.
A group called Pastors for Peace examines the state of Cuba and its people forty-plus years after the U.S. embargo began. Many ordinary citizens are interviewed and the film looks at the positive and negative aspects of life in Cuba. (Rev: SLJ 4/07)

Polar Regions

526 ● **Life in the Freezer** (9–12). 1993. 180 min. BBC Video. $14.98.
A spectacular tour — in six half-hour segments — of Antarctica's landscape and wildlife. The DVD of this 1993 BBC series was released in 2005. (Rev: VL 1–2/06)

United States

General History and Geography

527 ● **Geographic Perspectives: The United States of America** (7–12). 2006. 23 min. Series: Geography for Students. Schlessinger Media (dist. by Library Video Company). PPR. Closed captioned. ISBN 978-1-4171-0558-8. $39.95.
This part of a six-volume series that takes a broad view of geography looks at the United

States and its natural, physical, and cultural features, covering everything from topography and climate to ethnic groups and accents. Teacher's guide included. Also in this series: *Environment and Society, Human Systems, Physical Systems, Places and Regions,* and *The World in Spatial Terms.* (Rev: LMC 1/07; SLJ 6/06; VL 7/06)

528 📇 **Know Your USA** (3–12). EdWare Interactive Learning. Windows. $24.95 (home use), $299.95 (multi-PC school use). Download software from www.knowyourusa. net that allows you to explore the geography of the United States and test your knowledge. Oddly, it provides links to Wikipedia. Also available on CD-ROM. (Rev: LMC 3/07; SLJ 6/08; CTR 7/06)

529 ⊙ **10 Days That Unexpectedly Changed America** (10–12). 2006. 3 discs. 460 min. The History Channel (dist. by A&E Home Video). PPR. ISBN 978-0-7670-8930-2. $39.95.
Eschewing the obvious, this eclectic collection of 10 documentaries covers events ranging from Shays' Rebellion and the Scopes "Monkey Trial" to Elvis's 1956 appearance on the *Ed Sullivan Show,* in each case placing the event in historical context and showing its impact on American society. (Rev: BL 9/15/06; VL 9–10/06)

Historical Periods

NATIVE AMERICANS

530 ⊙ **Exploring Our Past: Native Peoples of North America** (3–5). 2006. 100 min. Mazzarella Bros. Productions. $189.95.
A five-part program focusing on the arrival of the earliest settlers to North America via a land bridge from Asia, the many diverse tribes that formed across the country, and the cultures that developed. Live-action re-creations illustrate early Native American customs. (Rev: BL 11-15/06)

531 ⊙ **The Powhatan Mystery** (7–12). 2006. 20 min. Jackson Associates. PPR. $125.
What exactly contributed to the near-disappearance of the Native Americans who were so populous in Virginia when the first English settlers arrived? Reenactments, interviews, and graphics look at all aspects of the mystery. (Rev: VL 7–8/07)

532 ⊙ **The Trail of Tears: Cherokee Legacy** (9–12). 2006. 115 min. Rich-Heape Films. PPR. $34.95.
A moving account, narrated by James Earl Jones, of this dark chapter in America's history, with reenactments and interviews with historians. (Rev: VL 1–2/07)

REVOLUTIONARY PERIOD AND THE YOUNG NATION (1775–1809)

533 ⊙ **The American Revolution for Students** (5–8). 2005. 5 discs. 115 min. Library Video Company. $199.75.
In five parts — Causes of the Revolution (1765–1774), Origins of Democracy (1688–1765), Declaring Independence (1775–1776), The Revolutionary War (1776–1783), and Creating a New Nation (1783–1791) — this is a comprehensive look at the Revolution with re-enactments, archival images, and interviews with historians. (Rev: BL 7/05)

534 ⊙ **Liberty's Kids** (K–5). 2004. 60 min. WHYY-TV/PBS. $79.95.
Animation and an appealing matter-of-fact presentation add to this overview of young people in the American Revolution, featuring historical and fictional characters.
⅄ ALA ALSC Notable Children's Videos 2005

535 ⊙ **Von Steuben's Continentals: The First American Army** (5–10). 2007. 60 min. Lionheart FilmWorks. $19.95.
How the homespun colonial army became war-worthy under Baron Von Steuben, who became Inspector General of the Continental Army in 1778. Historical reenactors make this a realistic program, full of interesting facts about life in the army. The first in a new series. (Rev: SLJ 12/07)

NINETEENTH CENTURY TO THE CIVIL WAR (1809–1861)

536 ⊙ **The Orphan Trains** (9–12). 2006. 60 min. Series: The American Experience. PBS Home Video. $24.98.
Tells the story of minister Charles Loring Brace's establishment in 1853 of the Children's Aid Society, and of the homeless and orphaned children the organization sent from slums in the east to work on farms in the west — and hopefully find a better life. Original letters from these children, photographs, and

interviews with people who experienced this relocation add to the moving presentation. (Rev: SLJ 1/97; VL 9–10/06)

CIVIL WAR (1861–1865)

537 ● **Civil War: Life and Times** (6–10). 2006. 35 min. Series: Incite! Learning. Don Johnston. ISBN 978-1-4105-0847-8. $149.99.
Four brief but effective segments featuring teen characters provide different views of the Civil War. Reenactments show young soldiers on the battlefield; civilians dealing with the hardships of war; and slaves running for freedom. Includes teacher's guide. (Rev: SLJ 4/07)

538 ● **Horses of Gettysburg** (9–12). 2006. 2 discs. 116 min. Series: Civil War Minutes. Inecom. PPR. Closed captioned. ISBN 978-1-59218-033-2. $39.95.
After a history of horses' cooperation with man in many facets of life, this compelling film looks at the close relationship between soldiers and their mounts and the brave contributions horses made during the Battle of Gettysburg — in which as many as 72,000 horses and mules died. (Rev: BL 9/15/06; VL 9–10/06)

539 ● **Smithsonian's Great Battles of the Civil War** (9–12). 2006. 3 discs. 537 min. Mastervision. ISBN 978-1-55919-564-5. $69.95.
This excellent nine-hour presentation from the National Museum of American History explores the major battles of the Civil War using dramatic re-enactments, eyewitness accounts read by well-known actors, period photographs and paintings, interviews, maps, and so forth. Narrated by Richard Dreyfuss. (Rev: VL 11–12/06)

RECONSTRUCTION TO WORLD WAR I (1865–1914)

540 ● **Transcontinental Railroad** (9–12). 2003. 120 min. Series: The American Experience. PBS Video. $24.98.
The story of the building of the railroad — contrasting the engineering triumphs and the incredible human costs — is placed in historical and social context using interviews, archival materials, and dramatic reenactments. Newly available on DVD. (Rev: VL 7/06)

BETWEEN THE WARS AND THE GREAT DEPRESSION (1918–1941)

541 ● **Hoover Dam: The Making of a Monument** (7–12). 1999. 60 min. Series: The American Experience. PBS Home Video. Closed captioned. $19.95.
The dramatic story of this huge engineering project is shown in archival footage and interviews with those involved. Newly available on DVD. (Rev: VL 7/06)

542 ● **Retro News, Vol. 2: History of Aviation/News of 1934** (4–8). 2006. 60 min. Series: Retro News. Small Planet. $29.99.
Hosted by Professor Whatsit, these two entertaining programs use historical footage to cover the main events in the history of aviation and in the year 1934. Lighthearted archival news clips (such as a marbles championship and a wedding performed in midair) give a feel for everyday life and the people of the times. Also in this series: *Retro News: The News of 1941* (2006). (Rev: SLJ 7/07)

WORLD WAR II

543 ● **Citizen Tanouye** (8–12). 2007. 58 min. WGBH Boston. ISBN 978-1-59375-760-1. $19.95.
Eight students at a high school in Torrance, California, host this award-winning program presenting their efforts to find out more about the Japanese American WWII hero Takayuki Tanouye, who attended their school. Tanouye was posthumously awarded the Medal of Honor in 2000. Interviews with WWII veterans and Tanouye's brother make this program that explores the internment of Japanese Americans even more powerful. (Rev: BL 1/1–15/08; SLJ 9/07)

544 ● **Japanese Americans in WWII: Going for Broke** (7–12). 2006. 25 min. New Dimension Media. PPR. ISBN 978-1-59522-288-6. $49 (single site), $189 (multi-site).
Hosted by Daniel Inouye and narrated by George Takei (of *Star Trek*), this is a compelling history of Japanese Americans, their internment during World War II, and the contributions of the Japanese Americans who did serve — voluntarily — in the American armed forces. Teacher's guide included. (Rev: SLJ 10/06; VL 7/06)

545 ⚫ **Rush to War: Between Iraq and a Hard Place** (11–12). 2007. 86 min. Echo Bridge Home Entertainment. Closed captioned. $19.99.

A harshly critical look at what led the United States into war with Iraq during George W. Bush's presidency. Famous and less-well-known Bush critics are interviewed, as are some Bush supporters. September 11, the Abu Ghraib prison photographs, and the Valerie Plame incident are also discussed. (Rev: SLJ 11/07; VL 11–12/07)

Regions

MOUNTAIN AND PLAINS STATES

546 ⚫ **America's National Monuments: Legacy of the Great Plains** (6–12). 2006. 4 discs. 118 min. Ambrose Video. PPR. $129.99.

This four-part series full of archival material, on-location footage, and expert commentary visits national monuments on the Great Plains and discusses their geologic and historical importance. (Rev: BL 9/15/06; SLJ 11/06; VL 9–10/06)

NORTHEASTERN AND MID-ATLANTIC STATES

547 ⚫ **Discoveries . . . America: Maryland** (8–12). 2006. 60 min. Bennett-Watt Entertainment. PPR. ISBN 978-1-932978-34-6. $24.95.

This well-filmed virtual tour takes in the amazing diversity of this small state — including the historic areas of Baltimore, the farmlands, the busy seaside at Ocean City, and the fishermen who bring in the crabs from the Chesapeake Bay. (Rev: VL 9–10/06)

548 ⚫ **Discoveries . . . America: Rhode Island** (10–12). 2006. 60 min. Bennett-Watt Entertainment. PPR. ISBN 978-1-932978-38-4. $24.95.

The smallest state proves to be full of interest to visitors in this review of its historic and tourist destinations. (Rev: VL 9–10/06)

549 ⚫ **Discoveries . . . America: Washington D.C** (6–12). 2005. 60 min. Series: Discover-

ies . . . America. Bennett-Watt Entertainment. PPR. ISBN 978-1-932978-33-9. $24.95.

Take a tour of the highlights of the nation's capital, from the many monuments and museums on the Mall to the zoo, the architecture of Georgetown, the historic canals, and the diverse offerings of the Eastern Market. (Rev: BL 3/16/06)

550 ⚫ **The Library of Congress: Volumes to Speak** (9–12). 2003. 27 min. Series: Great Museums. Cambridge Educational (avail. from Films Media Group). PPR. Closed captioned. ISBN 978-1-4213-2932-1. $49.95.

A look at the treasures housed in the world's largest library — such as Jefferson's draft of the Declaration of Independence, maps carried by Lewis and Clark, and Martin Luther King's typed script of the "I Have a Dream" speech — plus information on the building itself and interviews with the staff. (Rev: SLJ 5/06; VL 5–6/06)

551 ⚫ **New York** (K–4). 2004. 23 min. Series: U.S. Geography for Children. Library Video Company. ISBN 978-1-57225-903-4. $29.95.

In postcards, Miguel describes his travels around the Empire State; history, geography, natural resources, and important cultural sites are all covered. (Rev: BL 8/04)

PACIFIC STATES

552 ⚫ **Being Caribou** (7–12). 2006. 54 min. National Film Board of Canada (dist. by Bullfrog Films). ISBN 978-0-7722-1206-1. $250 (Rental: $85).

In response to President George Bush's implication that the Arctic National Wildlife Refuge is not worth preserving, a filmmaker and a park warden went there to document the beauty of the land and the lives of the animals there — caribou, wolves, grizzly bears, and so forth. (Rev: SLJ 10/06)

553 ⚫ **Chavez Ravine** (10–12). 2004. 24 min. JAM Flicks (dist. by Bullfrog Films). PPR. Closed captioned. ISBN 978-1-59458-246-2. $195.

This story of the destruction of a Mexican American community in Los Angeles during the 1950s — ostensibly to make way for a housing project although the land eventually housed Dodger Stadium — will prompt debate on today's eminent domain disputes. (Rev: VL 5–6/06)

♀ YALSA 2006 Selected Videos and DVDs

554 ◐ **Dig into History with California Jones: California Missions** (3–5). 2007. 23 min. Library Video Company. ISBN 978-1-604020-33-5. $49.95.
Explores the history of California missions, with discussion of food, livestock, games, and other related subjects. (Rev: BL 9/15/07; SLJ 9/07)

555 ◐ **Jump: A Frogumentary** (7–12). 2006. 67 min. Coolbellup Media. $22.
An entertaining history of the California frog-jumping contest inspired in 1928 by Mark Twain's short story "The Celebrated Jumping Frog of Calaveras County." (Rev: SLJ 1/07)

556 ◐ **Song of the Salish Sea** (1–12). 2006. 45 min. Earthwise Media. PPR. $29.95.
Puget Sound, the Strait of Georgia, and the Strait of Juan de Fuca make up the Salish Sea. This presentation looks at the geology and plant and animal life of the area. Teacher's guide and a bonus music video included. (Rev: VL 3–4/07)
♀ ALA ALSC Notable Children's Videos 2007

SOUTH

557 ◐ **Carousel of Memories** (8–12). 2006. 27 min. Cintia Cabib. $35.
All about the history of the carousel in Glen Echo Park near Washington, D.C., with interviews with those who enjoyed it during its heyday and with people who fought to have it restored after the park closed in the 1960s. (Rev: SLJ 2/07)

558 ◐ **Discoveries . . . America: Florida** (8–12). 2005. 60 min. Bennett-Watt Entertainment. PPR. ISBN 978-1-932978-22-3. $24.95.
The city of Miami, the Everglades, the Keys, and the Kennedy Space Center are only a few of the attractions featured in this survey of Florida's geography, economy, people, and culture. (Rev: VL 1–2/06)

Philosophy and Religion

World Religions and Holidays

General and Miscellaneous

559 **Chalo Festival Time** (K–6). 2006. 30 min. Hindi Kids. $14.95.
Children celebrate Indian festivals including Holi, Rakhi, Diwali, and Kolu. The traditions and purpose behind each celebration are explained. Narration is available in English, Hindi, Gujarati, and Punjab. (Rev: SLJ 8/07)

560 **The Great Bible Discovery Series, Vol. 1** (K–6). 2007. 75 min. Series: Great Bible Discovery. Creative Communications for the Parish (dist. by Vision Video). $19.99.
Animation and live action combine for a meaningful presentation covering creation, Noah's ark, and Abraham. Volume 2 covers Joseph, Ruth, and Passover, and volume 3 Jesus' life and parables. (Rev: VL 7–8/07)

561 **Jacob's Ladder, Episodes 1 and 2** (6–9). 2006. 60 min. Vision Video. $19.99.
A group of young teens are transported back to biblical times and become involved in events that are related in the Bible; these episodes deal with Gideon. (Rev: VL 7/06)

562 **Jacob's Ladder, Episodes 10–13** (6–9). 2006. 2 discs. 120 min. Vision Video. $19.99.
The final four episodes of this series tell the Biblical story of the end of King Saul's reign and the early days of David's kingship. Actors portray the characters well in this reenactment of Old Testament times. (Rev: SLJ 6/07)

563 **New Year in Ping Wei** (5–8). 2005. 30 min. Pearl River. $24.95.
Liu Yen Twin and her family prepare for the Chinese New Year in their rural town. The narration is in Chinese with English captions. (Rev: BL 3/1/06)

564 **The Story of God** (9–12). 2005. 3 discs. 180 min. Films Media Group. PPR. Closed captioned. ISBN 978-1-4213-4498-0. $399.95.
Three BBC programs — *Life, the Universe, and Everything*; *No God But God*; and *The God of the Gaps* — offer thought-provoking insights into religious beliefs over time and across cultures. (Rev: VL 1–2/07)

565 **Where Facts and Fiction Meet: The Biblical Christ in a Da Vinci Code Society** (9–12). 2005. 90 min. Ensign Media (dist. by Vision Video). $29.99.
A well-illustrated and well-researched examination of the biblical questions raised by Dan Brown's novel. (Rev: VL 5–6/06)

Christianity

566 **Advent Calendar on DVD: A Christmas Countdown for December** (3–9). 2006. 80 min. Vision Video. $14.99.
Traditions surrounding Advent and Christmas are explained in brief vignettes. Through art and photographs, religious topics (such as angels) and cultural traditions (such as

Rudolph the Red-Nosed Reindeer) are explored. (Rev: SLJ 3/07)

567 ● **The America of the Amish** (9–12). 2006. 54 min. Zoulou Compagnie (dist. by Films Media Group). Closed captioned. ISBN 978-1-4213-5566-5. $149.95.
The lives of Amish groups in Ohio and Pennsylvania are explained through interviews; footage of the Amish at work, worship, and play; and narration. (Rev: SLJ 4/07)

568 ● **Creature Comforts: Merry Christmas Everybody!** (6–12). 2005. 24 min. Sony Pictures Home Entertainment. Closed captioned. ISBN 978-1-4248-2566-0. $9.95.
This look at Christmas from an unusual and humorous point of view features British claymation animals discussing their traditions. (Rev: VL 11–12/06)

569 ● **The Mormons** (9–12). 2007. Approx. 240 min. Series: The American Experience. WGBH Boston. ISBN 978-1-4157-2745-4. $19.95.
This lengthy documentary looks at the Mormon faith, the history of the Church of Jesus Christ of Latter-day Saints, and the controversies surrounding some of its practices, including polygamy. (Rev: SLJ 10/07)

Islam

570 ● **The Battle for Islam** (9–12). 2005. 63 min. Films Media Group. PPR. Closed captioned. ISBN 978-1-4213-4191-0. $149.95.
A look at the Muslim faith in various parts of the world, with interviews of individuals living both secular and strictly traditional lives. This documentary, seen on the BBC in 2005, asks whether the traditional or the progressive Islam will prevail. (Rev: VL 11–12/06)

571 ● **Decoding the Past: Secrets of the Koran** (9–12). 2006. 91 min. The History Channel. PPR. ISBN 978-0-7670-9068-1. $24.95.
For high school students, this is a useful and thorough introduction to the Koran, with commentary, dramatic re-creations, maps, and on-location footage as well as a focus on the importance of the Koran in Middle Eastern politics. (Rev: BL 10/1/06; VL 9–10/06)

572 ● **Me and the Mosque** (9–12). 2005. 52 min. National Film Board of Canada. Closed captioned. $195.
An interesting exploration of modern mosques and the separation of genders during worship; director Zarqa Nawaz looks mainly at the situation in Canada and the United States, and captures viewers' attention with an opening comic skit. (Rev: VL 7/06)

Society and the Individual

Government and Political Science

General and Miscellaneous

573 🌐 **Democracy in the 21st Century** (10–12). 2006. 37 min. Series: Democracy in World History. Hawkhill Assocs. Closed captioned. ISBN 978-1-55979-205-9. $109.

Advanced students will benefit most from the ideas put forth in this presentation. The benefits of living in a democracy as well as the challenges faced by a post 9/11 world are covered, as is the role democracies may play in the future. (Rev: SLJ 1/07)

United States Government and Institutions

General and Miscellaneous

574 🌐 **The Journey of the One and Only Declaration of Independence** (2–5). 2007. 30 min. Weston Woods. Closed captioned. ISBN 978-0-439-02758-8. $59.95.

An iconographic adaptation of the book by Judith St. George that traces the convoluted path the Declaration of Independence has taken. The document will take on new meaning to students who view this film and see what it has been through. (Rev: SLJ 10/07)

The Constitution

575 🌐 **Bundle of Compromises** (6–9). 2007. 2 discs. 150 min. Find the Fun. $79.99.

This is a creative look at the Constitution and its precedents and historical and social context, with humorous segments explaining key vocabulary and concepts. (Rev: BL 4/15/07; SLJ 2/07)

576 🌐 **Cases in Controversy: The 14th Amendment** (9–12). 2003. 54 min. Jumby Bay Studios. ISBN 978-0-9744350-0-8. $39.95.

Presents 14 cases in which the Fourteenth Amendment to the Constitution (banning discrimination) figured prominently. (Rev: BL 2/15/04)

577 🌐 **A DVD History of the U.S. Constitution** (9–12). 2005. 4 discs. 210 min. Ambrose Video. ISBN 978-1-58281-308-0. $129.99.

This well-produced four-volume set gives thorough and balanced coverage of the events preceding and following the creation of the U.S. Constitution, and includes many archival images and contemporary location shots. The component parts are: The Seeds of the Constitution/Founding the Constitution, 1619–1774; Writing the Constitution and the Bill of Rights/Testing the Constitution, 1774–1803; The Constitution Survives/The Constitution Is Expanded, 1810–1918; The Constitution in a Changing World/Constitutional Reform and Controversy, 1919–2005. (Rev: BL 1/1–15/06; SLJ 1/06)

Federal Government, Its Agencies, and Public Administration

578 ◐ **The Dark Side** (9–12). 2006. 90 min. PBS Video. Closed captioned. ISBN 978-0-7936-9236-1. $29.99 ($59.95 w/PPR).
Vice President Cheney is the focus of this PBS "Frontline" investigation into the struggle within the administration for control of intelligence information in the years following the terrorist attacks of September 11, 2001. (Rev: VL 11–12/06)

The Law and the Courts

579 ◐ **Kids Go to Court** (2–6). 2000. 18 min. TMW Media Group. PPR. $64.95.
Using a mock trial as an example, this humorous introduction to the court system looks at the ways in which proceedings affect children and the reasons why children are usually involved (divorce, abuse, as a witness, and so forth). Key words are carefully defined. (Rev: BL 2/1/06; SLJ 2/06; VL 1–2/06)

580 🎲 **Phoenix Wright: Ace Attorney** (9–12). 2005. Capcom. Windows, Game Boy Advance, Nintendo DS. ESRB: T (blood, language, suggestive themes, violence).
As a beginning attorney at law, you must prove you have what it takes to be a lawyer. Defend your cases as you uncover the truth behind each, present evidence, and cross-examine witnesses.

581 ◐ **Raise the Bar** (10–12). 2005. 55 min. National Film Network. ISBN 978-0-8026-0304-3. $24.95.
California teens competing in the 2004 state mock trial championship illustrate skills of reasoning, speaking, and working as a team. (Rev: BL 3/1/06)

582 ◐ **Unintended Consequences: Eminent Domain** (10–12). 2006. 15 min. izzit.org. $9.99.
This documentary examines the power of eminent domain and the recent expansion of its use to transfer property from one owner to another.
♕ YALSA 2008 Selected DVDs and Videos

Politics

ELECTIONS

583 ◐ **Call It Democracy** (7–12). 2007. 74 min. Cinema Guild. ISBN 978-0-7815-1203-9. $99.95 (Rental: $65).
How Americans vote, from the founding of the country to the historic confusion of the 2004 elections. Concepts such as the Electoral College are clearly explained using graphics, interviews, film footage, and photographs. (Rev: SLJ 9/07)

584 ◐ **Swing State Ohio: A Journey to the Heartland of a Divided Nation** (7–12). 2006. 61 min. JLP Media. $16.95.
Presents interviews with citizens and politicians in a state whose voters are crucial to deciding national elections. (Rev: SLJ 9/07)

Citizenship and Civil Rights

General and Miscellaneous

585 **Dear Mr. President** (10–12). 2006. 60 min. Big Kids Productions. PPR. $29.95.
Five teenage girls from Israel and Palestine travel across the United States hoping to meet President Bush and present their hopes for peace. Although they do not succeed in their objective, they do talk with many people on their journey and convey thought-provoking insights. (Rev: BL 8/06; VL 9–10/06)

586 **What Is an American?** (3–5). 2005. 22 min. Series: My America: Building a Democracy. Sunburst. ISBN 978-1-885285-54-6. $49.95.
A lively production featuring animated characters Turkey and Eagle plus a diverse group of children who consider the question. Narration, photographs, and maps add background. (Rev: BL 11/15/05)

Civil and Human Rights

587 **The ACLU Freedom Files** (9–12). 2005. 2 discs. 280 min. The Disinformation Company. ISBN 978-1-932857-50-4. $24.95.
Half-hour programs cover a variety of legal issues — including religious freedom, voting rights, women's rights, and racial profiling — tackled by the American Civil Liberties Union; one segment looks at the composition and function of the Supreme Court. Commen-

tary by comics provides light relief. (Rev: VL 9–10/06)

588 **Equality: A History of the Women's Movement in America** (7–12). 1996. 30 min. Schlessinger Media. PPR. Closed captioned. $39.95.
Contemporary women of achievement — Gloria Steinem, Anna Quindlen, and others — introduce discussion and dramatizations of the lives of earlier women who struggled for equality — Abigail Adams, Susan B. Anthony, and Elizabeth Cady Stanton, among others. This well-received presentation has recently become available on DVD and has a Spanish-language track. (Rev: BL 4/1/97; SLJ 4/97; VL 3/96)

589 **February One** (10–12). 2004. 61 min. California Newsreel. PPR. Closed captioned. $49.95.
The story of the four black freshmen who challenged segregation by taking seats at a whites-only lunch counter in February 1960 is told through interviews, archival clips, and dramatic re-creations. (Rev: BL 2/1/05; VL 1–2/06)

590 **To Form a More Perfect Union: Milestones of the Civil Rights Movement** (8–12). 2005. 38 min. U.S. Allegiance (dist. by Library Video Company). PPR. $19.99.
The U.S. Postal Service's series of stamps called "To Form a More Perfect Union" serves to introduce — in 3- to 5-minute segments — key events of the civil rights movement, which are shown in an arresting blend of archival footage, photographs, articles,

interviews, and artifacts. (Rev: SLJ 7/06; VL 7/06)

591 ◉ **Voices of Civil Rights** (9–12). 2005. 2 discs. 243 min. The History Channel (dist. by A&E Home Video). PPR. Closed captioned. ISBN 978-0-7670-7668-5. $29.95.

Five documentaries — including *Crossing the Bridge* (about the violent assault on protesters by state troopers at a bridge in Selma) and *Mississippi State Secrets* (about government surveillance of activists) — look at the civil rights movement in the 1950s and 1960s.

Immigration

592 ◉ **Arirang** (9–12). 2003. 112 min. Tom Coffman Multimedia. PPR. $29.95 for individuals, $49.95 for institutions.

The events that buffeted Korea during the 20th century are a striking backdrop to the stories of Koreans who chose to migrate to the United States, many to prosper and some to face prejudice. (Rev: VL 5–6/06)

593 ◉ **Crossing Arizona** (9–12). 2006. 77 min. Cinema Guild. ISBN 978-0-7815-1155-1. $99.95.

A look at the immigration problem at the Mexico-Arizona border from many perspectives. Viewers will be shocked to learn how many immigrants have died crossing the desert, and will be moved to join in the search for an answer to this issue. (Rev: BL 3/1/07; SLJ 2/07)

594 ◉ **Golden Venture** (9–12). 2007. 70 min. New Day Films. ISBN 978-1-57448-152-5. $95.

The title comes from the name of a Chinese ship that arrived in New York in 1993 with 300 illegal immigrants on board. Through the stories of many of the passengers, viewers will come to see the human side of the immigration debate. (Rev: SLJ 6/07)

595 ◉ **A Great Wonder: Lost Children of Sudan** (9–12). 2004. 61 min. Two Shoes Productions (dist. by Bullfrog Films). ISBN 978-1-59458-041-3. $250.

Three young Sudanese refugees now living in Seattle describe the horrors they endured in their African homeland and the difficulties of adapting to their new lives in the United States. (Rev: BL 9/15/04; SLJ 10/04)

596 ◉ **Rain in a Dry Land** (7–12). 2006. 82 min. Anne Makepeace Productions (dist. by Bullfrog Films). ISBN 978-1-59458-523-4. $295.

This film tells the stories of two Bantu families who fled the civil war in Somalia and resettled in Georgia and Massachusetts, showing the hardships they suffered in Africa and the difficulties they have adjusting to American culture. (Rev: BL 2/1/07; SLJ 4/07)

Ethnic Groups and Prejudice

General and Miscellaneous

597 ◉ **Race — The Power of Illusion** (9–12). 2003. 57 min. California Newsreel. $99.

A thorough examination of all aspects of race, this documentary is composed of three episodes: "The Difference Between Us" — a look at genetics and physical traits; "The Story We Tell" — a discussion of the concept of race and the development of ideas of racial superiority; and "The House We Live In," which tackles contemporary assumptions and attitudes. (Rev: BL 3/15/04; SLJ 9/03; VL 9–10/03)

ဪ YALSA 2004 Selected Videos and DVDs

African Americans

598 ◉ **African American Lives** (10–12). 2006. 240 min. PBS Video. Closed captioned. ISBN 978-1-4157-1694-6. $34.99 ($64.95 w/PPR).

Henry Louis Gates Jr. and eight other well-known African Americans trace their family histories in this documentary that discusses the problems posed by record-keeping during slavery, and the new opportunities that DNA research offers in establishing long-ago roots. (Rev: VL 9–10/06)

599 🖳 **Exploring the World of Thomas Day** (4–12). 2004. Thomas Day Project / New

Hope Publications (www.thomasday.net). Windows, Macintosh. $149.95.

Search for clues that will free a young apprentice from jail in this interactive program set in the 19th century and highlighting African American history. Thomas Day (1801–1861) was a free African American cabinetmaker who lived in North Carolina from the early 1820s to the early 1860s and built a large furniture business. (Rev: SLJ 4/04)

ALA Notable Children's Software 2004

600 ● **A History of Black Achievement in America** (7–12). 2005. 4 discs. 216 min. Ambrose Video. PPR. $199.99.

This eight-part series documents African Americans' contributions to American society and culture, highlighting the lives and works of many key figures at the same time as it explains the obstacles that hampered this group's progress. (Rev: BL 2/1/06)

601 ● **The Pact** (7–12). 2006. 85 min. Spark Media (dist. by Thomas S. Klise). $79.99.

Based on the book *The Pact: Three Young Men Make a Promise and Fulfill a Dream* (2003), this documentary tells the story of three poor, disadvantaged African American men who beat the odds and make it to medical school. (Rev: SLJ 1/07)

Asian Americans

602 ● **My Brown Eyes** (4–8). 1994. 19 min. Master Communications. PPR. ISBN 978-1-888194-55-5. $60.

The child of Korean immigrants, Jun has trouble fitting in at his American school. This live-action short film will help children to empathize with those who are different. Discussion guide included. (Rev: BL 1/1–15/05; SLJ 1/05; VL 1–2/05)

Hispanic Americans

603 ● **A History of Hispanic Achievement in America** (8–12). 2006. 4 discs. 237 min. Ambrose Video. PPR. Closed captioned. $129.99.

Eight episodes introduce key Hispanic figures — from early explorers including Cortes and de Soto through individuals as diverse as Cesar Chavez, Joan Baez, and Roberto

Clemente — offering social and historical context throughout. (Rev: BL 1/1–15/07; SLJ 2/07; VL 1–2/07)

604 ● **Puerto Rican Heritage for Children** (K–4). 1997. 25 min. Series: American Cultures for Children. Schlessinger Video Productions (dist. by Library Video Company). PPR. Closed captioned. $29.95.

Tour the Commonwealth of Puerto Rico with host Phylicia Rashad and a group of children, hear about the contributions of famous Puerto Ricans to the mainland, and learn a few words in Spanish, a folktale, and an activity. Newly available on DVD, this series also includes *African-American Heritage, Arab-American Heritage, Central American Heritage, Chinese-American Heritage, Irish-American Heritage, Japanese-American Heritage, Jewish-American Heritage, Korean-American Heritage, Mexican-American Heritage, Native American Heritage,* and *Vietnamese-American Heritage*. (Rev: SLJ 7/05; VL 7/06)

605 ● **Valley of Tears** (9–12). 2007. 77 min. Cinema Guild. ISBN 978-0-7815-1189-6. $99.95 (Rental: $65).

The plight of Mexican American farm workers in Texas is chronicled, beginning with a strike in 1979 over low wages and continuing through 2002, when the workers had united to try to improve their situation. An interesting look at issues of immigration, workers' rights, and prejudice. (Rev: SLJ 8/07)

Native Americans

606 ● **Homeland: Four Portraits of Native Action** (10–12). 2005. 88 min. Katahdin Productions (dist. by Bullfrog Films). PPR. Closed captioned. ISBN 978-1-59458-267-7.

Four cases illustrate Native Americans' continuing struggles to preserve their land and resources from exploitation. (Rev: VL 1–2/06)

YALSA 2007 Selected Videos and DVDs

607 ● **Native American Teens . . . Who We Are** (7–12). 2006. 29 min. Series: In the Mix. Castle Works. ISBN 978-1-931843-10-2. $69.95.

With an emphasis on modern Native Americans who are succeeding in U.S. culture as well as remembering their Native roots, this presentation will open the eyes of many students. (Rev: BL 4/15/07; SLJ 3/07)

Other Ethnic Groups

608 ⬥ **Whose Children Are These?** (9–12). 2007. 28 min. Filmakers Library. $295 (Rental: $65).

A look at three teenagers whose families were separated following 9/11, when the U.S. government deported many Muslim men who were not American citizens. This expensive program is also available as a rental. (Rev: SLJ 7/07)

♉ YALSA 2007 Selected Videos and DVDs

Social Concerns and Problems

General and Miscellaneous

609 🌏 **Tales of Sand and Snow** (11–12). 2006. 48 min. National Film Board of Canada. $149.

Examines two isolated cultures — one in Africa, the other in Canada — and the changes they are experiencing in an age of globalization. In French with English subtitles. (Rev: SLJ 1/07)

Environmental Issues

General and Miscellaneous

610 🌏 **America's Lost Landscape: The Tallgrass Prairie** (7–12). 2006. 60 min. Bullfrog Films. ISBN 978-1-59458-383-4. $250 (Rental: $85).

The sad story of the vast areas of tallgrass prairie that have disappeared in the last century is told in archival images and beautiful film, with details of the plants and animals that have been lost. (Rev: SLJ 11/06)

611 🌏 **Black Diamonds** (7–12). 2006. 72 min. Bullfrog Films. ISBN 978-1-59458-612-5. $275 (Rental: $95).

The history of coal mining and the coal industry, with an emphasis on the effects that surface mining has had on the landscape and economy of West Virginia and the rest of Appalachia. Interviews, vintage film, and

music enhance the presentation. (Rev: SLJ 4/07)

612 🌏 **Cowboys, Indians and Lawyers** (9–12). 2006. 57 min. Walking Shadows Productions (dist. by Bullfrog Films). ISBN 978-1-59458-379-7. $250.

The story of a conflict in Colorado over the building of a dam. The Native American Ute tribe disagrees with environmentalists about the possible effects of the dam, and the filmmakers present both points of view. (Rev: SLJ 3/07)

613 🌏 **Dimming the Sun** (9–12). 2006. 56 min. WGBH Boston. Closed captioned. ISBN 978-1-59375-566-9. $19.95.

Students studying global warming will be intrigued by this presentation, which looks at a phenomenon that scientists feel may contribute to the problem: sunlight blocked by air pollution. This "NOVA" program features scientists explaining their research in detail. (Rev: LMC 3/07; SLJ 4/07)

614 🌏 **Earth's Natural Resources** (4–8). 2007. 20 min. Series: Natural Resources. Visual Learning. PPR. ISBN 978-1-59234-169-6. $89.95.

An introduction to renewable and nonrenewable resources, including solar energy, fossil fuels, and mineral resources. The importance of recycling and reusing is stressed. The other three programs in the series are *Everyday Natural Resources, Energy Resources,* and *Sustainability and Natural Resources.* (Rev: SLJ 10/07)

615 ● **Ecology Fundamentals** (3–5). 2006. 15 min. Visual Learning. ISBN 978-1-59234-149-7. $79.95.
In sections titled "Ecology," "Organisms, Population, Community," "Ecosystem," "Habitat and Niche," "Ecosystem Roles," and "Food Chains and Food Webs," viewers will learn about the interrelationship between living things and the surrounding environment. Teacher's guide included. (Rev: SLJ 10/06)

616 ● **Fire on the Land/Beaver Steals Fire** (7–12). 2007. Confederated Salish and Kootenai Tribes (dist. by Univ. of Nebraska Press). ISBN 978-0-8031-1371-8. $19.95.
This DVD-ROM and DVD set combines information about the use of fire by Native Americans with a Salish folktale about how fire came to be used by humans. The DVD-ROM is packed with information about the use of fire for land management and the history of Native Americans. (Rev: SLJ 5/07)

617 ● **Freeze, Freeze, Fry: Climate Past, Present, and Future** (9–12). 2007. 90 min. Midwest Tape. $50.
With the help of images and graphs, Harvard professor Daniel P. Schrag presents a lesson on global warming to a group of high school students. Following the lesson, the students interview the professor regarding his career, and in a final segment Schrag addresses teachers and offers tips. (Rev: BL 12/1/07; SLJ 10/07)

618 ● **Global Warming: Science and Solutions** (6–12). 2006. 2 discs. 58 min each. Centre Communications and the National Center for Atmospheric Research (dist. by Ambrose Video). $79.99.
This set of two DVDs (*The Science of Global Warming* and *Global Warming: Solutions*) features scientists discussing what has caused the problem and what can be done to end or reverse it. Graphics and animations add to the presentation. (Rev: SLJ 3/07)

619 ● **Global Warming: The Storm Rising** (9–12). 2007. 2 discs. 114 min. Ambrose Video. $79.99.
In two parts — *Warnings from a Warm Planet; Predictions for a Warmer Planet* — this program looks at the evidence of harm already done by global warming and then explores scientific predictions for the future. Teacher's guide included. (Rev: SLJ 9/07)

620 ● **Going Green: Every Home an Eco-Home** (5–8). 2005. 24 min. Green Planet Films (dist. by Library Video Company). $27.95.
Middle-school students take a tour of an ecologically sound house in Los Angeles, examining its solar collectors, water recycling system, composting, and so forth; discussion centers on practical and inexpensive ways to lead a "green" life. (Rev: BL 1/1–15/07; VL 1–2/07)

621 ● **Greenhouse Effect: Climate Change and Global Warming** (7–12). 2006. 25 min. Distribution Access. PPR. $99.
This program examines the evidence for climate change in an objective overview. The presentation is accessible to middle-schoolers, and an additional advanced version that is also included goes into greater detail. (Rev: SLJ 2/08)

622 ● **How to Save the World: One World, One Cow, One Planet** (10–12). 2007. 103 mins. Green Planet Films. $29.95.
A persuasive argument for organic farming, based on the harm caused to the environment by farming practices in India and the United States. The globalization of farming is at the root of the problem, and the film looks at biodynamic agriculture as the answer to pollution and food shortages. (Rev: SLJ 9/07)

623 ● **An Inconvenient Truth** (9–12). 2006. 96 min. Paramount. $29.99.
Former Vice President Al Gore presents his award-winning exploration of global warming, an indictment of those who deny the dangers it poses. (Rev: BL 4/15/07; LMC 10/07; VL 11–12/06)

624 ● **Power Shift: Energy and Sustainability** (7–12). 2004. 26 min. WorldLink Media (dist. by the Video Project). PPR. $89.95.
Cameron Diaz hosts this investigation of all the alternatives we have — solar, wind, and so forth — to the fossil fuels on which we currently depend and discusses the pollution and other dangers we face. (Rev: SLJ 6/05; VL 11–12/04)
♙ YALSA 2005 Selected Videos and DVDs

625 ● **Solar Energy: Saved by the Sun** (9–12). 2007. 60 min. WGBH Boston. ISBN 978-1-59375-721-2. $19.95.
The benefits and limitations of the use of solar power are explained by scientists and others in this "NOVA" presentation. Viewers will come away with an understanding of how solar power works and how it may help to slow global warming. (Rev: BL 12/1/07; SLJ 10/07)

626 ● **Swim for the River** (6–12). 2007. 56 min. Bullfrog Films. ISBN 978-1-59458-534-0. $250.
The story of why and how Christopher Swain swam the entire length of the Hudson River in 2004 in an attempt to raise awareness of the river's beauty and its need for preservation. (Rev: BL 4/15/07; SLJ 9/07)

627 ● **Water Detectives** (4–7). 2007. 12 min. National Film Board of Canada. $95.
The story of students in Matamoros, Mexico, who succeeded in getting their whole town to reduce its water consumption. (Rev: SLJ 3/1/08)
♻ ALA ALSC Notable Children's Videos 2008

Pollution

628 ● **Smog: The Sweet Smell of Success?** (9–12). 2006. 30 min. Series: Late Lessons from Early Warnings: Cultivating Environmental Foresight. Films for the Humanities and Sciences (dist. by Films Media Group). ISBN 978-1-4213-4371-6. $129.95.
Our changing attitudes toward pollution are traced in this fascinating film that looks at the smog of the early 20th century — when smoke was viewed as a necessary part of industrial progress; the mid-century, when the effects of the smoke become apparent; the continued growth in pollution through the 1970s; and the final move toward emissions controls. (Rev: SLJ 12/06)

629 ● **'Til the River Runs Clear** (9–12). 2007. 30 min. Kunhardt Productions (dist. by PBS Home Video). Closed captioned. ISBN 978-0-7936-9365-8. $14.99.
The story of the *Clearwater*, a boat that folk singer Pete Seeger used in the 1960s to travel the Hudson River and spread his message of respect for the environment. (Rev: SLJ 10/07)

Recycling

630 ● **Respect Yo' Mama: Here Comes Mr. Recycle Man!** (6–8). 2005. 35 min. Garbage In. $14.95.
This look at garbage and recycling will fascinate those devoted to environmental issues as well as anyone interested in machines, the whole process of recycling, and the range of end products. (Rev: BL 2/1/06)

Population Issues

General and Miscellaneous

631 ● **Aruba** (6–12). 2006. 12 min. National Film Board of Canada. $129.
The sad life of a disadvantaged inner-city boy who resorts to taking his drug-dealing father's gun to school to confront a bully. Teacher's guide available. (Rev: SLJ 5/07)
♻ YALSA 2007 Selected Videos and DVDs

632 ● **Exploring Communities and Its Workers** (K–3). 2007. 10 min. Mazzarella Media. ISBN 978-1-934119-09-9. $39.95.
Takes a look at the needs of communities and the workers who respond to these needs. This is part of an interesting series that explores the differences between urban and rural communities, rules and laws, and other aspects of human society. The other titles are: *Exploring Communities Alike and Different, Exploring Communities and Geography, Exploring Communities Long Ago,* and *Exploring Communities' Rules and Laws.* (Rev: BL 8/07; SLJ 7/07)

633 ● **If the World Were a Village** (2–5). 2007. 24 min. Story Entertainment (dist. by Visual Education Centre). PPR. $59.99.
An animated version of the award-winning 2002 book by David Smith that reduces the world's population to just 100. In an engaging way, Smith presents statistics about the world and its people in a way that even young children will understand and appreciate. (Rev: SLJ 9/07)

634 ● **The Perfect Life: Growing Up in Urban America** (10–12). 2007. 82 min.

Choices Inc. ISBN 978-1-933724-12-6. $99.95.

Five teenagers living in a dangerous section of New York City discuss their prospects for the future. Sadly, most of them end up in bad situations at the end of the film. The viewer also sees footage of the teens as carefree children at a summer camp in the country, adding to the tragedy. (Rev: BL 8/07*; SLJ 9/07)

635 ◉ **Scared Sacred** (9–12). 2005. 105 min. National Film Board of Canada. PPR. $195.
Man's ability to see continuing hope and humanity despite disaster and long-term stress is examined by director Velcrow Ripper; stock footage and interviews detail dire conditions and human resilience in countries including Bosnia, Cambodia, and Afghanistan. (Rev: VL 5–6/06)

636 ◉ **Surviving Peer Pressure: You Can Do It!** (7–12). 2006. 22 min. Human Relations Media. PPR. $119.95.
Presenting common teen peer pressure scenarios, a teacher discusses coping strategies and the importance of being prepared for these difficult situations. Teacher's guide included. (Rev: LMC 8–9/06; SLJ 2/06; VL 1–2/07)

Crime, Gangs, and Prisons

637 ◉ **Every Mother's Son** (10–12). 2004. 53 min. AndersonGold Films (dist. by New Day Films). PPR. ISBN 978-1-57448-128-0. $150.
In interviews with the mothers who lost their sons, filmmakers Tami Gold and Kelly Anderson explore the circumstances of three young men killed erroneously by the police in the United States — Amadou Diallo, Anthony Baez, and Gary Boskey. (Rev: VL 5–6/06)
⛉ YALSA 2006 Selected Videos and DVDs

638 ◉ **Fighting for Life in the Death-Belt** (10–12). 2005. 52 min. National Film Network. ISBN 978-0-8026-0433-0. $29.95 ($179.95 w/PPR).
Efforts to spare two men on death row in Georgia are explored in a thought-provoking production that includes expert opinions on the importance of adequate legal representation. (Rev: VL 1–2/07)

639 ◉ **I Am Not a Target!** (3–8). 2004. 49 min. BFS Entertainment. ISBN 978-0-7792-5738-6. $14.98.
Provides advice on coping with a variety of potentially dangerous situations; includes security camera footage of an abduction and some controversial self-defense techniques. (Rev: VL 5–6/06)

640 ◉ **It's Not About Sex** (10–12). 2007. 23 min. Educational Video Center. $150, $75 (schools).
An exploration of sexual assault in the United States, the large percentage of rapes of people under 18, and the reasons for low rates of reporting of these crimes.
⛉ YALSA 2008 Selected DVDs and Videos

641 ◉ **Juvies** (10–12). 2004. 66 min. Chance Films Incorporated. $19.95.
A disturbing look at the juvenile justice system in the United States.
⛉ YALSA 2008 Selected DVDs and Videos

642 ◉ **Reckless Indifference** (10–12). 2006. 94 min. Choices Inc. ISBN 978-1-933724-04-1. $49.95.
A disturbing look at a case in California in 1995 that resulted in four young men being convicted of murder. Interviews with people involved in the case, as well as news footage and reenactments, encourage sympathy for the defendants. (Rev: BL 1/1–15/07; SLJ 1/07)

643 ◉ **Teens at Risk: Youth and Guns** (8–12). 2005. 18 min. TMW. $64.95.
A look at violence in Los Angeles, in which former gang members talk about their experiences and the shootings that caused their injuries. Students try role-playing and discuss ways to keep out of danger. (Rev: BL 1/1–15/06)

644 ◉ **Vandalism on Display** (8–12). 2006. 23 min. Gordon-Kerckhoff Productions (dist. by Library Video Company). PPR. $64.95.
This effective program presents instances of vandalism in five different settings — city, school, car, computer, and cemetery — and emphasizes the variety of motivations and the impact on innocent victims. Teacher's guide included. (Rev: VL 9–10/06)

645 ◉ **Voices from Inside: Incarcerated Teens Speak Out** (8–12). 2006. 20 min.

Series: In the Mix. Castle Works. ISBN 978-1-931843-63-8. $69.95.

An interesting survey of teens' reactions to incarceration, revealing how hard life behind bars can be, but also the pride some gang members derive from the experience. (Rev: BL 10/15/06; SLJ 12/1/06; VL 11–12/06)

Social Action, Social Change, and Futurism

646 ● **Community Service: Service Learning** (5–12). 2007. 15 min. Learning ZoneXpress. Closed captioned. ISBN 978-1-57175-470-7. $49.95.

A brief look at what opportunities are available for young people who want to (or are required to) perform volunteer work. (Rev: SLJ 10/07)

Social Customs and Holidays

647 ● **La Quinceanera** (10–12). 2007. 42 min. Laquinceaneradocumentary.com. PPR. $79.95.

A loving look at the custom of celebrating a girl's 15th birthday as a coming-of-age event. Ana Maria, who is the youngest girl in a Mexican family, discusses her feelings as she prepares for the big day. Her mother explains the significance of the tradition in this fascinating look at modern Mexican culture. In Spanish with English subtitles. (Rev: SLJ 12/07; VL 12/11/07)

648 ● **Prom Night in Kansas City** (10–12). 2002. 54 min. Zeitgeist Films. $24.99.

Filmmaker Hali Lee returns to her hometown to document how students at different schools prepare for and celebrate the all-important prom night, revealing a wide range of diversity. (Rev: BL 3/15/04; VL 9–10/05)

⊙ YALSA 2004 Selected Videos and DVDs

Terrorism

649 ● **Al Qaeda After 9/11** (9–12). 2006. 30 min. Discovery School. ISBN 978-1-59380-554-8. $69.95.

An often-frightening look at how Al Qaeda has adapted and spread following 9/11. Interviews with terrorism experts and footage of Al Qaeda training camps show the threat posed by this group and others like it. (Rev: SLJ 1/07)

650 ● **9/11: The Flight that Fought Back** (9–12). 2006. 56 min. Discovery School. ISBN 978-1-59527-836-4. $69.95.

A reenactment of what may have happened on United Airlines flight 93 on 9/11. Students will be moved by the account, which is gleaned from telephone calls, the cockpit recorder, news reports, and interviews. Teacher's guide included. (Rev: SLJ 2/07)

Economics and Business

General and Miscellaneous

651 ❁ **Economics, 3rd Edition** (9–12). 2005. 6 discs. 1,080 min. Series: Great Courses. The Teaching Company. ISBN 978-1-59803-127-0. $149.95.
In 36 half-hour lectures, Dr. Timothy Taylor shares his enthusiasm for economics in two parts, the first covering microeconomics and the second macroeconomics. (Rev: VL 7/06)

652 🎲 **Toy Shop** (3–6). 2008. Majesco. Nintendo DS. Players: 1. ESRB: E.
As the granddaughter or grandson of a toy store owner, the player must bring the shop back to profitability, creating toys and anticipating customer demand. This game combines entertainment with basic business information. (Rev: CTR 2/08)

Labor Unions and Labor Problems

653 ❁ **Maquilapolis** (10–12). 2006. 68 min. California Newsreel. PPR. Closed captioned. $49.95.
Portrays the lives of women who work in Tijuana's factories under terrible conditions and for little pay. Far from helpless victims, the women are organizing to improve their situation and live healthier lives. The presentation is mainly in Spanish with English subtitles. (Rev: VL 5–6/07)

Money and Trade

654 ❁ **Buyer Be Fair: The Promise of Product Certification** (9–12). 2006. 57 min. Fox-Wilmer (dist. by Bullfrog Films). ISBN 978-1-59458-347-6. $250 (Rental: $85).
The advantages that "fair trade" and certified products present for the environment, the producer, and the concerned consumer are discussed along with imbalances in world trade and competitive opportunities. (Rev: SLJ 11/06)

Marketing and Advertising

655 ❁ **Cracking the Advertising Code** (6–9). 2006. 15 min. Learning ZoneXpress. Closed captioned. ISBN 978-1-57175-240-6. $49.95.
This is a fascinating look at the world of advertising, showing how advertisers influence buying decisions. Includes teaching materials. (Rev: BL 1/1–15/07)

Guidance and Personal Development

Education and Schools

General and Miscellaneous

656 ⌖ **BrainPOP** (3–8).
www.brainpop.com
Engaging and informative Flash-based content is the draw to this innovative, award-winning Web site hosted by orange robot called Moby and his teen sidekick Tim. Movies cover a wide range of topics spanning the curriculum and enjoyable interactive quizzes, experiments, and activities reinforce key concepts and facts. Also available: *BrainPOP en Español* and *BrainPOP Jr.* for grades K–3. (Rev: *BrainPOP*: CTR Fall 04; LMC 3/05; MM&IS 1–2/05; SLJ 1/08; *BrainPOP en Espanol*: LMC 11–12/06; *BrainPOP Jr.*: CTR 10/06; LMC 10/07)

657 ◉ **Building Adolescent Readers** (7–12). 2005. 2 discs. 97 min. Stenhouse Publishers. PPR. ISBN 978-1-57110-430-4. $295.
High school teacher Kelly Gallagher describes strategies that succeed both in motivating students to read and in helping them understand what they are reading. Discussion guide included. (Rev: VL 5–6/06)

658 ◉ **Connect the Dots: How School Skills Become Work Skills** (6–8). 2006. 20 min. Human Relations Media. Closed captioned. ISBN 978-1-55548-017-2. $119.95.
A good answer to the question, "What will I ever use this for?" On-the-job skills such as meeting deadlines are related to school situations and subjects. Includes teacher's guide. (Rev: LMC 8–9/07; SLJ 2/07)

659 ◉ **Far from Home** (7–12). 2006. 40 min. Women Make Movies. $89.
African American high school senior Kandice reveals the social and academic pressures she faces in this film that shows the changes as she is bussed each day from her home in Boston to a school 45 minutes away in a mainly white suburb. (Rev: SLJ 12/06)
⚉ YALSA 2007 Selected Videos and DVDs

660 ▦ **Garfield's Typing Pal** (2–8). 2003. De Marque (www.typingpal.com). Windows. $19.95.
Learn to type the easy way with Garfield the cat, enjoying entertaining text and games.
⚉ ALA Notable Children's Software 2004

Development of Academic Skills

Study Skills

661 ◉ **The 5 Steps for Study Skills Success** (5–8). 2007. 18 min. Smith Show Media Productions. $29.99.
Host Antonio Smith helps two struggling young students, offering tips on note-taking, using the SQ3R (survey, question, read, recite, and review) method, concentrating, taking tests, and so forth. (Rev: BL 4/15/07; SLJ 6/07)

662 ◉ **Great Homework and Study Skills for Middle School and High School** (7–11). 2007. 85 min. Dan Sperling Video & Film

Productions (dist. by Five Star Educational). ISBN 978-1-59382-027-5. $59.95.

Four teenagers learn study skills from a tutor in this presentation that acknowledges the many demands on high school students. Time management and organization are stressed. (Rev: SLJ 9/07)

663 ◐ **Information Literacy: The Perils of Online Research** (8–12). 2006. 21 min. Cambridge Educational (dist. by Films Media Group). ISBN 978-1-4213-5719-5. $89.95.

Avoiding the pitfalls of plagiarism and bad information, a young woman conducts research online. Teacher's guide available. (Rev: LMC 8–9/07; SLJ 5/07)

Tests and Test Taking

664 ◐ **New SAT Prep** (10–12). 2005. 6 discs. 212 min. Series: Standard Deviants. Goldhil Entertainment. PPR. ISBN 978-1-59443-020-6. $160.98.

An upbeat review of strategies for test taking. The set includes six programs that are also available individually: "Introduction to the SAT and Sentence Completion," "Critical Reading and Vocabulary," "The Writing Section," "Introduction to the Math Section," "Algebra," and "Geometry." (Rev: SLJ 12/05; VL 1–2/06)

665 ◐ **Test-Taking Strategies: Reading** (2–4). 2007. 45 min. Rock 'n Learn (dist. by Big Kids Productions). ISBN 978-1-934312-00-1. $19.95.

Marco the pencil offers test-taking tips in this animated program that uses a breezy style to

help students feel confident when faced with reading tests. (Rev: SLJ 8/07)

Writing and Speaking Skills

666 🖥 **Essay Express: Strategies for Successful Essay Writing** (4–8). 2005. FableVision. Windows, Macintosh. Single site, $89.95; 5 copy lab pack, $320.

The Rotten Green Peppers rock band and a robot named BOTEC help to emphasize important aspects of this appealing guide to effective essay writing. (Rev: LMC 8–9/06; SLJ 1/06)

Ȣ ALA Notable Children's Software 2006

667 ◐ **Making the Speech: From Last Year's Loser . . . to This Year's Winner** (8–11). 2005. 63 min. VAT 19. $29.95.

Stanley progresses from the disgrace of last year's failed speech to an award-winning success during this program full of helpful information on speech writing and giving. (Rev: BL 9/15/05)

668 ◐ **Writing for Students: Editing and Proofreading** (4–10). 2006. 23 min. Schlessinger Media (dist. by Library Video Company). PPR. Closed captioned. ISBN 978-1-4171-0306-5. $39.95.

Hosts Julie and Nick emphasize the importance of these skills — for future journalists, screenwriters, and even songwriters — and demonstrate the basics of good prose. (Rev: LMC 10/06; VL 5–6/06)

Academic Guidance

General and Miscellaneous

669 ❀ **The Gender Chip Project** (9–12). 2006. 54 min. Women Make Movies. $89.
A look at a student support group at Ohio State University for young women interested in careers in math and science. The students discuss the challenges they face in their fields and how they have managed to overcome them. (Rev: SLJ 6/07)

Colleges and Universities

670 ❀ **Cracking College: The 7 Secrets of Savvy Students** (10–12). 2007. 36 min. College Crossroads. $69.95.

This program hosted by a recent college graduate offers practical advice for college-bound students, some of it rather obvious, but with the benefit that he is sharing his own experiences. He stresses the importance of developing good relationships with professors and taking advantage of free tutoring opportunities. (Rev: BL 11/15/07; SLJ 8/07)

671 ❀ **How to Get Into the College of Your Choice** (10–12). 2005. 24 min. Human Relations Media. PPR. Closed captioned. ISBN 978-1-55548-063-9. $139.95.
Provides practical strategies for success in the admissions process, plus interviews with recent high school graduates, a dean of admissions, and a guidance counselor. Teacher's guide included. (Rev: SLJ 1/06; VL 5–6/06)

Careers and Occupational Guidance

General and Miscellaneous

672 ● **Job Survival: Keeping and Advancing in Your Job** (9–12). 2005. 23 min. Linx Educational Publishing. PPR. ISBN 978-1-891818-71-4. $108.

Scott and Sabrina are young workers with bad work habits, which are pointed out and corrected in the course of the program. Communication skills, punctuality, respect, and a positive attitude are among the attributes stressed. Teacher's guide included. (Rev: SLJ 2/06; VL 3–4/06)

673 ● **The Virtual Job Interview: Practice and Preparation for Getting the Job You Deserve** (11–12). 2006. 30 min. Daniel Peters Productions (dist. by Victory Multimedia). $29.98.

Students who are nervous about interviewing for jobs will glean a great deal from this film. In four sections ("Preparation," "The Day Of," "Illegal Questions," and "Mr. Aitchar"), the basics of preparing for an interview are presented. The final section is a practice interview, and the interviewee is hired or rejected based on his or her responses. (Rev: SLJ 4/07)

674 ⌂ **Vocational Biographies** (7–12). www.vocbiosonline.com/index.php

Users can explore more than 1,000 occupations by reading "career biographies" — lengthy descriptions of individual jobs, focusing on the experiences of one individual and including educational requirements, work experience, benefits, job description, and insights on daily enjoyments and frustrations.

Careers

General and Miscellaneous

675 ● **Career Assessment: Finding a Career That Fits** (10–12). 2005. 24 min. Linx Educational Publishing. PPR. ISBN 978-1-891818-73-8. $108.

Assessing your own skills and interests, and writing a career mission statement are the first two steps recommended. Study guide and instructor's guide included. (Rev: VL 1–2/06)

676 ● **Confessions of a Fashion Designer** (6–12). 2007. 13 min. Learning ZoneXpress. Closed captioned. ISBN 978-1-57175-448-6. $79.95.

Students interested in the world of fashion will get the scoop on what it takes to get into this field and what a typical day is like for the hands-on owner of a dress company. (Rev: LMC 11–12/07; SLJ 8/07)

677 ● **Confessions of an Interior Designer** (6–12). 2007. 12 min. Learning ZoneXpress. Closed captioned. ISBN 978-1-57175-446-2. $79.95.

An experienced interior designer gives the scoop on what it takes to get into this field and what a typical day is like — both the ups and the downs. (Rev: LMC 11–12/07; SLJ 8/07)

678 ⊗ **Confessions of Chefs and a Restaurateur** (6–9). 2007. Learning ZoneXpress. Closed captioned. ISBN 978-1-57175-444-8. $79.95.
Viewers visit a College of Culinary Arts and a restaurant to learn more about the requirements and training for a culinary career, salary ranges, and how a typical day progresses. (Rev: BL 6/1–15/07; LMC 11–12/07; SLJ 8/07)

679 ⊗ **Future Stars: An Inside Look at Modeling** (9–12). 2005. 50 min. Blue Wood. $24.95.
This presentation gives aspiring models and actors a view inside a modeling school and a realistic assessment of the profession and an individual's chances of success. (Rev: BL 5/1/06; SLJ 6/06)

680 ⊗ **Get a Life!** (9–12). 2007. 70 min. Janson. ISBN 978-1-56839-291-2. $24.95.
A hip look at career options for teens, containing interviews with people in a variety of professions (such as musician, poet, and teacher), describing their responsibilities, challenges, and pressures. (Rev: BL 9/15/07; SLJ 7/07)

681 ⊗ **Interview Performance** (11–12). 2006. 26 min. VEA. $89.95.
This useful video, produced in Australia, covers how to prepare for a job interview, answer questions skillfully and honestly, and present yourself in the best possible light. (Rev: SLJ 8/07)

682 ⊗ **Make Me a Model** (9–12). 2005. 103 min. NFI. $24.95.
Sara and Aja learn about modeling in this informative program full of beauty tips and practical information about how to become a model. (Rev: BL 4/15/06)

683 ⊗ **Matching Your Skills, Talents and Ambitions to a Dream Career** (7–12). 2006. 20 min. Human Relations Media. Closed captioned. ISBN 978-1-55548-030-1. $139.95.
The training, skills, and talents needed to become a doctor, a teacher, a photographer, and a pilot are outlined. Students are encouraged to determine for themselves what their own "dream jobs" may be. (Rev: SLJ 1/07)

684 ⊗ **Now What? Non-College Opportunities for High School Grads** (7–12). 2006. 20 min. Human Relations Media. Closed captioned. ISBN 978-1-55548-028-8. $139.95.
Students looking for alternatives to college will be interested in this film, which shows a variety of trades and business positions that can be pursued directly after high school. The military option is also explored. Includes teacher's guide. (Rev: SLJ 3/07)

685 ⊗ **Pet Vet 3D: Wild Animal Hospital** (3–6). 2007. Viva Media. Windows. ISBN 978-1-934088-46-3. $29.99.
Players can simulate setting up a veterinary practice in an African wildlife park. They are responsible for all aspects, including the business side. A great program for children interested in animal care, Africa, and entrepreneurship. (Rev: SLJ 9/07)

686 ⊗ **Ten Things Not to Do in an Interview** (10–12). 2006. 30 min. VEA. $89.95.
A few major things: Don't arrive late, don't forget your resume, and don't dress inappropriately. The message comes across loud and clear in this enjoyable informational film. (Rev: SLJ 8/07)

687 ⊗ **What Type of Person Am I? Personality and Careers** (6–8). 2006. 20 min. Human Relations Media. Closed captioned. ISBN 978-1-55548-018-9. $119.95.
Are you a doer, a thinker, a creator, a helper, a persuader, or an organizer? This introduction to personality types will get middle-schoolers thinking about what careers may best suit their personalities. Includes teacher's guide. (Rev: SLJ 2/07)

688 ⊗ **Women Entrepreneurs** (7–12). 2007. 15 min. Series: Women in Nontraditional Careers. Her Own Words. Closed captioned. ISBN 978-1-877933-73-8. $95; resource guide: $45.
A simple, no-frills introduction to 25 women who run their own businesses, both large and small. Discussion questions are included. (Rev: SLJ 4/07)

Arts, Entertainment, and Sports

689 ⊗ **Careers in Arts: Careers in Television** (6–8). 2006. 56 min. Discovery School. ISBN 978-1-59380-527-2. $69.95.
Students looking to break into TV will be impressed by the variety of options presented in this DVD. Food stylists, producers, and

puppeteers are only some of the occupations included. Includes teacher's guide. (Rev: SLJ 3/07)

690 Careers in the Performing Arts (6–8). 2006. 2 discs. 112 min. Series: Careers in Arts . Discovery School. ISBN 978-1-59527-999-6. $99.95.
Students interested in the arts will be pleased to learn of the varied careers that are available to them. Performers of many backgrounds and with different talents discuss their work. Discussion questions are included. This set consists of *Careers on Stage and on Air* and *Careers in Song and Dance.* (Rev: SLJ 2/07)

691 Get Into Hollywood: Breaking Into Television (10–12). 2005. 90 min. PDF Productions. PPR. $59.95.
Writer, director, actor, producer, and cinematographer are among the careers explored in this presentation, hosted by actors Michael Dorn and Jane Hajduck, that gives plenty of practical tips. Teacher's guide included. (Rev: SLJ 2/06; VL 1–2/06)

Law, Police, and Other Society-Oriented Careers

692 I Want to Be a . . . Firefighter (9–12). 2005. 42 min. Explore a Career. $19.99.
A clear presentation of the work of a firefighter, covering history, duties, and physical and educational requirements. (Rev: BL 10/15/05; SLJ 1/06; VL 11–12/05)

Medicine and Health

693 Trauma Center: Second Opinion (8–12). Atlus. Nintendo DS, Wii. Players: 1. ESRB: T (blood, mild language, mild violence).
Work in a hospital trauma center as you, the intern, diagnose illnesses, treat patients, and help perform surgery.

YALSA Top 50 Core Recommended Collection Titles

Science and Engineering

694 Careers in the Physical Sciences (5–12). 2007. 26 min. Series: Careers in the Sciences. Cambridge Educational. ISBN 978-1-4213-5951-9. $89.95.
Students will see real scientists and other workers on the job in varied positions that involve the physical sciences. They will find out what it takes to land these jobs and the satisfaction that they offer. Also in the series: *Careers in the Earth Sciences* and *Careers in the Life Sciences.* (Rev: LMC 11–12/07; SLJ 8/07)

Technical and Industrial Careers

695 Women in Electronics (8–12). 2007. 15 min. Series: Women in Nontraditional Careers. Her Own Words. Closed captioned. ISBN 978-1-877933-41-7. $95.
Nine women with careers in electronics discuss what drew them to the field and what their jobs are like. The diverse positions described include engineer, technician, and technical writer. A resource guide is available. (Rev: SLJ 5/07)

696 Women in the Automotive Industry (6–12). 2006. 15 min. Series: Women in Nontraditional Careers. Her Own Words. Closed captioned. ISBN 978-1-60118-005-6. $95.
Nine women with careers in the automotive industry discuss what drew them to the field and what their jobs are like. The diverse positions described include mechanic, repair-shop owner, and salesperson. A resource guide is available. (Rev: SLJ 7/07)

Personal Finances

Managing Money

697 ◉ **Financial Fitness for Young Adults: Protecting Your Identity** (9–12). 2005. 25 min. Film Ideas. ISBN 978-1-57557-674-9. $195.
Young people are apparently the most likely victims of identity theft, and this production explains how it happens and how to avoid it and why a good credit rating is so important. (Rev: SLJ 3/06)

698 ◉ **In Debt We Trust: America Before the Bubble Bursts** (10–12). 2007. 52 min. Media Education Foundation. $125 (high schools and nonprofits), $34.95 (public libraries).
A look at Americans' dependence on credit card and other forms of debt despite the burden this places on individuals' budgets — and the national economy, with discussion of the new federal bankruptcy laws and efforts to offer more protection for consumers. Presented by former ABC News and CNN producer Danny Schechter. (Rev: VL 7–8/07)
♉ YALSA 2008 Selected DVDs and Videos

699 ◉ **It's Your Money: Financial Flight School** (10–12). 2006. 20 min. Learning ZoneXpress. PPR. Closed captioned. ISBN 978-1-57175-235-2. $49.95.
Budgeting, savings, credit cards, and car ownership are among the topics addressed in this program aimed at older teens. Teacher's guide included. (Rev: VL 9–10/06)

Health and the Human Body

General and Miscellaneous

700 🌐 **Fit for Life . . . Eat Right and Exercise** (8–11). 2005. 29 min. Series: In the Mix. Castle Works. $69.95.

Teen hosts guide viewers through healthy choices at mealtime and leisure time. (Rev: BL 9/1/05)

701 🌐 **Tell Me Why, Vol. 31: Food, Diet and Exercise** (4–8). 2006. 30 min. TMW Media. $29.95.

A lively question-and-answer format is used to convey information on nutrition, vitamins, body size, and fitness. Teacher's guide included. (Rev: SLJ 11/06)

Aging and Death

702 🌐 **Kids Talkin' About Death** (4–7). 2006. 20 min. National Film Board of Canada. $99 (Rental $40).

Children ages 9 to 12 describe death in their own words. Some have little experience with death, while others are acquainted with grief. The differing points of view will spur discussion among students. Teacher's guide available. (Rev: LMC 4–5/07; SLJ 1/07)

Alcohol, Drugs, and Smoking

703 🌐 **Addiction and the Human Brain** (7–12). 2005. 28 min. Human Relations Media. ISBN 978-1-55548-068-4. $139.95.

Presenting the belief that the teen brain is more vulnerable to irreversible damage from the abuse of drugs than the adult brain, this program features animations of the brain's function, testimony by teens about their drug habits, and interviews with experts. Includes teacher's guide and student handouts. (Rev: SLJ 2/06)

704 🌐 **Athletes, Alcohol, and Steroids: What's Wrong with This Picture?** (9–12). 2005. 22 min. Human Relations Media. PPR. Closed captioned. ISBN 978-1-55548-058-5. $139.95.

An informative look at the reasons why some teen athletes risk their health and chances of success by using alcohol and steroids. Teacher's guide included. (Rev: SLJ 2/06; VL 4/4/06)

705 🌐 **Drinking and Driving Kills** (7–10). 2006. 20 min. New Dimension Media. $49.

This effective presentation tells the story of Jayme Webb, a college honor student who drove after a night of drinking, causing an accident that left one man dead and three others injured. Photographs, 911 tapes, statistics, and interviews with medical professionals demonstrate how dangerous drinking can be. (Rev: BL 1/1–15/07)

706 ✇ **The End of Silence: Teens Talk to Teens About Methamphetamine Abuse** (7–12). 2003. 58 min. Knott & Serrie. $95.
A video produced by students at Anderson Valley High School in Mendocino County, California, in which they interview young addicts, ex-addicts, and others affected by methamphetamines. (Rev: BL 5/1/04; SLJ 5/04)

707 ✇ **Four More Days** (7–12). 2007 (revised edition). 18 min. Norwood Community TV (dist. by Film Ideas). ISBN 978-1-57557-957-3. $150.
The joy of four high school seniors' final days of school turns to grief after a drunken-driving accident results in death, injury, and arrest for the driver. (Rev: SLJ 11/07)

708 ✇ **Getting Stupid: How Drugs Damage Your Brain** (6–12). 2004. 23 min. Human Relations Media. PPR. Closed captioned. ISBN 978-1-55548-197-1. $99.95.
The impact of drugs and alcohol on the teenage brain are shown through MRIs and 3-D animations. Includes teacher's guide. (Rev: SLJ 6/03; VL 1–2/06)

709 ✇ **Huffing: The Latest Facts About Inhalant Abuse** (6–9). 2006. 20 min. Human Relations Media. Closed captioned. ISBN 978-1-55548-007-3. $119.95.
Students will learn just how dangerous "huffing" (inhaling substances such as aerosol cleaners) is. Parents of children who have died give harrowing accounts. Teacher's guide included. (Rev: SLJ 9/07)
ஃ ALA ALSC Notable Children's Videos 2008

710 ✇ **Natural Highs and the Truth About So-Called "Natural" Drugs** (7–12). 2006. 18 min. Human Relations Media. Closed captioned. ISBN 978-1-55548-020-2. $139.95.
A discussion of the natural highs derived from a variety of activities (sports and arts, in particular) and the differences between these highs and the ones that result from the use of drugs like marijuana. Teens talk about their addictions and about ways to get drug-free highs. Teacher's guide included. (Rev: LMC 8–9/07; SLJ 3/07)

711 ✇ **Rushing, Crashing, Dying: The Meth Epidemic** (7–12). 2006. 25 min. Human

Relations Media. Closed captioned. ISBN 978-1-55548-023-3. $139.95.
Former addicts give firsthand accounts of the devastation that meth can cause. Vivid descriptions of the drug's effects on the brain and on families and communities will further discourage teens who might have considered experimenting with meth. Teacher's guide included. (Rev: SLJ 1/07)

712 ✇ **Ryan** (10–12). 2004. 14 min. Copper Heart Entertainment in association with the National Film Board of Canada. $99.
Canadian animator Ryan Larkin's descent into alcoholism, drug abuse, and life on the street is chronicled in this unusual animated documentary. (Rev: VL 9–10/05)
ஃ YALSA 2006 Selected Videos and DVDs

713 ✇ **Steroids: True Stories** (7–12). 2006. 20 min. Blake Works. $99.99.
Craig and Nate discuss steroid use from two points of view: Craig as a former user, and Nate as star athlete who has never used the drugs. Discussion questions are included in this presentation hosted by Red Sox player Curt Schilling. (Rev: SLJ 2/07)

714 ✇ **A Talk with Your Kids About Smoking** (4–12). 2005. 38 min. Patrick Reynolds (dist. by Victory Multimedia). ISBN 978-0-9711567-1-5. $19.95 (PPR version available for $75 from www.tobaccofree.org).
Patrick Reynolds, the grandson of tobacco chief R. J. Reynolds, talks about the ways in which tobacco companies have persuaded children to start smoking. This presentation complies with CDC guidelines and provides a formula for saying no and clear examples. (Rev: VL 11–12/06)

715 ✇ **Teen Danger Zone: Teens at Risk** (9–12). 2007. 47 min. Cambridge Educational. Closed captioned. ISBN 978-1-4213-5419-4. $89.95.
Teenagers who have been harmed by using drugs, alcohol, and practicing other destructive behaviors describe how their lives have been affected. The documentary style of the film will have a big impact on viewers. (Rev: SLJ 9/07)

716 ✇ **Tobacco and Death: Perfect Together** (7–12). 2006. 27 min. Human Relations

Media. Closed captioned. ISBN 978-1-55548-022-6. $139.95.

After viewing this presentation, which gives accounts of young people who have died or been disfigured from tobacco use, teens will think twice about using any form of tobacco. Includes teacher's guide. (Rev: SLJ 3/07)

717 ☻ **Too Much: The Extreme Dangers of Binge Drinking** (9–12). 2006. 20 min. Human Relations Media. Closed captioned. ISBN 978-1-55548-019-6. $139.95.

Relying on teens' love of satire, this presentation opens with a tongue-in-cheek spoof of a 1950s filmstrip on the dangers of drinking. It then gets serious and addresses the tempations that teenagers face today, with tales of deadly drinking binges and an explanation of what alcohol does to the brain. Fun alternatives to drinking are also given. (Rev: SLJ 1/07)

718 ☻ **Top Ten Myths About Alcohol and Drugs** (7–12). 2006. 18 min. Human Relations Media. Closed captioned. ISBN 978-1-55548-021-9. $139.95.

Former addicts discuss misconceptions about using alcohol and drugs (for example, "prescription drugs are not harmful") in this breezy, entertaining presentation. Teacher's guide available. (Rev: SLJ 5/07)

719 ☻ **Uppers and Downers: The Facts About Stimulants and Depressants** (7–12). 2006. 16 min. Human Relations Media. Closed captioned. ISBN 978-1-55548-024-0. $139.95.

The devastating effects of the misuse of these drugs is made clear. Former addicts give firsthand accounts of what addiction is like, and experts discuss how uppers and downers harm the body and mind. Includes teacher's guide. (Rev: SLJ 3/07)

720 ☻ **Weighing the Risks** (9–12). 2006. 30 min. Discovery School. ISBN 978-1-59527-812-8. $69.95.

Teens who have overcome addiction, as well as those whose lives have been forever changed by alcohol or drugs, will give students much to think about in this presentation. Adults also offer advice on dealing with peer pressure and making healthy decisions. (Rev: SLJ 1/07)

Diseases and Illnesses

721 ☻ **The Age of AIDS** (9–12). 2006. 240 min. PBS Video. PPR. Closed captioned. ISBN 978-0-7936-9223-1. $69.95.

In the early 1980s, awareness grew that a fatal disease was spreading. This "Frontline" documentary looks at the history of the epidemic, the social controversies, the evolution in treatment methods, and the price of treatment in the West and in developing nations. (Rev: VL 11–12/06)

722 ☻ **Battling Eating Disorders** (9–12). 2006. 29 min. Meridian Education (dist. by Films Media Group). Closed captioned. ISBN 978-1-4213-5574-0. $69.95.

Several young people (including one young man) discuss how eating disorders such as anorexia and bulimia harmed their bodies and their lives. Viewers will be motivated to get help for themselves or others with eating disorders after seeing this film, which is narrated by Jamie-Lynn Sigler of *The Sopranos*, who has overcome anorexia. (Rev: LMC 10/07; SLJ 4/07)

723 ☻ **A Day So Beautiful** (11–12). 2004. 15 min. National Film Board of Canada. $89.

Christopher, a young man suffering a terminal illness, shows his strength as he copes with isolation and searches for joy and meaning in what remains of his life.
� YALSA 2006 Selected Videos and DVDs

724 ☻ **The Lice Busters** (K–3). 2004. 13 min. KidSafety of America. ISBN 978-1-884413-68-1. $49.95.

An introduction to head lice, with information on symptoms, treatment, and prevention. (Rev: BL 11/15/04; SLJ 11/04)

725 ☻ **Living with Chronic Illness** (9–12). 2003. 30 min. PBS/In the Mix. $69.95.

Teens speak frankly about dealing with a variety of chronic illnesses, including asthma, Crohn's disease, sickle cell anemia, and cancer.
♛ YALSA 2004 Selected Videos and DVDs

726 ☻ **Living with Slim: Kids Talk About HIV/AIDS** (7–12). 2004. 28 min. Shosholoza Productions. $25 for individuals; $50 for institutions.

Seven African children infected with HIV/AIDS (often called "slim") tell how they got the disease and describe how it has affected their lives. (Rev: VL 7/06)

727 ● **The Origins of AIDS** (10–12). 2003. 43 min. National Film Board of Canada. PPR. $195.
This thought-provoking film presents the controversial view that AIDS was the result of a scientific experiment that went wrong; other theories are also discussed. (Rev: VL 5–6/06)

728 ● **A Tale of Two Teens** (7–12). 2006. 52 min. Susan Walker Productions (dist. by Cinema Guild). ISBN 978-0-7815-1136-0. $99.95.
Viewers learn about the scale of the HIV/AIDS problem in South Africa and are reminded that the danger still exists in the United States. A shorter, 34-minute version is also available. (Rev: SLJ 11/06)

729 ● **Understanding HIV and AIDS** (5–8). 2006. 27 min. Human Relations Media. Closed captioned. ISBN 978-1-55548-008-0. $119.95.
How is HIV different from AIDS? Rapper Bow Wow explains this and more in this informative presentation that includes interviews with HIV-positive teenagers, doctors, and others, with an emphasis on prevention. Includes teacher's guide. (Rev: SLJ 3/07)

Genetics

730 ● **The Family That Walks on All Fours** (9–12). 2007. 56 min. WGBH Boston. ISBN 978-1-59375-658-1. $19.95.
Why would a family in Turkey walk on "all fours" rather than upright? Scientists debate the possible causes of this strange phenomenon in this "NOVA" program. Genetic, neurological, and evolutionary possibilities are discussed. Aspects of the program may be disturbing to some. Teacher's guide included. (Rev: SLJ 4/07)

731 ● **Genes and Heredity** (5–8). 2006. 23 min. Series: Human Body in Action. Schlessinger Media (dist. by Library Video Company). PPR. $39.95.
This is a clear, comprehensive overview of genetic concepts, covering how traits such as eye and hair color are passed from one generation to the next. Teacher's guide included.

This is part of a 10-volume series that also includes *The Brain and the Nervous System, Cells, Circulatory and Respiratory Systems, Digestive and Excretory Systems, Health and Nutrition, The Immune System, Interrelationship of the Body Systems, Reproductive and Endocrine Systems,* and *Skeletal and Muscular Systems.* (Rev: LMC 10/06; SLJ 10/01)

732 ● **Traits and Heredity** (3–5). 2006. 15 min. Visual Learning Co. ISBN 978-1-59234-151-9. $79.95.
Animations and an appealing presentation make the information on chromosomes, inherited traits, and so forth easy for young students to understand. Includes teacher's guide. (Rev: LMC 2/07; SLJ 10/06; VL 11–12/06)

Grooming, Personal Appearance, and Dress

733 ● **Body Image Obsession** (6–12). 2006. 17 min. Series: Self-Esteem. CWK Network (dist. by New Dimension Media). ISBN 978-1-59522-293-0. $49.
Young people discuss how the pressure to be "perfect" has affected their lives. Eating and body-image disorders are discussed, and one young woman talks about the botched plastic surgery that has left her with lifelong afflictions. Includes teacher's guide. (Rev: SLJ 3/07)

734 ● **Wet Dreams and False Images** (10–12). 2003. 11 min. Jesse Epstein (dist. by New Day Films). PPR. ISBN 978-1-57448-111-2. $99.
A young Brooklyn barber called Dee-Dee is much disappointed to learn that the sexy and glamorous pin-ups on his wall are the results of skillful retouching. A humorous look at the importance of body image, with some raw language. (Rev: VL 1–2/05)
ᵍ YALSA 2005 Selected Videos and DVDs

735 ● **The Zit** (4–8). 2005. 5 min. Pipsqueak Films. PPR. $39.95.
A zit takes center stage in this funny/gross computer-animated short about a teenager tackling a serious problem. (Rev: VL 5–6/06)
ᵍ YALSA 2006 Selected Videos and DVDs

The Human Body

General and Miscellaneous

736 ◕ **All Systems Go Again!** (9–12). 2006. 30 min. VEA. $89.95.
How the body's systems work together to use energy is the focus of this film. Footage of athletes in action adds interest to the in-depth information. (Rev: SLJ 8/07)

737 ◕ **Beethoven's Hair** (10–12). 2005. 84 min. Rhombus Media (dist. by Bullfrog Films). PPR. ISBN 978-1-59458-354-4. $295.
The fascinating story of the travels of a lock of Beethoven's hair over a period of two centuries and its eventual testing to see if it can provide clues to Beethoven's various ills. (Rev: BL 11/1/06; SLJ 7/07; VL 9–10/06)

Digestive and Excretory Systems

738 ◕ **Systems of the Body: Digestion** (5–9). 2006. 18 min. Human Relations Media. Closed captioned. ISBN 978-1-55548-010-3. $119.95.
Animation and live action combine to help students understand how food moves through and is used by the body. Teacher's guide available. (Rev: SLJ 6/07)

Musculoskeletal System

739 ◕ **All About Bones and Muscles** (K–4). 2006. 23 min. Series: Human Body for Children. Schlessinger Media (dist. by Library Video Company). PPR. $29.95.
A close-up look at the composition of bones and muscles, plus their functions and importance to a healthy life. Part of an eight-volume series that also includes *All About Blood and the Heart, All About Health and Hygiene, All About Nutrition and Exercise, All About Cells and Body Systems, All About the Brain, All About the Human Life Cycle,* and *All About the Senses.* Teacher's guide included.

740 ◕ **Standard Deviants School: Anatomy** (6–8). 2004. 27 min. Cerebellum. $215.93 (for complete series).
An entertaining introduction to the bones that make up the human skeleton, giving their names, locations, terminology, usefulness,

and interesting facts. Part of a series that also includes *Muscles, The Nervous System, Eyes and Ears, The Circulatory System, The Lymphatic and Respiratory System, The Digestive and Urinary Systems,* and *The Endocrine and Reproductive Systems.* (Rev: BL 12/1/04)

Teeth

741 ◕ **Smiles for a Lifetime** (K–6). 2007. 80 min. Library Video Company. $29.95.
An informative presentation by Jamie Johnson, a dentist and mother, on good dental hygiene. Segments are divided by age level, and cover everything from correct brushing and flossing techniques to a visit to the dentist and orthodontics. (Rev: BL 10/15/07; SLJ 11/07)

Hygiene and Physical Fitness

742 ◕ **Brush Up on Hygiene** (3–6). 2007. 20 min. Human Relations Media. ISBN 978-1-55548-320-3. $99.95.
A lighthearted look at the importance of cleanliness in keeping illness and offensiveness at bay, featuring a combination of live action and animation. Teacher's guide and activity sheets included. (Rev: SLJ 12/07)

743 ◕ **Classical Pilates: Kids and Young Adults** (K–12). 2006. 75 min. Classical Pilates (dist. by Bayview Entertainment). $19.99.
Pilates workouts are presented in four sections — for ages 5 to 7, 8 to 10, 10 to 12, and 12 to 17. (Rev: SLJ 10/06)

744 ◕ **Empowering Pilates: Exercise Video for Teens** (8–12). 2007. 57 min. Shamrock Film Productions. $74.99.
For young people interested in vigorous activity, this presentation describes the basics of Pilates and takes them through a workout. (Rev: BL 9/1/07; SLJ 9/07)

745 ◕ **Get Active with Stinky Shoe and Coach LaRoo** (1–5). 2004. 30 min. A.L.L. For Kids. $17.95.
Cartoon characters Stinky Shoe and Coach LaRoo take young viewers to Camp Imagination, where camp counselors and campers

demonstrate exercises and stretching. (Rev: BL 9/15/04; SLJ 6/04)

746 💿 **Get Fit with Sqedunk** (K–2). 2005. 40 min. Sqedunk. $13.

Sqedunk is a large pink pig mascot that helps in the demonstration of 14 exercises set to lively music. (Rev: BL 4/1/06)

747 💿 **Mighty Me Training Camp** (K–2). 2007. 36 min. Mighty Me Productions (dist. by Midwest Tapes). $14.95.

A group of children get active with trainer Brian Donovan, who encourages youngsters to feel strong and powerful through exercise. Animation and funny clips make this a light-hearted presentation. (Rev: SLJ 11/07)

748 💿 **Pilates Week: Five 15-Minute Work-outs for the Busy Teen** (8–12). 2007. Sham-rock Film Productions. $79.99.

Part of the Empowering Pilates for Teens series, this program is for young athletes who would like to incorporate a new form of exercise into their routines. Teenagers demonstrate each move on two levels: beginning and more difficult. Also in the series: *Toning Pilates for Teens.* (Rev: SLJ 9/07)

749 💿 **Team Up! For Your Toddler's Health** (K). 2007. 30 min. The 3 Squares (dist. by AV Café). Closed captioned. $19.95.

Simple exercises set to favorite childhood tunes make this a fun video for parents and toddlers to enjoy together. The program reminds parents and children to "Eat Right, Play with Might, and Sleep Tight to Be Big, Healthy, and Strong!" (Rev: BL 9/1/07; SLJ 11/07)

750 💿 **Wii Fit** (K–12). 2008. Nintendo. Wii. ESRB: E (comic mischief).

This exercise game uses the Balance Board peripheral, which is controlled by the player's movements. Yoga, strength training, balance games (including ski jumping and slaloms), and aerobics are the major activities, and there are about 40 different selections. Players can track their body mass index over time. (Rev: CTR 6/08)

Mental Disorders and Emotional Problems

751 💿 **C.A.G.E. the Rage** (6–9). 2007. 23 min. Cambridge Educational. ISBN 978-1-4213-6216-8. $89.95.

A helpful program for teenagers who need to manage their anger, this film uses the C.A.G.E. process: Calm down, Assess the situation, Gauge alternatives, Empower yourself. Teacher's guide included. (Rev: SLJ 9/07)

752 💿 **Chill: Empowering Teens to Manage Stress** (7–12). 2006. 4 discs. 120 min. Comprehensive Health Education Foundation. $499.95.

Four teenagers produce a documentary about dealing with stress at school as well as pressure from friends, family, and society. Includes teacher's guide, lessons, and handouts. The individual discs — *Chill: In the System, Chill: Playing the Part, Chill: Family Ties,* and *Chill: Keeping It Real* — are available for $149.95 each. (Rev: SLJ 2/07)

753 💿 **Eternal High: A Teenager's Experience with Depression and Suicide That Will Change Your Life** (8–12). 2006. 30 min. Aquarius Health Care Media. $150.

Brian, 17, discusses his struggle with depression and suicidal thoughts, which were conquered with the help of medication and therapy. The positive outcome shows that depression can be managed. (Rev: SLJ 2/07)

754 💿 **From Depression to Discovery: A Teenager's Guidebook** (7–12). 2005. 25 min. Cambridge Educational (dist. by Films Media Group). ISBN 978-1-4213-2691-7. $49.95.

The symptoms — and treatment — of depression are revealed as three teens detail their experiences; one — a young Asian American man — attempted suicide. The importance of seeking adult help is emphasized. Includes teacher's guide. (Rev: SLJ 1/06)

755 💿 **Understanding Brothers and Sisters on the Autism Spectrum** (K–12). 2007. 94 min. Coulter Video. $39.99.

There are four sections on this DVD: one for ages 4 to 7, one for ages 7 to 12, one for 12 to adult, and one for parents. Each addresses the issues involved in having an autistic sibling (or child) in an age-appropriate way. The segment for the youngest children uses puppets. (Rev: SLJ 11/07)

Nutrition and Diet

756 ◉ **Food Safari: Lunch** (K). 2003. 30 min. Yum Yum Studios. $12.99.

Young children learn how wheat grows and bread is made in this appealing presentation about nutrition featuring bear puppets and an animated monkey called Couscous. Also available: *Lunch.* (Rev: BL 1/1–15/04)

757 ◉ **Getting Youth Fired Up About What Their Culture Feeds Them** (7–12). 2006. 4 discs. 30 min. Series: FUEL. Comprehensive Health Education Foundation. $499.95 ($149.95 each).

This tool in the fight against childhood obesity takes the stance that by eating right, exercising, and avoiding unhealthy products, teens are standing up to a consumer culture. The four DVDs include *Fuel: Skin Deep; Fuel: Energy for Action; Fuel: The Perfect Machine;* and *Fuel: Taking on the World.* Teacher's guide, lessons, and handouts included. (Rev: SLJ 1/07)

758 ◉ **Junk Food Wars** (7–10). 2005. 30 min. Cambridge. ISBN 978-1-4213-1939-1. $89.95.

Viewers will learn why it is important to eat properly and how to make well-informed food choices. (Rev: BL 11/15/05)

759 ◉ **The Lunch Lady's Guide to the Food Pyramid** (2–6). 2005. 18 min. Thinkeroo Studios. PPR. $39.95.

A trendy lunch lady explains the food pyramid using an entertaining studio show format. (Rev: VL 5–6/06)

760 ◉ **My Pyramid: Choosing Nutritious Food and Healthy Activities** (K–2). 2007. 21 min. SchoolMedia (dist. by 100% Educational Videos). ISBN 978-1-58541-922-7. $39.95.

What makes a food healthy? Children explore the answer to this question and learn how to choose healthy foods. Includes teacher's guide. (Rev: SLJ 11/07)

761 ◉ **My Pyramid: Simple Steps to Healthy Living** (9–12). 2006. 15 min. Discovery School. ISBN 978-1-59527-846-3. $69.95.

The FDA's new pyramid is explained, along with tips for choosing healthy foods and incorporating exercise into one's life. (Rev: SLJ 2/07)

762 ◉ **MyPyramid.gov: Steps to a Healthier You** (6–9). 2005. 16 min. Learning ZoneXpress. ISBN 978-1-57175-104-1. $49.95.

A look at the component parts of the food pyramid, with animated drawings, views of recommended foods, and practical tips; an adult narrator fields questions from high school students. (Rev: BL 10/15/05)

763 ◉ **The New Food Pyramid: It's All About You!** (6–9). 2005. 23 min. New Dimension Media. Closed captioned. ISBN 978-1-59522-218-3. $49 (single site), $159 w/PPR.

Middle-schoolers give advice on eating well and keeping in shape. (Rev: BL 4/15/06)

764 ◉ **Nutrition** (2–4). 2006. 14 min. Visual Learning. PPR. Closed captioned. ISBN 978-1-59234-155-9. $79.95.

A basic overview of essential nutrients and the ways the body uses what we ingest. Teacher's guide included. (Rev: VL 1–2/07)

765 ◉ **Nutrition** (1–6). 2005. 23 min. Series: Health for Children. Schlessinger Media (dist. by Library Video Company). PPR. Closed captioned. $29.95.

All about eating right, this presentation stresses the importance of variety, moderation, and portion control in staying healthy and strong. Other titles in this series are *Dealing with Feelings, Decisions and Conflicts, Drugs and Disease, Environmental Health, Personal Health and Hygiene, Safety Awareness,* and *Staying Safe: Strangers, Cyberspace and More.* (Rev: VL 5–6/05)

766 ◉ **Nutrition and the New Food Pyramid** (3–5). 2007. 18 min. SchoolMedia (dist. by 100% Educational Videos). ISBN 978-1-58541-923-4. $39.95.

A lighthearted look at the food pyramid and at nutrition in general, featuring a finicky eater named Josh and a comic book hero, Energy Man, who springs to his aid to explain the merits of a balanced diet. Teacher's guide included. (Rev: SLJ 9/07)

767 🔾 **Nutrition and You** (5–8). 2007. 80 min. Visual Learning. Closed captioned. ISBN 978-1-59234-165-8. $299.

An introduction to eating right, with four segments: "Nutrition Basics," "Balanced Diet," "Healthy Eating Habits," and "A Healthy Body." Plenty of questions help to engage the viewer. Includes teacher's guide and reproducible masters. (Rev: LMC 1/08; SLJ 11/07)

768 🔾 **Nutrition for Life One: Pregnancy, Infancy and Childhood** (10–12). 2006. 39 min. VEA. $89.95.

This program covers the nutrition needed to help the human body grow in the earliest stages of life. Also available: *Nutrition for Life Two: Youth, Adulthood and Late Adulthood* (2006). (Rev: SLJ 8/07)

769 🔾 **Obesity in a Bottle** (5–12). 2006. 21 min. Learning ZoneXpress. ISBN 978-1-57175-324-3. $79.95.

Teenagers may be surprised to learn that what they drink can make them fat, but after viewing this presentation they will be fully aware of the amount of sugar and calories in sodas, energy drinks, and other popular beverages. Includes teacher's guide. (Rev: SLJ 3/07)

770 🔾 **Overweight in America: Why Are We Getting So Fat?** (7–12). 2005. 21 min. Human Relations Media. ISBN 978-1-55548-067-7. $139.95.

Overweight teens describe their lives and their feelings, and experts discuss the causes (large portions, fast food, lack of exercise, and so forth) and recommend ways to lose weight sensibly. Includes teacher's guide. (Rev: SLJ 4/06)

771 🔾 **Portion Distortion: Seeing the Healthy Way to Eat** (2–6). 2005. 20 min. Human Relations Media. Closed captioned. $99.95.

In a combination of live action and animation, this presentation offers lots of healthy information, with real kids doing the persuading. (Rev: LMC 11/05; SLJ 7/06)

🔾 ALA ALSC Notable Children's Videos 2006

772 🔾 **Snack Attack** (9–12). 2006. 22 min. Meridian Education (dist. by Films Media Group). Closed captioned. ISBN 978-1-4213-5085-1. $69.95.

Teens will learn what is unhealthy about much snack food. They will visit a high school that has eliminated junk-food vending machines and hear teens' questions about nutrition answered by dietitians. Quizzes are included to keep students on their toes. (Rev: SLJ 4/07)

773 🔾 **Teen Nutrition: What's the Big Debate?** (6–12). 2007. 26 min. Learning ZoneXpress. ISBN 978-1-57175-513-1. $79.95.

Two teenagers preparing for a debate about nutrition review the food pyramid, how to read food labels, and the importance of exercise. (Rev: SLJ 10/07)

Physical Disabilities and Problems

774 🔾 **Dealing with Disabilities** (9–12). 2006. 30 min. Discovery School. ISBN 978-1-59527-807-4. $69.95.

Three young people living with varied disabilities (asthma, spina bifida, and cancer) discuss what they can and cannot do in a presentation that stresses respect for those with physical limitations. (Rev: SLJ 2/07)

Reproduction and Child Care

775 🔾 **A Doula Story: On the Front Lines of Teen Pregnancy** (10–12). 2004. 60 min. The Kindling Group. Closed captioned. $99.99.

Loretha Weisinger is a labor coach, or "doula," working with pregnant teens in Chicago. This appealing documentary shows how she guides the girls through pregnancy, birth, and the necessary adjustments that follow. Spanish-language version available. (Rev: BL 1/1–15/06; VL 7/06)

776 🔾 **From Conception to Birth** (9–12). 2006. 25 min. Discovery School. ISBN 978-1-59380-555-5. $69.95.

The experiences of five expecting couples show the wide range of options and outcomes relating to pregnancy. One couple did not intend to become pregnant; another relies on artificial insemination. Pregnancy loss is also discussed. (Rev: SLJ 2/07)

777 ✪ **How I Learn: Ages and Stages of Child Development** (9–12). 2006. 17 min. Learning ZoneXpress. ISBN 978-1-57175-246-8. $49.95.

Teenagers will learn more about the babies and children they babysit or care for in this short program hosted by a teenaged childcare worker. (Rev: SLJ 5/07)

778 ✪ **Journey into Life: Human Reproduction** (7–12). 2006. 25 min. New Dimension Media. ISBN 978-1-59522-564-1. $49.

Seven segments using photography, graphics, and live action discuss how babies are made and born. Photographs of an embryo growing inside the womb provide a fascinating look at the beginnings of human life. This presentation is for older students who are prepared to see the process of birth. Teacher's guide available. (Rev: SLJ 5/07)

779 ✪ **Three Girls I Know . . .** (9–12). 2004. 54 min. No Excuses Productions (dist. by Film Library). $125 (public libraries), $195 (institutional).

Focuses on the lives of three diverse teenage girls, talking about their everyday stresses as well as teen sexuality, pregnancy, and HIV/AIDS. (Rev: BL 5/15/04; SLJ 10/04; VL 5–6/04)

Safety and First Aid

780 ✪ **Asleep at the Wheel: The Dangers of Drowsy Driving** (7–12). 2006. 15 min. Human Relations Media. ISBN 978-1-55480-322-4. $139.95.

Drivers under the age of 25 make up only 19 percent of all drivers, but they are responsible from more than half of crashes caused by driving while sleepy. This program emphasizes the danger, the warning signs of drowsiness, and the strategies to stay awake that simply don't work. Teacher's guide included. (Rev: SLJ 12/06)

781 ✪ **The Choking Game** (5–9). 2006. 19 min. Human Relations Media. Closed captioned. ISBN 978-1-55548-009-7. $119.95.

The dangers of recreational asphyxiation are made real through interviews with the brother and mother of a boy who died playing this "game." Tips on resisting peer pressure, signs that someone might be experimenting with choking, and other useful information make this a valuable resource. Teacher's guide included. (Rev: LMC 8–9/07; SLJ 1/07)

782 ✪ **Disney's Safety Hits, Volume 1** (1–6). 2004. 29 min. Disney Educational Productions. PPR. Closed captioned. ISBN 978-1-932644-68-5. $59.95.

Bike Safety with Bill Nye the Science Guy and *I'm No Fool on Wheels* are both live-action features, the first for older children and the second for younger (it covers roller-skating and skateboarding as well as cycling). Teacher's guide included. Volume 2 features *Winnie the Pooh's Great School Bus Adventure* and *Too Smart for Strangers*. (Rev: VL 5–6/05)

783 ✪ **From A to ZZZZ's: What Teens Need to Know About Sleep** (7–12). 2005. 23 min. Human Relations Media. ISBN 978-1-55548-071-4. $139.95.

Teens generally get less sleep than they need — partly because of their school starting times. This program stresses the dangers of sleep deprivation, especially when teens begin driving. (Rev: SLJ 4/06)

784 ✪ **Just Yell Fire: Empowering Girls to Protect Themselves** (6–12). 2007. 45 min. Just Yell Fire/Maggie Jessup. Free upon request.

Girls learn self-defense in this compelling presentation that includes typical scenarios in which danger lurks.
✽ ALA ALSC Notable Children's Videos 2008

785 ✪ **Road Skillz** (10–12). 2006. 24 min. Crazy Car Films (dist. by Pro-Active Entertainment Group). $19.95.

A race car driver hosts this program that aims to impress on students the dangers of driving. It looks at common hazards and the ways drivers should react. Teacher's guide included. (Rev: SLJ 12/06)

786 ❀ **Stranger Safety** (K–3). 2005. 42 min. AV Café. ISBN 978-0-9765640-0-3. $19.98.
The host — the perky Safe Side Superchick — uses humor and color-coded shirts while teaching children to recognize different kinds of people; "Hot Tips" reinforce the 12 short lessons. (Rev: BL 10/15/05; SLJ 11-12/05)

787 ❀ **The Sun Show** (1–3). 2005. 20 min. Sun Safety for Kids. PPR. Closed captioned. $19.95.
Hosted by children, this is an effective guide to the dangers of exposure to the sun, with practical tips and catchy cautionary phrases. Comes with a teacher's guide; a companion production is aimed at children in grades 4 to 6. (Rev: SLJ 7/06; VL 9–10/06)

788 ❀ **Teens and Tanning: Sun Safety Update** (7–12). 2005. 14 min. Learning ZoneXpress. PPR. ISBN 978-1-57175-100-3. $49.95.
The dangers of tanning are the focus of this informative presentation that gives some historical perspective as well as recommending safe alternatives. Includes teacher's guide. (Rev: SLJ 1/06; VL 1–2/06)

Sex Education and Sexual Identity

789 ❀ **Breaking the Silence: Lesbian, Gay, Bisexual, Transgender, and Queer Foster Youth Tell Their Stories** (10–12). 2006. 30 min. National Center for Lesbian Rights. $25.
Young people who spent time in foster care and who identify themselves as homosexual, bisexual, or transgender talk about their experiences.
⚥ YALSA 2007 Selected Videos and DVDs

790 ❀ **Let's Talk Puberty** (4–7). 2007. 25 min. Disney Educational Productions. $89.
Targeted at younger students, these two animated programs — *Let's Talk Puberty for Girls* and *Let's Talk Puberty for Boys* — describe the physical and emotional changes for girls and boys during puberty. The importance of nutrition, hygiene, and stress management are also discussed. Reproduction itself is not covered. A teacher's guide is included. (Rev: BL 10/15/07; LMC 3/08; SLJ 11/07)

Human Development and Behavior

Psychology and Human Behavior

General and Miscellaneous

791 🌐 **Every Teen Has Challenges** (7–12). 2007. 79 min. Dan Sperling Video & Film (dist. by Victory Multimedia). ISBN 978-1-59382-047-3. $59.95.
Students will realize they are not alone in facing hardships while viewing this program. Teens answer questions about the challenges they face in their lives (divorce, disabilities, and drinking, for example) and how they are dealing with them. (Rev: SLJ 9/07)

792 🌐 **The Grace Lee Project** (9–12). 2005. 68 min. Women Make Movies. $295, rental $90.
Korean American filmmaker Grace Lee investigates a concept that has long puzzled her — are all the women with her name really as meek and dutiful as they are portrayed by their acquaintances? — and discovers Grace Lees of many personalities. This is an entertaining exploration of identity.
 ♕ YALSA 2008 Selected DVDs and Videos

793 🌐 **The Guarantee** (10–12). 2007. 11 min. New Day Films. PPR. $99, rental $65.
Watch comic book artist Robert Castillo sketch illustrations to accompany the humorous story of a ballet dancer with a big nose who is urged to have plastic surgery to enhance his career. Will the new nose guarantee success? (Rev: VL 1–2/08)
 ♕ YALSA 2008 Selected DVDs and Videos

794 🌐 **Inside Out: Introduction to Psychology** (9–12). 2006. 6 discs. 660 min. Intelecom.

PPR. Closed captioned. ISBN 978-1-58370-078-5. $899.
Twenty-two half-hour lessons offer a comprehensive introduction to psychology plus a fascinating overview of the ways in which psychology is incorporated in fields ranging from marketing to criminal profiling. (Rev: VL 1–2/07)

795 🌐 **Let's Get Real** (7–9). 2004. 35 min. New Day Films. $99.
Middle school students talk about the prejudice, bullying, disabilities, and sexual identity issues they experience. (Rev: BL 4/15/04; SLJ 8/18/04; VL 7–8/04)
 ♕ ALA ALSC Notable Children's Videos 2005; YALSA 2005 Selected Videos and DVDs

Emotions and Emotional Behavior

796 🌐 **The Real Deal on Love, Relationships, and Marriage** (11–12). 2005. 90 min. Center for Educational Media. ISBN 978-1-888933-16-1. $79.
This program accepts the power of young love but advocates caution when making important decisions based on this emotion. (Rev: BL 7/05)

797 🌐 **Time Out on Anger Management: Learning Self-Control** (K–5). 2006. 20 min. Human Relations Media. PPR. Closed captioned. ISBN 978-1-55548-093-6. $99.95.
Dramatized vignettes illustrate situations that tend to stimulate anger, and tactics to stop the

anger and behave in a positive manner are suggested and reinforced. (Rev: VL 11–12/06)

Ethics and Moral Behavior

798 ❂ **Profiles in Honesty** (8–11). 2005. 25 min. Human Relations Media. Closed captioned. $139.95.

Teens discuss honesty and the difficulties honesty poses, and look at examples of honesty in history and news clips. Part of a series that looks at other qualities such as courage and perseverance. (Rev: BL 3/15/06)

Etiquette and Manners

799 ❂ **The Courtesy Challenge** (6–9). 2007. 21 min. Learning Learning ZoneXpress. ISBN 978-1-57175-438-7. $79.95.

Using a wall-climbing competition as its framework, this presentation looks at basic good manners; the acronym CLIMB takes viewers through Common courtesies, Language, Introductions, Mealtime manners, and Beyond the basics. (Rev: BL 7/07; LMC 11–12/07)

800 ❂ **The (Netiquette) Edge** (6–12). 2007. 21 min. Learning ZoneXpress. ISBN 978-1-57175-435-6. $79.95.

Teens learn the etiquette surrounding the use of STEPS (Surfing, Text messaging, E-mailing, cell Phones, and Social networking sites) while they organize a ballroom dancing club. A useful resource to help kids remember that their actions can have repercussions — even online. Teacher's guide included. (Rev: SLJ 8/07; VL 7–8/07)

801 ❂ **You're Rude, Dude!** (2–6). 2007. 20 min. Human Relations Media. ISBN 978-1-55548-361-6. $99.95.

Don't be rude, say the stars of this fun guide to being polite and thoughtful in all aspects of life. Teenagers demonstrating how not to be polite will have viewers laughing. Teacher's guide and activity sheets included. (Rev: SLJ 12/07)

Personal Guidance

802 ❂ **Abusive Relationships: Get Help, Get Out** (7–12). 2006. 27 min. Series: In the Mix. In the Mix (dist. by Castle Works). $69.95.

Teenagers describe how they became involved in abusive relationships (some physically abusive, others emotionally) and what it took to break free of their abusers. (Rev: SLJ 1/07)

803 ❂ **Are You a Bully?** (3–6). 2005. 20 min. Series: Bully Smart. Human Relations Media. Closed captioned. ISBN 978-1-55548-082-0. $99.95.

This program, the first installment in a four-part series — $349.95 (ISBN 1-55548-086-1) — shows the various forms that bullying may take. The other three parts are: *Five Ways to Stop a Bully, Don't Stand By*, and *Help! I'm a Bully*. Includes teacher's guide and student handouts. (Rev: SLJ 2/06)

804 ❂ **Becoming an Organized Student** (6–10). 2007. 20 min. Human Relations Media. $119.95.

Need a little organization? Here are tips (for middle-schoolers in this case) for making your school and social life much less stressful. (Rev: SLJ 12/07)

♟ ALA ALSC Notable Children's Videos 2008

805 ❂ **Caution: Teenager Under Construction** (6–9). 2007. 16 min. Human Relations Media. Closed captioned. ISBN 978-1-55548-040-0. $119.95.

Teenagers talk about the issues they dealt with (mainly emotional and social) as they made the transition from childhood to adolescence. Teacher's guide included. (Rev: LMC 11–12/07; SLJ 10/07)

806 ❂ **Cliques, Phonies and Other Baloney** (2–6). 2006. 30 min. Comical Sense Co. ISBN 978-0-9787783-0-9. $14.99.

An animated presentation with a lesson about being true to one's friends and oneself, rather than being "phony" just to fit in. Skye learns that friendship with Jack can be more meaningful than membership in Brittany's group. Host/animator Trevor Romain interacts with the characters. (Rev: SLJ 4/07)

807 ❂ **Cyberbullying: Cruel Intentions** (9–12). 2007. 41 min. ABC News (dist. by Films Media Group). Closed captioned. ISBN 978-1-4213-5931-1. $129.95.

Depression, eating disorders, and even suicide can result when teenagers are not careful when they're online, according to this ABC Primetime program. Viewers are told how to avoid being bullied as well as how not to inadvertently become cyberbullies themselves. (Rev: SLJ 12/07)

808 ● **Developing Self-Confidence** (5–7). 2007. 20 min. Human Relations Media. ISBN 978-1-55548-438-5. $119.95.
The key to self-confidence is avoiding putting yourself down, according to this video, which encourages viewers to replace negative thoughts with positive ones. Teacher's guide and activity sheets included. (Rev: SLJ 12/07)

809 ● **Dominoes** (4–12). 2006. 10 min. Series: ShowPeace. National Film Board of Canada (dist. by Bullfrog Films). ISBN 978-0-7722-1211-5. $150 (Rental: $30).
An animated program on conflict resolution that features a domino seeking to join a group of four other dominoes but initially being rebuffed. The message of the film may be lost without discussion following viewing. (Rev: SLJ 6/07)

810 ● **Drama Queens and Tough Guys: Helping Teens Handle Emotions** (7–12). 2006. 18 min. Human Relations Media. Closed captioned. ISBN 978-1-55548-090-5. $119.95.
Four scenarios show unnecessarily dramatic and/or aggressive reactions to situations and suggest ways to avoid these pitfalls and cope with life's traumas. Teacher's guide included. (Rev: VL 7/06)

811 ● **The Five Life Strategies for Successful Teens** (7–12). 2006. 26 min. Human Relations Media. PPR. ISBN 978-1-55548-066-0. $139.95.
Goal-setting, discipline, communication, organization, and a willingness to take positive risks are the five strategies recommended in this program that features real-life examples and teen narrators. Teacher's guide included. (Rev: SLJ 1/06; VL 9–10/06)

812 ● **Girls' Business: Friendship and Bullying in Schools** (7–9). 2007. 26 min. VEA. $89.95.
A look at bullying, gossiping, ostracizing, and other cruelties that girls may inflict on one another, and the harm they can cause. The positive aspects of healthy friendship are discussed as well. (Rev: SLJ 9/07)

813 ● **The Harassment Workshop** (7–12). 2006. 20 min. Human Relations Media.

Closed captioned. ISBN 978-1-55548-033-2. $139.95.
A group of teenagers shares their experiences with being harassed. The presentation addresses online harassment, or "cyber-bullying," as well as the more traditional forms of teasing and molestation that teenagers may encounter. Includes teacher's guide. (Rev: LMC 8–9/07; SLJ 3/07)

814 ● **Holding an Effective Meeting** (9–12). 2006. 18 min. Library Video Network. $99.
Stressing the importance of agendas, focus, correct behavior, and a positive attitude, this brief program uses a boring meeting as its framework. (Rev: VL 7/06)

815 ● **Lake Tahoe: Cliff Jumping** (5–12). 2006. 18 min. Series: Ultimate Choice 1; Ultimate Choice 2. Media Kids (dist. by Media Pro). $59.
Part of a 10-DVD series for grades 5 to 8 that illustrates values such as teamwork, trust, and conflict resolution through participation in sports (often extreme). Teens discuss their feelings before participating in obstacle courses, water challenges, flying trapezes, and so forth; and there are group discussions afterward about life skills learned. The companion series Ultimate Choice 2 (11 DVDs) does the same for grades 8 to 12. Teacher's guides are available for both series. (Rev: SLJ 4/07)

816 ● **Love Shouldn't Hurt: Recognizing Dating Violence** (9–12). 2006. 18 min. Series: In the Mix. In the Mix (dist. by Castle Works). ISBN 978-1-931843-97-3. $69.95.
The warning signs of dating violence are illustrated in three vignettes performed before a high school audience. Teacher's guide included. (Rev: SLJ 12/06)

817 ● **Making Good Choices: Keys to Good Decisions** (7–12). 2006. 18 min. Human Relations Media. Closed captioned. ISBN 978-1-55548-096-7. $199.95.
Dramatizations show teens in situations where making the right choice is critical to their well-being. Teacher's guide included. (Rev: SLJ 11/06)

818 ● **The Power Trip: Bullying in School** (5–9). 2006. 20 min. Human Relations Media.

Closed captioned. ISBN 978-1-55548-006-6. $119.95.

Adult host Michael Carpenter talks with young people who have been bullied or been bullies, and they offer practical suggestions to prevent or stop bullying, both online and at school. Includes teacher's guide. (Rev: LMC 10/07; SLJ 3/07)

819 ● **Real Character, Real People: Profiles in Respect** (7–12). 2005. 20 min. Human Relations Media. PPR. Closed captioned. $139.95.

Part of a series on character development, this program explores the importance of respect and how to earn it and acknowledge it, using both teen and adult models. Teacher's guide included. Also in the series: *Profiles in Citizenship, Profiles in Courage, Profiles in Honesty,* and *Profiles in Responsibility.* (Rev: SLJ 3/06; VL 3–4/06)

820 ● **Stop Bullying . . . Take a Stand!** (7–10). 2005. 30 min. Series: In the Mix. Castle Works. ISBN 978-1-931843-95-9. $69.95.

Hosted by a former Miss America who herself was once a victim of bullying, this effective program looks at various kinds of bullying — including cyberbullying — and at ways of avoiding and dealing with bullies. (Rev: BL 2/1/06; SLJ 1/06; VL 3–4/06)

821 ● **Stressball Sally and Friends: Bullying** (2–5). 2005. 32 min. The Stressball Sally Company. PPR. $24.95.

An animated portrayal of Sally's efforts to deal with unpleasant bullying. She seeks adult help and learns physical and mental relaxation techniques that help her cope with difficult situations; includes a Spanish-language track. (Rev: VL 5–6/06)

822 ● **Taking a Stand** (7–12). 2006. 3 discs. 54 min. Series: Bullying Prevention. Meridian Education (dist. by Films Media Group). Closed captioned. ISBN 978-1-4213-4474-4. $199.95.

Three videos — *Bullies, Cyberbullying,* and *Bully Girls* — explore the harm done by bullies (extreme examples being bullied students who themselves turn violent), ways to prevent bullying, virtual bullying, and girls' methods of bullying. (Rev: SLJ 11/06)

823 ● **Wise Owl Says: Don't Be a Bully Bystander** (K–2). 2006. 10 min. Series: Wise Owl Bully Stopper Kit. Human Relations Media. Closed captioned. ISBN 978-1-55548-097-4. $99.95.

This presentation encourages kids to take action when they see someone being bullied, using specific prevention techniques. Includes teacher's guide, posters, activity cards, and stickers. Also in this series: *Wise Owl Says: I See a Bully* and *Wise Owl Says: You Can Stop a Bully.* (Rev: SLJ 1/07)

Social Groups

Family and Family Problems

824 ● **In My Shoes: Stories of Youth with LGBT Parents** (7–12). 2005. 31 min. COLAGE Youth Leadership and Action Program (dist. by Frameline Distribution). $100.

Five teens describe their lives with parents who are lesbian, gay, bisexual, or transgender. There is a focus on everyday activities and the normalcy of these unconventional families. (Rev: SLJ 7/06; VL 7/06)

825 ● **The Scoop on Blended Families** (8–11). 2006. 16 min. Learning ZoneXpress. PPR. Closed captioned. ISBN 978-1-57175-242-0. $49.95.

The Scoop Group — who meet at an ice cream shop and whose name is an acronym for supportive respect, communication, a "double-scoop" of optimism, and patience — helps its members cope with new siblings, new living arrangements, and other problems associated with newly blended families. (Rev: BL 10/1/06; SLJ 8/06; VL 9–10/06)

826 ● **Taking the "Duh" Out of Divorce** (1–5). 2005. 45 min. The Comical Sense Company. PPR. ISBN 978-0-9762843-8-3. $14.99.

Twelve-year-old Skye refuses to accept her parents' divorce but in a detailed dream sequence involving a court trial arrives at a degree of acceptance and understanding; music and humor add to this Trevor Romain title. (Rev: SLJ 12/05; VL 1–2/06)

Physical and Applied Sciences

General and Miscellaneous

827 ⊙ **The Ascent of Man** (10–12). 2001. 5 discs. 676 min. Ambrose Video. $149.99.
Created by the BBC and Time-Life Films in 1973, this award-winning 13-volume series — newly available on five DVDs — is a wide-ranging survey of history and science, showing how mankind has progressed through the ages. (Rev: BL 12/1/01; VL 9–10/06)

828 ⊙ **Classifying Life** (5–8). 2006. 20 min. Series: Classification of Life. Visual Learning. ISBN 978-1-59234-137-5. $89.95.
Classifying Life introduces scientific classification systems and explains their history, their evolution, and the continuing controversies. Also in this series: *Classifying Monerans and Protists, Classifying Plants and Fungi,* and *Classifying Animals.* (Rev: BL 7/06; SLJ 7/06; VL 9–10/06)

829 ⊙ **Great Scientific Ideas That Changed the World** (10–12). 2007. 6 discs. 1,080 min. The Teaching Company. PPR. ISBN 978-1-59803-304-5. $149.95.
A sweeping overview on 6 discs, with 36 lectures by Dr. Steven L. Goldman of Pennsylvania's Lehigh University. After looking at the great thinkers of ancient Greece and Rome, Goldman then covers the Middle Ages, the Renaissance, the origins of modern scientific thought, and the breakthroughs of the 19th and 20th centuries. Printable course guide included. (Rev: BL 12/1/07)

830 ⊙ **Planet Earth: The Complete Series** (7–12). 2006. 5 discs. 550 min. BBC Video. ISBN 978-1-4198-4936-7. $79.98.
A beautiful program displaying the natural beauty of the earth and the variety of life — plant, animal, and human — that it holds, with a message of conservation. Eleven 50-minute segments. (Rev: SLJ 1/08)

831 ⊙ **Rock-On** (4–6). 2005. 30 min. Tapeworm. $19.95.
A lively, music-filled introduction to a number of key topics — the planets, weather, the water cycle, for example — that will catch students' attention and encourage them to explore further. (Rev: BL 12/1/05)

832 ⊙ **Science as Inquiry in Action** (5–8). 2000. 23 min. Schlessinger Media (dist. by Library Video Company). PPR. Closed captioned. $29.95.
This excellent introduction to the scientific process features a student who is guided by eminent thinkers including Franklin and Curie in his efforts to create a science fair project. Newly available on DVD, this includes a teacher's guide. (Rev: BL 12/1/00; LMC 2/07; VL 7/06)

833 ⊙ **Science, Please** (K–8). 2003. 40 min. National Film Board of Canada. $89.
A collection of 26 brief segments, suitable for a range of grade levels, that cover interesting scientific phenomena in an entertaining fashion using animation and archival images. Among questions answered are "What makes ice slippery?" and "How does a light bulb

work?" (Rev: LMC 11–12/04; SLJ 8/04; VL 7–8/04)

☿ ALA ALSC Notable Children's Videos 2005

834 ⊗ **Tools in Science** (4–8). 2006. 80 min. Visual Learning. PPR. Closed captioned. ISBN 978-1-59234-147-4. $299.
Four 20-minute programs — Lab Equipment Safety, Measuring Mass and Volume, Measuring Length and Temperature, and The Microscope — cover tools used in the science lab. Teacher's guide included.

835 ▦ **The Way Cool Game of Science: Populations and Ecosystems** (4–8). 2007. Disney Educational Productions. Windows, Macintosh. ISBN 978-1-59753-142-9. $49.95.
Bill Nye the Science Guy hosts this interactive science game that asks randomly chosen multiple choice questions about populations and ecosystems, followed by a clip from Nye's TV show giving the correct answer. Also use *The Way Cool Game of Science: Structure and Function in Living Systems.* (Rev: BL 6/1–15/07; LMC 7/07; SLJ 112/07)

Astronomy and Space Science

General and Miscellaneous

836 ◉ **Core Astronomy** (5–7). 2007. 38 min. Ambrose Video. ISBN 978-1-58281-317-2. $49.99.

An informational program covering major discoveries made in astronomy (in chronological order from the time of Ptolemy onward) and noted scientists in the field. Illustrations, charts, graphics, photographs, and music add to the presentation. (Rev: BL 12/1/07)

837 ◉ **Exploring Earth, Sun, and Moon** (3–6). 2006. 15 min. Visual Learning. ISBN 978-1-59234-157-3. $79.95.

An excellent introduction to our planet, its moon, and its sun, with live-action footage and computer graphics. Teacher's guide included. (Rev: SLJ 10/06)

838 ◉ **Exploring Space: The Quest for Life** (9–12). 2006. 120 min. PBS Video. PPR. Closed captioned. ISBN 978-0-7936-9199-9. $59.95.

This wide-ranging and accessible survey uses computer-animated images and interviews with scientists to explain what we know about the origins of life on Earth and about the possible existence of life on other planets. (Rev: VL 11–12/06)

839 ◉ **Monster of the Milky Way: A Super-massive Black Hole** (7–12). 2007. 60 min.

WGBH Boston. Closed captioned. ISBN 978-1-59375-652-9. $19.95.

The difficult concept of a supermassive black hole — and, in this case, right in our galaxy — is presented in an interesting program featuring interviews with astronomers, animation, and graphics to aid understanding. (Rev: LMC 10/07; SLJ 6/07)

840 ▣ **Starry Night: Complete Space and Astronomy Pack** (4–12). 2005. 90 min. Imaginova. Windows, Macintosh. $49.95.

This planetarium program includes 50 guided tours to the universe. Viewers can inspect the sky from any point on Earth, controlling time, location, elevation, and so forth, and can travel beyond the Milky Way by spaceship. 192-page illustrated book included.

⚱ ALA Notable Children's Software 2005

841 ◉ **Understanding the Universe: An Introduction to Astronomy, 2nd ed.** (10–12). 2007. 16 discs. 2,880 min. Series: Great Lectures. The Teaching Company. PPR. ISBN 978-1-59803-274-1. $329.95.

Ninety-six lectures by astronomy professor Alex Filippenko of the University of California at Berkeley begin with basic concepts and move on to fascinating details about the universe and its galaxies. (Rev: BL 5/15/07)

842 ▧ **The Way Cool Game of Science: The Solar System and Space** (4–8). 2007. Disney Educational Productions. Windows, Macintosh. ISBN 978-1-59753-145-0. $49.95.

Students answer questions about space after seeing episodes of "Bill Nye the Science

Guy." The game can be played on the TV screen or on the computer. Segments include "Cause and Effect," "Fact or Fiction," "Fill-It-In," "Lab Vocab," "Where's Bill," and "Scientists at Work." (Rev: SLJ 11/07)

Astronautics and Space Exploration

843 ● **Project Mercury: A New Frontier** (9–12). 2005. 6 discs. 1,440 min. Spacecraft Films. $84.99.
A fascinating, thorough, and chronological record of the 1960s rocket program, with lots of re-mastered original footage. (Rev: VL 11–12/06)

844 ● **Space Exploration** (5–8). 1999. 23 min. Series: Space Science in Action. Schlessinger Media (dist. by Library Video Company). PPR. Closed captioned. $29.95.
Newly available on DVD, this presentation uses two aspiring astronauts as a focal point as it gives a history of man's exploration of space and looks at topics of particular interest — including diet and bathrooms. There is an activity, lots of NASA footage, and a teacher's guide. This is part of a series that also includes *Astronomy, Earth, Earth's Atmosphere, Moon, Planets and the Solar System, Stars, Sun,* and *Universe*. (Rev: SLJ 4/00; VL 7/06)

Stars

845 ● **The Mystery of Shooting Stars** (K–5). 2007. 50 min. Fogware. $19.99.
An entertaining introduction to shooting stars, using animation, live-action segments, and interviews with children, supplemented by brief information on the science. (Rev: BL 12/1/07; SLJ 9/07)

846 ● **Stars! Stars! Stars!** (K–6). 2005. 11 min. Weston Woods. PPR. ISBN 978-0-439-80460-8. $59.95.
An award-winning, fact-filled, animated introduction to astronomy that is both entertaining and educational. Based on the 2002 picture book by Bob Barner; study guide included. (Rev: VL 5–6/06)
♂ ALA ALSC Notable Children's Videos 2006

Sun and the Solar System

847 ● **Why Is the Sun So Hot? Heads Up! Part 3** (5–10). 2007. 28 min. Landmark Media. $195.
Scientist Bob McDonald takes viewers on a tour of U.S. observatories to talk with the astronomers there about the sun. Five segments discuss the nature of the sun and how it is studied. (Rev: SLJ 11/07)

Biological Sciences

General and Miscellaneous

848 🔘 **Best of Nature: Silver 25th Anniversary Collection** (9–12). 2007 86 min. Questar. ISBN 978-1-59464-282-1. $24.99.
Highlights of the popular PBS series include fascinating footage of animals hunting, mating, eating, and playing. (Rev: VL 9–10/07)

849 🔘 **In One Yard: Views Through a Microscope and Up Close** (5–10). 2006. 71 min. Warren Hatch Productions. ISBN 978-1-884195-53-2. $30.
Host Warren Hatch examines thirty plants and animals that live in his backyard (which has a pond) in Portland, Oregon. A longtime teacher, Hatch examines them using a microscope in his basement, illustrating respective size and offering various facts. Water lillies, frogs, bees, and crustaceans are only a few of the specimens viewers will see in this presentation suited to use in brief segments. Teacher's guide available. (Rev: SLJ 5/07)

850 🔘 **Squibs — Inside: Cells, DNA, and Adaptation** (4–12). 2005. 36 min. Ignite! Learning (dist. by Big Kids Productions). PPR. $29.95.
Learn facts about cells, cell reproduction, genetics, and so forth in an appealing format that includes music and animation and will appeal to a variety of ages, presenting lots of information in easily digestible mouthfuls. Part of a series that covers other scientific topics. (Rev: VL 3–4/06)

Botany

Foods, Farms, and Ranches
GENERAL AND MISCELLANEOUS

851 🔘 **All About Cowboys . . . for Kids, Part 1** (3–7). 2004. 45 min. TM Books & Video. ISBN 978-1-932291-18-6. $14.95.
Viewers learn about cowboy life through live-action footage and archival material, supported by cowboy music. They visit a 7-year-old cowboy and his pony, learn to tame a wild horse, and view a rodeo. Also available: *All About Cowboys . . . for Kids, Part 2.* (Rev: BL 6/1–15/04; SLJ 6/04)

852 🔘 **Ever Wondered About Food?** (9–12). 2006. 6 discs. 30 min. each. Meridian Education. ISBN 978-1-4213-4377-8. $349.95.
Fascinating information about foods that we eat, including cooking techniques, how different cultures have used foods, and recipes. Includes the following DVDs ($69.95 each): *Ever Wondered About Eggs?*, *Ever Wondered About Seafood?*, *Ever Wondered About Cheese?*, *Ever Wondered About Mushrooms?*, *Ever Wondered About Chicken?*, and *Ever Wondered About Potatoes?* (Rev: SLJ 3/07)

853 🔘 **Frankensteer** (10–12). 2006. 48 min. Paradigm Productions (dist. by Bullfrog Films). ISBN 978-1-59458-345-2. $250 (Rental: $85).
The overuse of antibiotics and hormones, giant feedlots, dangerous infections — all these problems plague the beef industry in North America. This evenhanded documen-

tary covers them all and is sure to spark discussion. You may want to avoid beef for dinner the day you watch it. (Rev: SLJ 10/06)

854 ◑ **Growing Our Food** (K–5). 2006. 23 min. Series: Agriculture for Children. Schlessinger Media (dist. by Library Video Company). PPR. Closed captioned. ISBN 978-1-4171-0636-3. $29.95.
Viewers learn farm vocabulary and procedures as they visit farms that use various techniques. An appealing presentation that will hold attention. Teacher's guide and Spanish language track included. Also in this series: *What Is Agriculture?*, *From Farm to Table*, and *Where Food Is Grown*. (Rev: VL 11–12/06)

855 ▦ **Harvest Moon: A Wonderful Life Special Edition** (3–12). Natsume. Windows, PlayStation 2, PSP, GameCube, Nintendo DS, Wii. Players: 1. ESRB: E.
Players learn how to maintain a farm and livestock as well as how to work and live with friends and neighbors.
☘ YALSA Top 50 Core Recommended Collection Titles

Plants and Flowers

856 ◑ **Coordination and Control Two: Plants** (10–12). 2006. 19 min. VEA. $89.95.
Plants have hormones, too, and this film discusses how they help plants respond and adapt to their environments. For advanced biology students. Teacher's guide included. (Rev: SLJ 9/07)

Zoology

General and Miscellaneous

857 ◑ **All About Animal Life Cycles** (PreK–3). 2006. 23 min. Series: Animal Life for Children. Schlessinger Media (dist. by Library Video Company). Closed captioned. ISBN 978-1-4171-0161-0. $29.95.
Narrated by children, this fact-filled installment in the 13-volume series covers the life cycles of a variety of animals — mammals, birds, reptiles, and insects — and looks in particular at fish, frogs, and butterflies. Teacher's guide included. (Rev: VL 7/06)

858 ▦ **Animal Genius** (K–6). 2007. Activision. Nintendo DS. ESRB: E (comic mischief). Elementary children can learn facts about animals in a number of ways playing these varied and enticing games. Scholastic also publishes a Leapster version. (Rev: CTR Leapster: 6/06; Nintendo DS: 12/07)

859 ▣ **Birds** (4–8). 2004. Form Wild (www.formwild.com). Windows, Macintosh. $12.50.
Birds is just one of 25 CDs containing full-color printable cutouts that fold into three-dimensional creatures, accompanied by facts and an activity.
☘ ALA Notable Children's Software 2004

860 ◑ **Core Biology: Animal Sciences** (6–9). 2007. 30 min. Ambrose Video. ISBN 978-1-58281-316-5. $49.99.
Covers animal sciences, with information on animal classification, kingdoms, behavior, communication, and so forth. Also in this series: *Plant Sciences*, *Environmental Sciences*, and *Microbiology and Genetics*. (Rev: BL 12/1/07)

861 ◑ **Journey to Planet Earth: The State of the Planet's Wildlife** (6–12). 2006. 25 min./55 min. Screenscope in assn. with South Carolina Educational Television. $149.
Available in two lengths, this is an excellent overview of the challenges facing wildlife around the world, with clear coverage of the root causes. Teacher's guide included. (Rev: SLJ 10/06)

Amphibians and Reptiles

GENERAL AND MISCELLANEOUS

862 ◑ **Amphibians** (5–8). 1999. 23 min. Series: Animal Life in Action. Schlessinger Media. $29.95.
An eye-catching, fact-filled introduction to amphibians and their life cycles, characteristics, habitat, and so forth. Includes an experiment and a teacher's guide. Part of a 16-volume series recently made available on DVD. (Rev: BL 6/1–15/00; LMC 4/5–07)

TORTOISES AND TURTLES

863 ◑ **Journey of the Loggerhead** (4–10). 2004. 30 min. Box Lunch Media. $89.95.
The fascinating life of the endangered loggerhead turtle is shown in excellent footage,

accompanied by discussion with experts. (Rev: BL 3/1/05; SLJ 4/05; VL 5–6/05)

☒ ALA ALSC Notable Children's Videos 2005

864 ◉ **Last Journey for the Leatherback?** (6–12). 2004. 30 min. Sea Turtle Restoration Project. PPR. ISBN 978-0-9761654-0-8. $10. This beautifully filmed account of the life of the massive, endangered leatherback turtle is accompanied by a strong environmental message. (Rev: VL 1–2/06)

Animal Species

GENERAL AND MISCELLANEOUS

865 ◉ **Branches on the Tree of Life: Molluscs** (9–12). 2006. 17 min. BioMEDIA Assocs. ISBN 978-1-930527-30-0. $68. Everything biology students need to know about this phylum of animals, which includes snails, clams, and other invertebrate creatures. Fascinating video captures the features of these organisms, and the presentation also covers how mollusks have evolved. (Rev: SLJ 3/07)

866 ◉ **Hanging with the Sloth** (5–8). 2006. 30 min. Choices Inc. ISBN 978-1-933724-07-2. $49.95. All about the behavior and habitats of sloths, with a visit to the Aviarios Sloth Rescue Center in Costa Rica to learn more about how these gentle creatures can be saved from extinction. (Rev: BL 12/1/06)

867 ◉ **Tall Blondes** (10–12). 2005. 60 min. Questar. Closed captioned. ISBN 978-1-59464-048-3. $19.99. Giraffes — the "tall blondes" of the animal world — star in this fact-filled documentary with great footage filmed in Africa, South America, and Colorado, where viewers watch a baby giraffe being born. (Rev: BL 4/15/05; VL 1–2/06)

APE FAMILY

868 ◉ **The Last Great Ape** (10–12). 2007. 56 min. WGBH Boston. Closed captioned. ISBN 978-1-59375-713-7. $19.95. The territory and survival of bonobos, a group of primates that live in the jungles of the Congo, are threatened by the encroachment of humans. Scientists studying their behavior have found them to be a peaceful,

matriarchal, and highly sexual group. Educators should note that there is footage of the animals' sexual behavior in this "NOVA" program. Teacher's materials available. (Rev: BL 8/07; SLJ 7/07; VL 9–10/07)

CATS (LIONS, TIGERS, ETC.)

869 ▨ **Tigre dientes de sable/Sabertooth Cat** (K–4). 2007. Capstone Press. Windows, Macintosh. ISBN 978-0-7368-7910-1. $14.95. With English text at the top of the page and Spanish at the bottom, this bilingual facsimile presentation of a Helen Frost book provides basic information on the sabertooth tiger. Users can click on highlighted (potentially difficult) words to see a definition, and the audio reading can be turned off so that students can read to themselves. (Rev: LMC 8–9/07; SLJ 9/07)

COYOTES, FOXES, AND WOLVES

870 ◉ **Living with Wolves** (9–12). 2007. 2 discs. 83 min. Image Entertainment. $14.99. A Discovery Channel program about Jim and Jaime Dutcher, who raise and photograph wolves in Idaho. A fascinating look at these animals in a beautifully wild setting. (Rev: VL 9–10/07)

Birds

GENERAL AND MISCELLANEOUS

871 ◉ **Alaska's Coolest Birds** (K–6). 2006. 55 min. Wonder Visions (dist. by Instructional Video). $24.99. A young narrator named Zachary adds to the appeal of this presentation of more than 70 different birds that can be found in Alaska. The stunning photography will astound young viewers. (Rev: SLJ 3/07)

BEHAVIOR

872 ◉ **How Birds Eat** (8–12). 2006. 37 min. NatureFlix Productions. PPR. $20. Excellent video footage shows the wide variation in birds' eating techniques and ability to spot food; a guide to birds is included. (Rev: BL 1/1–15/06; VL 1–2/07)

DUCKS AND GEESE

873 ◐ **Ride of the Mergansers** (1–8). 2004. 11 min. National Film Network. ISBN 978-0-8026-0513-9. $19.95. ($99.95 w/PPR).
A fascinating look at baby merganser ducks as they hatch and take an amazing first flight and swim (to Wagner's "Ride of the Valkyries"). (Rev: BL 10/1/06)

PENGUINS

874 ◐ **March of the Penguins** (6–12). 2005. 80 min. Warner. $28.99.
The fascinating, beautifully filmed story of the emperor penguins' mating and breeding ritual that involves an extraordinary migration. (Rev: VL 1–2/06)

Insects and Arachnids

GENERAL AND MISCELLANEOUS

875 ◐ **Dragonflies: A Complete Insect Life Cycle** (4–8). 2005. 12 min. Series: Big World of Insects, Spiders and Bugs. New Dimension Media. PPR. $49 (single site), $189 (multi-site).
Fascinating dragonfly facts are presented in this description of the insects' life cycle. Includes teacher's guide. (Rev: VL 1–2/06)

876 ◐ **Life in the Undergrowth** (9–12). 2005. 2 discs. 250 min. BBC Video. Closed captioned. ISBN 978-1-4198-2919-2. $34.98.
Hosted by David Attenborough, this beautifully photographed two-disc set introduces all kinds of bugs and gives details of their life cycles, mating, reproduction, behavior, and so forth. David Attenborough guides the viewer through a miniature universe teeming with life, never normally seen, yet all around us. New technology reveals surreal vistas and their extraordinary inhabitants. Though small, these creatures are ferocious. (Rev: VL 7/06)

BEES AND WASPS

877 ◐ **City of Bees** (1–6). 2005. 30 min. Frejas Born Film and Sound (dist. by Choices, Inc.). PPR. ISBN 978-1-933724-02-7. $49.95.
Explore the lives of bees and their social and work systems along with 6-year-old Oliver and his friends; features great close-up footage and a photo gallery. (Rev: SLJ 8/06; VL 9–10/06)

Marine and Freshwater Life

GENERAL AND MISCELLANEOUS

878 ✦ **Endless Ocean** (1–12). 2008. Nintendo. Wii. Players: 1. ESRB. E.
Encounter marine life — and some treasures — as you swim through a 3D world in this information-packed game. (Rev: CTR 2/08)

879 ◐ **Sponges** (7–12). 2005. 15 min. Series: Branches on the Tree of Life. BioMEDIA Associates. PPR. ISBN 978-1-930527-20-1. $68.
This is a short but solid introduction to the characteristics and behavior of sponges, with good information on relevant scientific concepts. (Rev: VL 5–6/06)

880 ◐ **The State of the Ocean's Animals** (10–12). 2007. 55 min. Series: Journey to Planet Earth. Screenscope. $149.
This sometimes-disturbing documentary hosted by Matt Damon looks at the state of the world's ocean inhabitants. Entire species are disappearing, it reports, due to overfishing, climate change, and unwise ecological practices. This is also available in a 25-minute version that can be used with younger students. (Rev: SLJ 8/07)

CORALS AND JELLYFISH

881 ◐ **Rainbows in the Sea** (6–12). 2005. 28 min. Earthwise Media. Closed captioned. $22.50.
A beautiful look at coral reefs around the world, with emphasis on their endangered status. (Rev: VL 11–12/05)
♗ ALA ALSC Notable Children's Videos 2006

FISHES

882 ◐ **Cuttlefish: Kings of Camouflage** (6–12). 2007. 56 min. WGBH Boston. Closed captioned. ISBN 978-1-59375-751-9. $19.95.
The strange and wonderful cuttlefish is the star of this "NOVA" presentation. Excellent photography of the creatures in their natural habitat and their ability to disguise themselves will engage viewers of all ages. (Rev: SLJ 12/07)

WHALES, DOLPHINS, AND OTHER SEA MAMMALS

883 🔘 **Ocean Odyssey** (9–12). 2006. 116 min. BBC Video. ISBN 978-1-4198-4297-9. $19.98.
This story of the life of a sperm whale, presented in realistic computer graphics and live-action footage, also captures the murky world of the deep ocean. (Rev: VL 3–4/07)

Pets

GENERAL AND MISCELLANEOUS

884 🔘 **How to Pick the Right Reptile for You** (4–8). 1997. 45 min. Third Point Productions. PPR. $19.95.
Newly available on DVD, this presentation discusses the suitability as pets of various snakes, lizards, tortoises, and looks at factors including diet and longevity. (Rev: VL 3/4/97)

CATS

885 🔘 **Understanding Cats with Roger Tabor** (9–12). 1998. 80 min. PBS Home Video. $29.99.
Cat expert Tabor looks at cats and kittens and how to understand them and care for them in segments titled "Understanding Your Cat," "Choosing Your Cat," "Kittens Learning About the World," "The Territorial Cat," "Communicating Cat," "Breaking Bad Habits," "Cat Care," and "The Mystery of the Cat." Newly released on DVD. (Rev: VL 7/06)

DOGS

886 🔘 **Clicker Puppy: Kids and Puppies Learning Together** (4–12). 2006. 48 min. Doggone Crazy (dist. by Instructional Video). $24.95.
Teaches dog owners to train their pets using a clicker, a training tool used to modify behavior. While this is geared to children, the importance of family involvement is emphasized. Basic commands and behaviors are covered. (Rev: SLJ 11/07)

Zoos, Aquariums, and Animal Care

887 🎲 **Animal Hospital** (3–8). 2006. Series: Pet Vet 3D. Viva Media. Windows. ESRB: E. $29.99.
Players run their own animal hospital, examining animals (horses, ponies, dogs, cats, rabbits, and pigs) and diagnosing problems as well as managing the business itself. There are three levels of difficulty, and participants learn about planning, problem solving, and practical math while also becoming familiar with animal care. (Rev: CTR 11/06)

888 🔘 **Jim Knox's Wild Zoofari at the National Aquarium in Baltimore** (1–4). 2006. 30 min. Series: Jim Knox's Wild Zoofari. CustomFlix. $14.98.
Endorsed by the Association of Zoos and Aquariums, this presentation emphasizes the animal rescue and rehabilitation programs that go on at the National Aquarium in Baltimore. Knox guides a group of children through the aquarium, where they talk with a dolphin trainer and visit workers in the Marine Animal Rescue Program. (Rev: SLJ 3/07)

Chemistry

A look at the uses for metalloids will help students see some of the real-life applications of chemistry. As silicon, one of the metalloids, is used in computer chips, the end of the video is about how computers have evolved and how important they have become in everyday life. (Rev: SLJ 3/07)

Geology and Geography

Earth and Geology

890 ◉ **Global Tectonics: Competing Theories** (7–12). 2006. 22 min. VEA. $89.95.
Plate tectonics or global expansion: Which is responsible for the formation of the earth as we know it today? This film looks at both possibilities and encourages viewers to consider that scientific theories may change over time. (Rev: SLJ 12/07)

891 ◉ **A Journey Through Geologic Time** (5–9). 2005. 20 min. Series: Geologic History. Visual Learning. $89.95.
An interesting discussion of geologic time (absolute versus relative), the geologic eras, and the evolution of Earth, with computer animation, quizzes, and reviews of material. Also in this series: *Earth's Changing Surface, Fossils,* and *Geology of North America.* Teacher's guide included. (Rev: BL 12/1/05)

892 ◉ **The Miracle Planet** (7–12). 2005. 5 discs. 250 min. Ambrose Video. PPR. $129.99.
Narrated by Christopher Plummer, this wideranging, fact-filled program on Earth's evolution features excellent animation, on-location footage, and interviews with scientists. The five parts are: "The Violent Past," "Snowball Earth," "New Frontiers," "Extinction and Rebirth," and "Survival of the Fittest." Produced by the National Film Board of Canada and NHK Japan. Teacher's guide included. (Rev: VL 7/06)

893 ◉ **The Nature of Earth: An Introduction to Geology** (10–12). 2006. 6 discs. 1,080 min. The Teaching Company. PPR. ISBN 978-1-59803-221-5. $114.95.
Dr. John J. Renton of West Virginia University speaks on 12 topics — Earth's origins, plate tectonics, minerals, rocks, volcanism, mass wasting, soils, erosion, groundwater, rock deformation, earthquakes, and mountains. (Rev: VL 3–4/07)

894 ◈ **The Way Cool Game of Science: Earth Structure and Processes** (4–8). 2007. Disney Educational Productions. Windows, Macintosh. ISBN 978-1-59753-144-3. $49.95.
Students answer questions about earth science after seeing episodes of "Bill Nye the Science Guy." The game can be played on the TV screen or on the computer. Segments include "Cause and Effect," "Fact or Fiction," "Fill-It-In," "Lab Vocab," "Where's Bill?," and "Scientists at Work." (Rev: SLJ 11/07)

Earthquakes and Volcanoes

895 ◉ **Earthquake Tsunami: Wave of Destruction** (7–12). 2007. 30 min. VEA. $89.95.
Produced in Australia, this program's focus is why tsunamis can be so deadly — and what causes them. Relief workers discuss the tsunami that claimed so many lives in 2004. Teacher's guide included. (Rev: SLJ 9/07)

896 ● **Expedition EarthScope** (7–12). 2006. 27 min. Earth Images Foundation (dist. by Bullfrog Films). Closed captioned. ISBN 978-1-59458-451-0. $195 (Rental: $45).
See scientists in action as a part of Earth-Scope, a National Science Foundation-funded program for the study of earthquakes and volcanoes in North America. Students studying these phenomena or interested in careers in the earth sciences will be fascinated. (Rev: SLJ 7/07)

897 ● **Mystery of the Megavolcano** (7–12). 2007. 60 min. WGBH Boston. Closed captioned. ISBN 978-1-59375-650-5. $19.95.
Could a "megavolcano" have exploded 75,000 years ago? In this "NOVA" program, scientists are shown collecting data and samples from around the world that support this theory. Graphics show how volcanoes erupt and the damage they can cause. (Rev: SLJ 4/07)

898 ● **Volcano** (2–5). 2006. 35 min. DK Eyewitness DVD. ISBN 978-0-756-62371-5. $12.99.
Journey around the world and explore the destructive force of volcanoes; newly available on DVD. (Rev: VL 9–10/06)

Rocks, Minerals, and Soil

899 ● **Rock and Mineral** (2–5). 1995. 35 min. DK Eyewitness DVD. ISBN 978-0-756-62368-5. $12.99.
Adapted from the popular series of DK books, this presentation shows the importance of rocks and minerals in our planet and the ways in which they change over time; newly available on DVD. (Rev: VL 9–10/06)

Mathematics

General and Miscellaneous

900 🖳 **Calculation Skills** (2–8). 2004. 4 discs. Core Learning. Windows. $19.95 (single site), $249 (school site).

Students learn and practice math concepts, often using timed tests. The four volumes are: Vol. 1: Addition and Subtraction, Basic Level (ISBN 1-897016-81-6); Vol. 2: Multiplication and Division, Basic Level (ISBN 1-897016-82-4); Vol. 3: Addition and Subtraction, Advanced Level (ISBN 1-897016-83-2); Vol. 4: Multiplication and Division, Advanced Level (ISBN 1-897016-84-0). Also available in French and Spanish. (Rev: SLJ 3/06)

901 🖳 **Cosmic Math** (1–5). 2006. LeapFrog. Leapster. $17.99.

Use your spaceship to blast away the correct answers in this four-level game that can be played by two children at different levels. Opportunities to play an arcade game pop up after a series of problems. (Rev: CTR 6/06)

902 🌐 **Fractions: Concepts and Operations** (4–8). 2006. 23 min. Series: Math for Students. Schlessinger Media (dist. by Library Video Company). PPR. Closed captioned. ISBN 978-1-4171-0602-8. $39.95.

Practical, real-life examples add to the appeal of this fast-paced overview that assumes some basic understanding. Spanish-language track and teacher's guide included. (Rev: LMC 8–9/07; VL 1–2/07)

903 🌐 **The Joy of Mathematics** (9–12). 2007. 4 discs. 720 min. The Teaching Company. PPR. ISBN 978-1-59803-310-6. $109.95.

Twenty-four lectures — including many simple math tricks — by Arthur T. Benjamin of Harvey Mudd College will inspire high school students to find the fun in math and to recognize the connections between mathematical disciplines. (Rev: VL 9–10/07)

904 🎲 **Math Missions: The Amazing Arcade Adventure** (3–5). 2003. Scholastic. Windows, Macintosh. ESRB: E. $49.99.

Players learn math skills as they solve real-life problems in Spectacle City, where Randall Underling is trying to drive all the stores out of business. Also use (for grades K–2) *Math Missions: The Race to Spectacle City.* (Rev: CTR 9/03)

🏅 ALA Notable Children's Software 2004

905 🌐 **Meaning from Data: Statistics Made Clear** (9–12). 2006. 4 discs. 720 min. Series: Great Courses. The Teaching Company. ISBN 978-1-59803-146-1. $109.95.

Twenty-four lectures introduce students to statistics — how they are compiled and organized, and so forth — and to their application in many important and varied parts of our lives. The dangers of misleading and biased numbers are underlined. (Rev: VL 7/06)

906 🌐 **Measuring** (2–5). 2006. 14 min. Visual Learning. PPR. Closed captioned. ISBN 978-1-59234-153-5. $79.95.

The importance of understanding measurement is highlighted in this brief overview of systems for measuring length, mass, volume, and temperature. Teacher's guide included. (Rev: VL 11–12/06)

Algebra, Numbers, and Number Systems

907 🌐 **Algebra for Students: Analyzing Inequalities** (7–12). 2007. 23 min. Series: Algebra for Students. Schlessinger Media (dist. by Library Video Company). PPR. Closed captioned. ISBN 978-1-4171-0807-7. $39.95.

This volume in the series looks at inequalities using the real-life example of purchasing concert tickets. A Spanish language track is included. Other titles in the series include: *Exponential Functions, Functions and Relations, Linear Equations and Slope, Patterns and Formulas, Polynomials, The Pythagorean Theorem and Right Triangles, Quadratic Functions, Systems of Linear Equations,* and *Variables, Expressions and Equations.* Teacher's guide included. (Rev: LMC *Linear Equations and Slope:* 3/08; VL 9–10/07)

908 🌐 **The Metric System** (4–8). 2006. 4 discs. 80 min. Visual Learning. Closed captioned. ISBN 978-1-59234-135-1. $299.

In four parts that include many real-life situations, this excellent presentation covers the basics of the metric system and how it differs from the English and American systems; metric length and temperature, metric mass and volume, and conversions from one system to another. Teacher's guide included, as well as review quizzes. (Rev: LMC 10/06; SLJ 7/06; VL 7/06)

Mathematical Games and Puzzles

909 🌐 **Cyberchase: Starlight Night** (3–7). 2004. 55 min. Paramount Home Entertainment. Closed captioned. ISBN 978-1-4157-0497-4. $16.99.

Two episodes of the PBS Kids animated series in which three kids use logic and math skills to fight Hacker and keep Cyberspace safe. (Rev: VL 1–2/05)

910 🎲 **2Simple Math Games 1** (4–7). 2007. 2Simple USA. Windows. Players: 1.

Six games reinforce basic math skills. (Rev: CTR 8/07)

Meteorology

General and Miscellaneous

911 ◉ **Climate Change and Our Future** (9–12). 2006. 50 min. Series: Classroom Encounters with Global Change Scientists. Classroom Encounters. $50.
A professor at Tufts University explains the phenomenon of climate change to a group of high school students; interaction between professor and students, images, and a question-and-answer segment add to the presentation. (Rev: SLJ 6/07)

912 ◉ **Popular Mechanics for Kids: Lightning and Other Forces of Nature** (1–6). 2006. 88 min. Koch Vision. ISBN 978-1-4172-2934-5. $14.98.
In entertaining episodes on "Ice," "Water," Earth Power," and "Electricity," viewers learn along with teen hosts Elisha and Tyler about some natural phenomena and how they can effect us. (Rev: VL 9–10/06)

913 ◉ **Weather** (2–5). 2006. 35 min. DK Eyewitness DVD. ISBN 978-0-756-62369-2. $12.99.
A whirlwind tour of extreme weather of all kinds; newly available on DVD. (Rev: VL 9–10/06)

914 ◉ **Weather Around Us** (3–5). 2007. Visual Learning. ISBN 978-1-59234-175-7. $79.95.
A basic introduction to weather and what causes it to change, including heat energy, air pressure, wind, and moisture. A quiz at the end can be used for assessment. Teacher's guide available. (Rev: SLJ 9/07)

915 ◉ **Weather on the Move** (3–5). 2007. 14 min. Visual Learning. ISBN 978-1-59234-177-1. $79.95.
An informative introduction to air masses, weather fronts, hurricanes, thunderstorms, lightning, and tornadoes. (Rev: BL 12/15/07; LMC 3/08; SLJ 8/07)

Storms

916 ◉ **Hurricane Katrina: The Storm That Drowned a City** (9–12). 2005. 56 min. WGBH Boston. PPR. Closed captioned. ISBN 978-1-59375-319-1. $19.95.
This "NOVA" production provides lots of information on hurricanes and their forecasting as well as covering the devastation caused by Katrina, historical information on the city and its location, and the failure to anticipate the dramatic damage to the city and its people. (Rev: VL 5–6/06)

917 ◉ **Hurricane! Katrina, Gilbert and Camille** (7–12). 2006. 2 discs. 120 min. WGBH Boston. $29.95.
Includes two "NOVA" episodes — *Hurricane Katrina: The Storm that Drowned a City* and *Hurricane* — that look at the impact of these three powerful storms. (Rev: VL 9–10/06)

918 ⬤ **Mystery of the Megaflood** (9–12). 2005. 56 min. WGBH Boston. PPR. Closed captioned. ISBN 978-1-59375-315-3. $19.95.

A sudden megaflood is posited as the cause of strange geological structures in a large area of Washington state; this "NOVA" production will serve as the starting point for conversation on many controversial topics. (Rev: LMC 10/06; SLJ 3/06; VL 5–6/06)

919 ⬤ **The Storm** (9–12). 2005. 60 min. PBS Video. Closed captioned. ISBN 978-0-7936-9098-5. $29.99 ($59.95 w/PPR).

With lots of archival footage and interviews, "Frontline" looks at the questions surrounding Hurricane Katrina — why the city was so unprepared and why the government's response was so inadequate — and provides lots of information on the Federal Emergency Management Agency. (Rev: VL 11–12/06)

Physics

General and Miscellaneous

920 ◐ **Core Physics** (9–12). 2007. 2 discs. 30 min. ea. Centre Communications (dist. by Ambrose Video). Closed captioned. $79.99 set, $49.99 ea.

This two-DVD set includes *Core Physics: Classical Physics* and *Core Physics: Modern Physics*. The major discoveries and theories concerning matter, energy, forces, space, and time — from 1814 through the discovery of quarks in 1964 — are clearly discussed with the aid of lots of images and diagrams. Teacher's guide included. (Rev: SLJ 12/07)

921 ◐ **Elements of Physics: Energy, Work, and Power** (9–12). 2006. 56 min. Discovery School. ISBN 978-1-59527-992-7. $69.95.

An overview of these basic physics concepts. Viewers will see energy at work in roller coasters, cars, and in other applications. A combination of animation and conventional footage adds interest. (Rev: SLJ 1/07)

922 ◐ **Everyday Simple Machines** (3–5). 2007. 14 min. Visual Learning. Closed captioned. ISBN 978-1-59234-167-2. $79.95.

We use levers, inclined planes, wedges, screws, wheels and axles, and pulleys every day, and this program explains their applications. A brief quiz at the end of this live-action film can be used as an assessment. Teacher's guide and reproducible masters included. (Rev: LMC 1/08; SLJ 9/07)

923 ◐ **The Ghost Particle** (9–12). 2006. 56 min. WGBH Boston. PPR. Closed captioned. ISBN 978-1-59375-561-4. $19.95.

Neutrinos are a mystery to most of us, and they baffled scientists for years. This "NOVA" program tells the story of scientists' search for these invisible particles. (Rev: VL 11–12/06)

924 🎮 **The Way Cool Game of Science: Matter** (4–8). 2007. Series: The Way Cool Game of Science. Disney Educational Productions. Windows, Macintosh. ISBN 978-1-59753-150-4. $49.95.

Students answer questions about matter after seeing episodes of "Bill Nye the Science Guy." The game can be played on the TV screen or on the computer. Segments include "Cause and Effect," "Fact or Fiction," "Fill-It-In," "Lab Vocab," "Where's Bill," and "Scientists at Work." (Rev: SLJ 8/07)

Energy and Motion

General and Miscellaneous

925 ◐ **Newton's Laws of Motion** (9–12). 2005. 26 min. VEA. PPR. $89.95.

Motion in motion! A creative and fun-filled look at the laws relating to inertia, acceleration, and reciprocal action. Live action with informative graphics. Teacher's guide included. (Rev: SLJ 9/07)

Light, Color, and Laser Science

926 ⊗ **Light** (3–5). 2004. 14 min. Visual Learning. ISBN 978-1-59234-091-0. $64.95.
A program covering light — its various properties and sources, its usefulness, and what life would be like without it — as well as the different types of electromagnetic waves, wavelengths, and the electromagnetic spectrum. A teacher's guide is included and there are many pauses for review of material. (Rev: BL 12/1/04; SLJ 9/04)

Technology and Engineering

Computers, Automation, and the Internet

927 🖳 **Anime Studio** (5–12). E-Frontier. Windows, Macintosh. $49.99.
Create 2D anime and cartoons using character templates, sketching your own art, or scanning in photographs and graphics. Allow the program to generate movement, and use its bone rigging system to bring life to figures.
♻ ALA Great Interactive Software for Kids Fall 2007

928 🌐 **Building Your Own Computer** (9–12). 2005. 171 min. Nebo Technical Institute. $19.99.
Yes, you can build a computer — if you have the right tools, materials, and instruction. This DVD is what you need, with a guide who gives very clear directions. (Rev: SLJ 1/07)

929 🌐 **Cyberstalking and Bullying** (6–12). 2006. CWK Network (dist. by New Dimension Media). ISBN 978-1-59522-303-6. $49.
Disturbing true stories of children who have been sexually abused will convince students of the dangers of communicating with strangers online. Other young people tell of being sent harassing e-mails by their peers. Viewers are told how they can avoid these situations and what to do if they are threatened to made to

feel uneasy while online. Teacher's guide available. (Rev: SLJ 6/07)

930 🌐 **The Great Robot Race** (6–9). 2006. 56 min. WGBH Boston. ISBN 978-1-59375-565-2. $19.95.
The exciting story of the competition to build a robotic vehicle that can cross 130 miles of desert and win a $2 million prize. John Lithgow narrates this well-presented "NOVA" program. (Rev: SLJ 12/06)
♻ ALA ALSC Notable Children's Videos 2007

931 🌐 **Online Predators: Invading My Space** (7–12). 2006. 20 min. Wildcatter Productions and Brain Trust Films (dist. by Wildcatter Productions). ISBN 978-1-57557-880-4. $79.95.
A cautionary film that explains how child molesters and others with evil intent may use the Internet to harass. Includes teacher's guide. (Rev: SLJ 3/07)

932 🖳 **Scratch** (3–12).
www.media.mit.edu
Developed at the MIT Media Lab, Scratch is a free program that facilitates the creation of interactive stories, games, music, and animations and allows the creator to share them on the Web. It can be downloaded at http://web.media.mit.edu/andresmh/tmp/download.html. (Rev: CTR 6/07)

Television, Motion Pictures, Radio, and Recording

933 ◆ **Start Editing Now (Classroom Workshop Edition)** (8–12). 2007. 3 discs. Videocraft Workshop. $129.95.
This three-DVD-ROM set includes one instructional disc and two that are to be used for hands-on practice of video editing. Teacher's guide included. (Rev: SLJ 10/07)

Transportation

Airplanes, Aeronautics, and Ballooning

934 ◆ **All About Airplanes and Flying Machines** (K–5). 2007. 45 min. TM Books & Video (dist. by Big Kids Prods). ISBN 978-1-932291-79-7. $14.95.
As the title states, this film looks at all sorts of flying vehicles, from hang gliders to hot air balloons, helicopters, airplanes, with information on historic flying machines. A segment on the Blue Angels is sure to be popular. (Rev: SLJ 5/07)

935 ◆ **The B-2 Stealth Bomber** (9–12). 2005. 56 min. Jumby Bay Studios/Vat19 Productions. PPR. $19.95.
An exciting and informative look at the "flying wing" and how it was conceived and engineered, with lots of history and explanations of the basic science of flight. Includes a tour of the plane and a brief feature on pilot training. (Rev: SLJ 1/06; VL 5–6/05)

936 🎲 **Microsoft Flight Simulator X** (5–12). 2007. Microsoft. Windows. Players: 1. ESRB: E.
This simulator provides a very realistic experience of flying aircraft of various types (18 are provided) at various altitudes and in varying conditions. You can view the plane's flight from the cockpit and can feel the effects of turbulence.

Automobiles and Trucks

937 ◆ **Adventures with Wink and Blink: A Day in the Life of a Garbage Truck!** (K–2).

2003. 30 min. Laurel Hill Entertainment. ISBN 978-0-9753885-1-8. $17.95.
Two costumed characters named Wink and Blink take kids for a look at the life of a garbage truck, from the factory where it's made to the landfill where it disposes of the garbage. Recycling tips and garbage truck safety are included. (Rev: BL 7/04; SLJ 6/04)

938 🎲 **Gary Gadget: Building Cars** (2–7). 2006. Viva Media. Windows, Macintosh. Players: 1. ESRB: E. $29.99.
Players help Gary build cars — realistic and fantastic — from the chassis up, using parts from his amazing junk pile. A challenging test drive follows. (Rev: SLJ 3/07; CTR 2/07)
🏆 ALA Notable Children's Software 2007

939 ◆ **Passing the Written DMV Test** (9–12). 2005. 45 min. Powell Productions. $19.95.
Prospective test-takers will find useful information and advice in this clear guide to safe driving and the rules of the road; many differences in state laws are listed. (Rev: SLJ 2/07; VL 7/06)

940 ◆ **Who Killed the Electric Car?** (10–12). 2006. 91 min. Sony. $26.99.
Why do we not have environmentally friendly electric cars? This documentary explores the history of the electric car — back to the early 20th century — and looks at political and economic factors that may have limited its viability. (Rev: VL 11–12/06)

Railroads

941 🎲 **Sid Meier's Railroads!** (8–12). 2006. Firaxis. Windows, Macintosh. ESRB: E. $39.99.
This sophisticated simulation/strategy game allows users to build their own railroad system, learning about the industry itself and its importance to society and the economy as a whole, and about techniques of fighting off competition. With outstanding graphics, the game features historical and fictional scenarios, real-time action, and of course trains (more than 30 diverse models) and great train audio. There are five levels of difficulty and multi-player options.
🏆 ALA Great Interactive Software for Kids Fall 2007

Ships and Boats

942 🖥️ **Charles W. Morgan: Voyages of the Past, Present and Future** (3–10). 2006. Mystic Seaport Museum (www.mystic seaport.org). Windows, Macintosh. $19.95.

This CD-ROM gives a tour of the *Charles W. Morgan*, a 19th-century whaling ship, and presents lots of information about the whaling industry, historic voyages, shipbuilding and so forth, with games, quests, quizzes, and music.

🏅 ALA Notable Children's Software 2006

943 🌐 **Shipping Out: The Story of America's Seafaring Women** (9–12). 2006. 56 min. Waterfront Soundings Productions. PPR. Closed captioned. $24.95.

Interviews with women who work on all kinds of merchant ships — as pilots and engineers, mates and cooks — reveal what attract-ed them to the traditionally masculine life on the high seas. This informative program looks at the dangers aboard ship and at the history of seafaring in America. (Rev: BL 4/1/06)

Weapons, Submarines, and the Armed Forces

944 🌐 **Underwater Dream Machine** (9–12). 2006. 56 min. WGBH Boston. PPR. Closed captioned. ISBN 978-1-59375-325-2. $19.95.

The machine of the title is a 6-man, $2 million submarine called the *Alicia* that is designed to navigate the deep sea. This "NOVA" program follows the design and construction of this vessel, which was built using only scavenged or off-the-shelf parts. (Rev: VL 5–6/06)

Recreation and Sports

Crafts, Hobbies, and Pastimes

General and Miscellaneous

945 🖳 **Collage Machine** (3–12). 2006. Proto-Zone Interactive. Windows, Macintosh. $24.95.

Users can draw on more than 500 photographs and images — or import their own — to create interesting collages, manipulating size and position with ease.

⛉ ALA Great Interactive Software for Kids Fall 2007

946 💿 **Fifty Greatest Kid Concoctions** (6–10). 2005. 70 min. Time Life. $14.95.

A selection of interesting projects — from cooking to music to science — involve ingredients found around the house. (Rev: VL 5–6/06)

947 💿 **Folklore** (K–6). 2004. 30 min. Chip Taylor Communications. Closed captioned. $89.99.

Five crafts — Paul Bunyan puppets, a turtle maraca, an eraser, a vest, and a towel — are inspired by North American folklore. (Rev: BL 12/15/04)

948 💿 **I Can Make Art Like: Kai Chan** (4–7). 2006. 12 min. Crystal Productions. PPR. $19.95.

Chinese sculptor Kai Chan demonstrates the art of making abstract sculptures from bamboo. (Rev: BL 11/1/06; VL 1–2/07)

949 💿 **I Can Make Art Like: Ron Noganosh** (4–7). 2006. 16 min. National Film Board of Canada (dist. by Crystal Productions). $19.95.

Ojibwa sculptor Ron Noganosh tells children about his culture and its influence on his work. He helps them make their own sculptures from found objects. Teacher's guide included. (Rev: SLJ 12/06)

950 🖳 **KaleidoDraw** (K–10). 2006. ProtoZone Interactive. Windows, Macintosh. $24.95.

Users can explore patterns and symmetry as they select colors and images and allow the drawing tool to work like a virtual kaleidoscope. (Rev: CTR 5/03)

⛉ ALA Great Interactive Software for Kids Fall 2007

951 🖳 **KaleidoPix** (K–10). 2006. ProtoZone Interactive. Windows, Macintosh. $24.95.

Create your own kaleidoscope using your own pictures or the many available on the disk; users learn about symmetry as they work. (Rev: CTR 2/07)

⛉ ALA Great Interactive Software for Kids Fall 2007

952 💿 **Puppet Circus Parade** (K–5). 2004. 120 min. Meunincks Media Methods. ISBN 978-0-939865-83-3. $29.95.

From simple finger puppets to rod-and-marionette creations, this DVD presents more than 20 puppet projects using everyday materials. The soundtrack is available in both English and Spanish, with or without subtitles, and a companion CD-ROM includes the patterns. (Rev: BL 7/04)

953 ● **Rainy Day Art 2** (3–6). 2005. 210 min. VAT 19. $19.95.
Art teacher Cherie Lynn Kassin presents 13 projects — a mosaic picture frame, a woven wall hanging, and so forth — that use readily available materials. (Rev: BL 8/05)

954 ● **Tie Dye 101: The Basics of Making Exceptional Tie Dye** (8–12). 2005. 87 min. TrueTieDye.com. PPR. ISBN 978-0-9763345-0-7. $24.95.
A step-by-step introduction to the art of tie-dye, offering advice on choosing fabrics, correct laundry procedures, and safety. (Rev: SLJ 6/06; VL 1–2/06)

955 ● **Winter Art Fun** (K–4). 2007. 2 discs. 120 min. Lightstone Video Productions. $24.95.
Ten winter-themed crafts include projects centered on snowmen, Christmas trees, and valentines. The techniques become more advanced as the presentation progresses, and practical tips are offered throughout. Materials are inexpensive and easy to find. (Rev: SLJ 9/07)

956 ● **World Art 2** (5–8). 2005. 150 min. VAT 19. $19.95.
Eleven projects with step-by-step instructions introduce arts and crafts from around the world, including Tibetan sand paintings, an African face mask, and a Navajo Indian blanket. (Rev: BL 11/1/05; SLJ 12/06)

Clay Modeling and Ceramics

957 ● **Art of Ceramics: Creating Animal Sculptures in Clay** (3–5). 2005. 29 min. Instructional Video. $29.95.
Humor and animation add appeal to the clear how-to instructions on the creation of real and imaginary animals. (Rev: BL 11/1/05)

958 ● **Gargoyles: How to Create Them** (7–12). 2007. 21 min. Crystal Productions. ISBN 978-1-56290-547-7. $29.95.
Learn to create medieval-looking gargoyles and chimeras (gargoyles are functional while chimeras are decorative) out of clay. The artist host discusses the history of gargoyles

and then takes the viewer through the process of shaping and firing. (Rev: SLJ 9/07)

959 ● **Making Dinosaurs Out of Clay** (K–4). 2006. 34 min. Crystal Productions. $29.95.
Learn to make a triceratops, a stegosaurus, a Tyrannosaurus rex, and a pteranodon out of clay, then to glaze them and fire them in a kiln. Presented by artist Mark Abilgaard. (Rev: SLJ 5/07)

Cooking

960 ● **Cooking for Kids** (5–8). 2006. 254 min. Title_set Distribution. ISBN 978-0-9726945-8-2. $39.95.
In these six episodes, culinary instructor Desirée Dorwart shows kids some basic techniques for cooking and baking, and guides them through the process of making chocolate chip cookies, various breakfast dishes, chocolate truffles, stir-fry meals, Italian dishes, and more. (Rev: BL 12/15/06; VL 6/12/07)

961 ● **Cooking with Kids: Exploring Chinese Food, Culture and Language** (4–8). 2006. 30 min. Ni Hao Productions (dist. by AV Café). ISBN 978-0-9779512-2-2. $19.95.
Three children plan a Chinese meal, buy the ingredients in San Francisco's Chinatown, then prepare egg flower soup, stir-fried chicken, and almond cookies. The recipes are included in the presentation so viewers can try them at home. Some Chinese words and phrases are defined. (Rev: SLJ 4/07)

962 ● **Creative Cakes, Parts 1 and 2** (9–12). 2007. 2 discs. 60 min. VEA. $89.95.
Part 1 teaches Basic Techniques and Part 2 Beyond the Basics. Viewers first learn to make simple decorations from frosting, then move on to more complex designs that give their cakes a professional look. (Rev: SLJ 9/07)

963 ● **Gingerbread Housemaking with the Gingerbread Lady** (3–12). 2006. 84 min. Patricia L. Hudson. PPR. ISBN 978-1-880928-04-2. $49.95.
Fancy a gingerbread house? Or just a cottage? The step-by-step instructions are here. (Rev: VL 11–12/06)

Costume and Jewelry Making, Dress, and Fashion

964 ❂ **Style Remix** (7–12). 2007. 100 min. Tri-Coast Studios (dist. by Leisure Arts). ISBN 978-1-60140-561-6. $19.95.
Teenage girls who are interested in fashion but don't want to spend a lot of money will enjoy this program. It instructs viewers on how to add interest to simple pieces, how to make the most of old or secondhand items, and how to transform clothes that are no longer in style. Some of the projects require some sewing, which is demonstrated. (Rev: SLJ 11/07)

Dolls and Other Toys

965 ❂ **I Love Toy Trains: The Final Show** (K–2). 2005. 55 min. TM Books & Video. ISBN 978-1-932291-29-2. $14.95.
Everything for the young fan of toy trains, including a visit to a collection, a Lego layout, and information on how the displays are constructed, all presented with appealing songs and sounds and live-action footage. (Rev: BL 11/15/05)

Drawing and Painting

966 🖥 **ArtRage 2.5** (5–12). 2007. Ambient Design. Windows, Macintosh. $25.
ArtRage is a versatile painting program that allows the user to choose media (oils, pencils, crayons, gold leaf, silver foil, and so forth), customize colors, use multiple layers, import images, and export the finished product in all the usual formats. Can be downloaded at www.artrage.com. (Rev: CTR 1/08)

967 ❂ **The Dance of Watercolor: Beginners and Beyond** (9–12). 2005. 64 min. Julie Cohn Productions. $19.99.
Watercolor with confidence following this program that features artist Julie Cohn. She encourages viewers to experiment with the use of water and to spend lots of time practicing and developing their skills and talent. Booklet included.

968 ❂ **Drawing Excitement with Thomas Kinkade** (5–8). 2004. 138 min. Instructional Video. $29.99.
Artist Thomas Kinkade presents 18 easy-to-follow art lessons, starting with how to combine lines to create objects, and then moving on to shapes, proportions, tone, texture, and so forth. A brief overview of art history and directions for drawing landscapes is also provided. (Rev: BL 4/15/04; SLJ 7/04)

969 ❂ **Drawing Power with Michael Moodoo: Pirate Drawing Adventure** (3–7). 2007. 80 min. Moodoo Productions. ISBN 978-0-9762454-6-9. $29.99.
The entertaining and talented Michael Moodoo helps young artists to draw a pirate ship and everything pirates need, such as a parrot and a treasure map. (Rev: SLJ 8/07)

970 ❂ **Drawing with Patricia Polacco** (K–3). 2005. 16 min. Art'SCool. $65.
Author/artist Polacco demonstrates how she works and provides tips on successful drawing. (Rev: BL 11/1/05)

971 ❂ **Easy 2 Draw Dolphins and Reef Animals with Cordi** (3–6). 2007. 120 min. Artragous Designs. $24.95.
Art instructor Cordi shows how to draw several aquatic animals using an easy three-step process; she also discusses supplies and environmental threats to coral reefs. (Rev: BL 5/1/07; SLJ 1/08)

972 ❂ **Easy 2 Draw Horses with Cordi** (4–8). 2004. 64 min. Artragous Designs. PPR. $24.95.
Cordi Bradburn presents six lessons on drawing realistic horses, showing the process of layout, line drawing, shading, and texturing, and using footage of real horses to illustrate her points. (Rev: BL 11/1/04; VL 11–12/04)

973 ❂ **Oodles of Doodles** (6–9). 2003. 60 min. Video Specialties. $29.95.
Learn to doodle effectively with the advice of cartoonist Mike Artell, who demonstrates how to make simple shapes — such as ovals, squares, and triangles — look like people, animals, insects, food, and so forth. (Rev: BL 6/1–15/04; SLJ 4/04)

Magic Tricks and Optical Illusions

974 ◐ **Learn Magic with Lyn** (3–7). 2007. 53 min. Magic of Lyn. $14.99.
Lyn Dillies, an experienced illusionist, takes viewers through 11 magic tricks — including objects that disappear, change color, and change form — carefully explaining each stage and the props necessary. (Rev: BL 6/1–15/07; SLJ 4/08)

975 ◐ **Optical Illusions: How to Create Them** (6–9). 2005. 24 min. Crystal Productions. $29.95.
Learn to create optical illusions using a ruler, paper, pencil, colored markers, and oil pastels. (Rev: BL 12/15/05)

Paper Crafts

976 ◐ **Origami, Vol. 2** (1–6). 2005. 48 min. DVK (dist. by Big Kids Productions). $24.95.
The construction of 17 origami figures — a penguin, a piano, a swan, and a star are among them — is shown in brief, clear segments with close-up shots that make the folds easy to see. (Rev: SLJ 3/06)

Sewing and Other Needle Crafts

977 ◐ **The Art of Knitting 4 Kids** (K–5). 2007. 99 min. TriCoast Studios (dist. by Leisure Arts). ISBN 978-1-60140-649-1. $19.95.

Children don't just learn to knit on this video — they also make their own knitting needles and visit an alpaca farm to see where yarn comes from. Children will be excited to start their own projects after viewing this program. (Rev: SLJ 10/07)

978 ◐ **Beading: 8 Easy Projects** (5–12). 2007. 40 min. On Air Video. $14.95.
Beading is a popular craft, and young beaders will enjoy tackling the eight projects featured on this program: a necklace, a bracelet, an ankle bracelet, an eyeglass chain, earrings, a zipper pull, a wine-glass charm, and a bib chain. A materials list is included. (Rev: BL 12/15/07; SLJ 11/07)

979 ◐ **The Great American Quilt Revival** (10–12). 2005. 58 min. Bonesteel Films (dist. by AV Café). PPR. $24.95.
An informative and attractive history of quilts and their evolving patterns and uses. (Rev: BL 12/15/06; VL 1–2/07)

980 ◐ **No-Rules Knitting! at the Teen Knit Café** (5–12). 2007. 98 min. TriCoast Studios (dist. by Leisure Arts). ISBN 978-1-60140-562-3. $19.95.
Did you know that you can dye yarn with Kool-Aid? That you can knit a bracelet? Middle-schoolers and high-schoolers will think differently about knitting after trying the funky projects featured here. (Rev: SLJ 10/07)

Jokes, Puzzles, Riddles, and Word Games

981 🎲 **Big Brain Academy: Wii Degree** (3–12). 2007. Nintendo. Wii. Players: 1–8. ESRB: E. $49.99.

Compete in multiple mentally challenging tests to determine who has the biggest brain. Categories are: identify, compute, analyze, memory, and logic. Also available in a Nintendo DS version ($19.99). (Rev: CTR 7/07)

⚇ ALA Great Interactive Software for Kids Fall 2007

982 🎲 **Bookworm Adventures** (3–12). 2007. PopCap Games. Windows. ESRB: E10+ (animated blood, mild cartoon violence). $19.99.

Children role-play, battle monsters, and earn treasures by spelling words, all to help a bookworm named Lex who is working to save the Great Library.

⚇ ALA Notable Children's Software 2007

983 🎲 **Bookworm Deluxe** (3–12). 2006. PopCap Games. Windows, Macintosh. ESRB: E. $19.95.

This game combines education and fun, with players spelling words to feed a ravenous bookworm named Lex.

⚇ ALA Notable Children's Software 2007

984 🎲 **Boom Blox** (K–12). 2008. Electronic Arts. Wii. Players: 1+. ESRB: E (cartoon violence, comic mischief).

Dexterity, problem solving, and creativity are at the heart of this game that uses the Wii controls to manage towers of blocks — either knocking them down or keeping them from falling. The physics of mass, angle, and so

forth become clear to players. (Rev: CTR 5/08)

985 🎲 **Brain Age 2: More Training in Minutes a Day** (5–12). 2007. Nintendo. Nintendo DS. Players: 1. ESRB: E.

Memory Sprint, Word Scramble, and Math Recall are just three of the 15 games included here. An initial test establishes your brain age in a range from 20 to 80 (the lower/younger score the better). (Rev: CTR 9/07)

986 🎲 **Bust-A-Move Bash** (6–12). 2007. Majesco Entertainment. Wii. Players: 1–8. ESBR: E.

A lively puzzle game in which players use the Wii Remote and Nunchuks to deal with an assault of bubbles; there are hundreds of puzzle levels. (Rev: VOYA 8/07; CTR 6/07)

987 🎲 **Crazy Machines 1.5** (3–10). 2007. Viva Media. Windows. Players: 1. ESRB: E. $19.99.

Brain-teasing entertainment involves inventing unusual Rube Goldberg-style contraptions and solving a variety of puzzles. An Inventor's Training Camp sets the new user on the right road. (Rev: CTR 4/07)

⚇ ALA Great Interactive Software for Kids Fall 2007

988 🎲 **I Spy Fantasy** (K–4). 2004. Scholastic. Windows, Macintosh. $19.95.

Excellent graphics add to the fun of this program in which players explore a castle, space, and the world beneath the sea solving riddles and playing scavenger hunt and other games. Based on the *I Spy* book, this game builds logic, memory, and reading skills. (Rev: CTR 9/03)

ALA Notable Children's Software 2004

989 **I Spy Mystery** (1–5). 2006. Scholastic. Windows, Macintosh. $19.99.
Thirteen mysteries and more than 50 riddles are combined in this eye-catching presentation that stimulates reading, writing, and problem-solving skills. (Rev: CTR 8/06)

ALA Notable Children's Software 2007

990 **I Spy Spooky Mansion Deluxe** (1–7). 2005. Scholastic. Windows, Macintosh. $19.95.
Solve 15 picture puzzles in order to escape from a haunted house in this award-winning interactive game based on the book *I Spy Spooky Night*, text by Jean Marzollo and photographs by Walter Wick. (Rev: CTR Summer 04)

ALA Notable Children's Software 2005

991 **Mercury Meltdown Remix** (6–12). 2006. Ignition Entertainment. PlayStation 2. Players: 1. ESRB: E.
Move blobs of mercury around mazes without losing any mercury while navigating various obstacles. Requires good hand and eye coordination. Memory card needed to save progress. (Rev: SLJ 2/07)

992 **New York Times Crosswords** (6–12). 2007. Majesco Entertainment. Nintendo DS. Players: 1–2. ESRB: E.
Solve more than 1,000 *New York Times* crosswords, with the ability to select difficulty and set time limits.

993 **Photo Puzzle Builder** (K–12). 2004. APTE Inc. Windows, Macintosh. $39.95 (single), $69.95 (school).
Build many different kinds of word and picture puzzles — crosswords, word searches, photo jigsaws, photo-scrambles, and so forth — using a photo library or by scanning in personal images. Teacher's guide included. (Rev: LMC 3/05; CTR Fall 04)

ALA Notable Children's Software 2005

994 **Puzzle Quest: Challenge of the Warlords** (6–12). 2007. D3 Publishers. Windows, PlayStation 2, PSP, Nintendo DS, Xbox 360, Wii. Players: 1–2. ESRB: E10+ (suggestive themes).
Players must undertake quests and deal with evil opponents as they strive to save the land of Etheria from the evil Lord Bane. Puzzles include a game of matching gems that earns money or other benefits. (Rev: SLJ 1/08; CTR 7/07)

Sports and Games

General and Miscellaneous

995 🔵 **A Child's Way to Yoga: Introducing Children to Yoga through Movement and Music** (K–2). 2007. 28 min. A Way to Yoga. $17.99.
A yoga instructor leads 10 children through eight simple yoga routines accompanied by original music and stories. (Rev: BL 9/1/07; SLJ 8/07)

996 🎲 **Mario Party 7** (3–8). 2006. Nintendo. GameCube. Players: 1–8. ESRB: E (comic mischief).
A board game featuring familiar Mario characters and a variety of choices depending on the cruise taken. (Rev: SLJ 7/06)

997 🔵 **Popular Mechanics for Kids: X-treme Sports and Other Action Adventures** (1–6). 2005. 92 min. Series: Popular Mechanics for Kids. Koch Vision. ISBN 978-1-4172-2766-2. $14.98.
Four episodes of a Canadian TV series feature energetic teenagers learning about extreme sports, with fascinating segments interspersed on topics such as athletic shoe and skateboard ramp design. (Rev: SLJ 5/05; VL 5–6/05)

998 🔵 **Profiles in Aspiration** (7–12). 2004. 45 min. Silver Productions. PPR. $15.
Female athletes from around the world discuss their aspirations and the sacrifices they have made to achieve excellence; excellent live footage of a wide variety of sports adds to the appeal. (Rev: SLJ 1/06; VL 5–6/05)

999 🔵 **What Color Is Your Butterfly?** (K–4). 2006. 36 min. Mamayo Co. $15.99.
Children are led through various yoga poses that will improve strength and balance in this program best suited to those with some previous yoga experience. (Rev: SLJ 6/07)

1000 🔵 **Yoga by Teens** (7–12). 2007. 40 min. Let It Go Yoga. $15.95.
An introduction to hatha yoga — focusing on standing, seated, and floor poses as well as deep-breathing and relaxation — hosted by three teenage sisters; including one with Down syndrome. (Rev: BL 5/1/07; SLJ 12/06)

1001 🔵 **Yomega Mania** (6–10). 2005. 210 min. Jumby Bay Studios (dist. by Vat19). PPR. $19.95.
From simple techniques to complex tricks, this is a comprehensive and practical resource for yo-yo enthusiasts. (Rev: VL 5–6/06)

Automobile Racing

1002 🎲 **Burnout Revenge** (5–12). Electronic Arts. PlayStation 2, Xbox, Xbox 360. Players: 1–6. ESRB: E10+ .
In this racing sequel to *Burnout 3*, the player gains points based on multiple factors including cars destroyed and maneuvers completed in oncoming traffic, as well as completing many other trick-based objectives.
👤 YALSA Top 50 Core Recommended Collection Titles

1003 ⊞ **Burnout 3: Takedown** (5–12). Electronic Arts. PlayStation 2, PSP, Xbox. Xbox 360. Players: 1–6. ESRB: E10+ (violence).
A racing game in which you can compete with your friends in many different modes of play. The focus is planning and completing the most elaborate stunts with the racing vehicle of your choice.
☒ YALSA Top 50 Core Recommended Collection Titles

1004 ⊞ **Gran Turismo 5 Prologue** (5–12). 2008. Sony Computer Entertainment. PlayStation 3. Players: 1–16 online. ESRB: E (mild suggestive themes).
The prologue to *Gran Turismo 5*, this new game brings better cars — Ferrari, BMW, Audi, and Nissan, for example — and better tracks plus a new in-cockpit view. Race in over 30 unlockable events on your way to the Gran Turismo championship. (Rev: CTR 5/08)

1005 ⊞ **Gran Turismo 4** (6–12). Sony Computer Entertainment. PlayStation 2. Players: 1–6. ESRB: E (mild lyrics).
In arcade mode, players race against the computer or other players, selecting from hundreds of different cars and 100 race tracks. In simulation mode, players qualify as racing drivers and each win brings new rewards. (Rev: SLJ 6/06; CTR Fall 05)

1006 ⊞ **Need for Speed: Most Wanted** (9–12). 2005. Electronic Arts. PlayStation 2, GameCube, Xbox, Xbox 360. Players: 1–2. ESRB: T (mild violence).
A popular street racing game in which the player must avoid capture by the police while competing against other cars in multiple styles of racing. (Rev: SLJ 10/06; CTR (PSP version) 4/06)

1007 ⊞ **Outrun 2006 Coast 2 Coast** (6–12). 2006. Sega of America. PlayStation 2, Xbox. Players: 1–8. ESRB: E.
Choose a car and then a mode to play this racing game that is set off the track. In Complete Race Missions, players progress from one race to another. In Heart Attack, Clarissa sets challenges that reward players with hearts. (Rev: SLJ 7/06)

Baseball

1008 ◉ **Hitting Drills and Techniques** (K–6). 2006. 34 min. Youth Sports Club. PPR. ISBN 978-0-9748517-9-2. $24.95.
Bat selection, proper grip, and stance and balance are emphasized in this presentation that shows drills, techniques, and strategies. (Rev: VL 11–12/06)

1009 ⊞ **It's the Big Game, Charlie Brown!** (2–5). 2007. Viva Media. Windows, Macintosh. ISBN 978-1-934088-64-7. $19.99.
Charlie Brown seeks players for his team, completing mini-games and learning baseball basics as he tours the neighborhood. (Rev: CTR 10/07)

1010 ◉ **Little League's Official How-to-Play Baseball DVD** (4–7). 2006. 70 min. MasterVision. ISBN 978-1-55919-996-4. $29.95.
In 19 brief segments, New Jersey Little League baseball players demonstrate easy-to-follow baseball techniques while two male coaches give advice and stress safety and other aspects. (Rev: BL 3/1/07; SLJ 5/07)

1011 ⊞ **MLB 08 The Show** (4–12). 2008. Sony Computer Entertainment. PlayStation 2, PlayStation 3, PSP. Players: 1+. ESRB: E.
Play as one of your favorite MLB teams as you compete to be world champion in this lifelike baseball video game. Play in season mode or against a friend.

Basketball

1012 ◉ **Antonio Smith's Fundamentals for Future Basketball All-Stars** (6–9). 2006. 30 min. Smithshow Sports. $29.99.
More than 30 basketball drills — covering ball handling, shooting, passing, agility, and conditioning — are introduced by high school basketball coach Antonio Smith, a former player on the Louisiana Tech University team. Educational study skills are also stressed. (Rev: BL 9/1/06)

1013 ● Driveway Basketball Drills (9–11). 2005. 30 min. Youth Sports Club. ISBN 978-0-9748517-4-7. $24.95.

Close-ups illustrate various basketball moves while a narrator explains the drills, which progress from simple dribbling to more complex skills. (Rev: BL 9/1/05)

1014 ● Harlem Globetrotters: The Team That Changed the World (9–12). 2005. 116 min. Warner Home Video. ISBN 978-1-4198-1752-6. $19.98.

A look at the entertaining all-black basketball team that introduced much of the world to the game; features include the 1948 match against the Minneapolis Lakers, the historic trip to Berlin in 1951, and interviews with players and fans. (Rev: VL 1–2/06)

1015 ● Kiss My Wheels (7–12). 2003. 56 min. Fanlight. $295.

Wheelchair basketball is the subject of this effective documentary focusing on the achievements of a coed, multiracial team called the Zia Hot Shots. (Rev: BL 7/03)
⚜ YALSA 2004 Selected Videos and DVDs

1016 ⌨ NBA Live 07 (5–12). 2007. EA Sports. Windows, PlayStation 2, PSP, Xbox, Xbox 360. Players: 1+. ESRB: E (mild violence).

Play as your favorite NBA team. Compete with a friend or against the computer in season mode. Part of an excellent, very popular NBA gaming series. *NBA Live 08* is the newest release and is available in the following formats: Windows, PlayStations 2 and 3, PSP, Xbox 360, Wii. (Rev: CTR 11/06)

1017 ● Swish 2: Learning and Coaching the Swish Method (5–10). 2005. 115 min. Breakthrough Sports (dist. by Youth Sports Club). PPR. ISBN 978-0-9724961-2-4. $29.95.

Coach Tom Norland shows how to ace basketball shooting, with demonstrations by players of varying ages and tips for players, coaches, and parents. (Rev: VL 1–2/07)

Camping, Hiking, Backpacking, and Mountaineering

1018 ● Deadly Ascent: The Dangers of Denali National Park's Mt. McKinley (9–12).

2006. 56 min. WGBH Boston. Closed captioned. ISBN 978-1-59375-559-1. $19.95.

A "NOVA" team looks at the particular dangers of this mountain — the highest in North America — that has claimed many lives. (Rev: VL 7/06)

1019 ● Farther Than the Eye Can See (9–12). 2004. 2 discs. 75 min. Serac Adventure Films. $29.95 for individuals; $59.95 for institutions.

An award-winning account of blind climber Erik Weihenmayer's ascent of Mount Everest. A 45-minute educational version is edited for student viewing. (Rev: BL 2/15/07)

1020 ● Minimum Impact: Take Only Photos, Leave Only Footprints (9–12). 2007. 24 min. VEA. $89.95.

How to be an ecologically responsible camper in everything from selecting the campsite to breaking camp and packing up. Filmed in Australia. Teacher's guide included. (Rev: SLJ 9/07)

Chess, Checkers, and Other Board and Card Games

1021 ⌨ Learn to Play Chess with Fritz and Chesster (3–8). 2003. Viva Media. Windows, Macintosh. $29.99.

Exploding toilets are only part of the fun as Fritz, son of King and Queen White, learns to play chess. The basics are presented in a series of effective mini-games. (Rev: CTR 5/03)
⚜ ALA Notable Children's Software 2004

1022 ⌨ Learn to Play Chess with Fritz and Chesster 2: Chess in the Black Castle (3–9). 2005. Viva Media. Windows. $29.99.

Bianca and Fritz hone their chess skills as they strive to rescue Chesster the Rat from the clutches of King Black. (Rev: CTR Winter 04)
⚜ ALA Notable Children's Software 2005

1023 ● Learning Chess the Easy Way: Chess for Absolute Beginners (3–6). 2005. 80 min. Susan Polgar Foundation. PPR. $22.95.

Animated chess pieces add to the appeal of this introduction presented by grand master Susan Polgar. (Rev: SLJ 1/07; VL 9–10/06)

177

Computer Games

General and Miscellaneous

1024 🎲 **Alien Hominid** (7–12). O3 Entertainment. GameCube, PlayStation 2, Xbox, Xbox 360 Live. Players: 1–4. ESRB: T (blood and gore, cartoon violence).
The FBI has located and fired upon an Alien aircraft, which causes the craft to crash to Earth. The player, as the Alien, will encounter many enemies along the way to reclaiming the aircraft and, finally, getting home. The player can unlock and play special mini games also.
🎲 YALSA Top 50 Core Recommended Collection Titles

1025 🎲 **Barnyard** (3–6). 2006. THQ. Windows, PlayStation 2, GameCube, Game Boy Advance, Wii. Players: 1. ESRB: E10+ (cartoon violence, comic mischief).
Barnyard animals get up to a variety of activities in this game that combines missions with arcade games such as "Tease the Mailman" and "Barnyard Darts." (Rev: SLJ 11/06; CTR 9/06)

1026 🎲 **Battlefield 2: Modern Combat** (9–12). 2005. Electronic Arts. PlayStation 2, Xbox. Players: 1–24. ESRB: T (language, violence).
A great and popular first-person shooter that offers both single-player mode and online multiplayer action. Play as a soldier in a war, selecting weapons from many different kits. Capture flags to earn points and, ultimately, victory for your team.

1027 🎲 **Chibi Robo** (5–12). Nintendo. GameCube. Players: 1. ESRB: E10+ (crude humor, mild cartoon violence).
Use Chibi, a robot, to perform multiple tasks for the family. Interact with other robots and humans to enhance the experience.
🎲 YALSA Top 50 Core Recommended Collection Titles

1028 🎲 **Diddy Kong Racing DS** (1–6). 2007. Nintendo. Nintendo DS. Players: 1–4. ESRB: E (mild cartoon violence).
A fast-paced racing game that offers lots of variety — including the ability to design your own tracks — and interesting characters. (Rev: CTR 3/07)

1029 🎲 **Donkey Kong Jungle Beat** (5–12). NAMCO. GameCube. Players: 1. ESRB: E10+ (cartoon violence).
A sequel to the classic Donkey Kong series, Donkey Kong Jungle Beat uses a set of bongos instead of a typical gaming controller. Easy to learn but more challenging as the game progresses, Donkey Kong Jungle Beat will appeal to gamers of all ages.
🎲 YALSA Top 50 Core Recommended Collection Titles

1030 🎲 **Elebits** (4–10). 2006. Konami. Wii. Players: 1–4. ESRB: E (cartoon violence).
During a strange electrical storm, 10-year-old Kai searches for small creatures called Elebits, exploring the house and then the neighborhood. Multiplayer mode allows for increased levels of sophistication. (Rev: VOYA 8/07; CTR 1/07)

1031 🎲 **Mario Kart: Double Dash!!** (3–12). Nintendo. GameCube. Players: 1–4. ESRB: E.
Race around 16 tracks facing opponents who plant traps and fire weapons.
🎲 YALSA Top 50 Core Recommended Collection Titles

1032 🎲 **Naruto: Clash of Ninja 2** (8–12). 2006. Tomy. Gamecube. Players: 1–4. ESRB: T (violence).
Based on an anime series, this is a typical fighting game with lots of battle options. (Rev: SLJ 1/07; CTR 9/07)

1033 🎲 **Okami** (9–12). Capcom. PlayStation 2, Wii. Players: 1. ESRB: T (crude humor, fantasy violence, suggestive themes, use of alcohol and tobacco, blood and gore).
Challenge your mind with quests and puzzles as you bring life back to a barren world; this attractive game is rooted in Japanese legends and mythological creatures.
🎲 YALSA Top 50 Core Recommended Collection Titles

1034 🎲 **Over the Hedge** (3–6). 2006. Activision. PlayStation 2, GameCube, Xbox. Players: 1. ESRB: E10+ (cartoon violence, crude humor).
Hammy the squirrel, Stella the Skunk, and the other characters from the popular comic strip and animated movie star in this game that challenges players to complete objectives and progress through levels, unlocking

178

comics, art, and music along the way. (Rev: SLJ 8/06)

1035 🎮 **Pikmin** (3–8). Nintendo. GameCube. Players: 1. ESRB: E.
Small astronaut Captain Olimar crashes his spaceship and must guide strange creatures he calls Pikmin through multiple tasks as he rebuilds it, racing against time in this game of strategy.
♟ YALSA Top 50 Core Recommended Collection Titles

1036 🎮 **Shark Tale** (6–9). 2004. Activision. Windows, PlayStation 2, GameCube, Xbox. Players: 1. ESRB: E (cartoon violence).
Based on the DreamWorks movie, this game offers players to take on the role of talented little fish Oscar and tackle a number of interactive challenges. (Rev: SLJ 8/06; CTR Fall 04)

1037 🎮 **Sid Meier's Civilization IV** (6–12). 2K Games. Windows, Macintosh. Players: 1–16. ESRB: E10+ (violence).
Create your own civilization and maintain its success through trading and combat with neighboring civilizations.
♟ YALSA Top 50 Core Recommended Collection Titles

1038 🎮 **Sly 3: Honor Among Thieves** (5–10). 2006. Sony Computer Entertainment. PlayStation 2. Players: 1–2. ESRB: E10+ (cartoon violence, comic mischief).
The final game in a trilogy starring Sly Cooper, a bad guy out to defeat a worse guy — Dr. M. (Rev: SLJ 7/06; CTR Summer 05)

1039 🎮 **Sonic Riders** (3–8). 2006. Sega of America. PlayStation 2, GameCube, Xbox. Players: 1–4. ESRB: E (comic mischief, cartoon violence).
The hedgehog and his friends are into airboard surfing here. Story mode gives some background for new players, tag mode provides one-on-one competition, and there are additional options. (Rev: SLJ 7/06)

1040 🎮 **Sonic Rush** (1–7). 2005. Sega of America. Nintendo DS. Players: 1–2. ESRB: E (mild cartoon violence).
A superfast game that features Sonic the Hedgehog and Blaze the Cat in lots of adventures; there are two difficulty levels and a two-player battle mode. (Rev: CTR 12/05)

1041 🎮 **Super Mario Sunshine** (3–8). Nintendo. GameCube. Players: 1. ESRB: E.
On an island vacation with Princess Peach, Mario finds himself in trouble — accused of causing destructive pollution.
♟ YALSA Top 50 Core Recommended Collection Titles

1042 🎮 **Super Paper Mario** (3–12). Nintendo. Wii. Players: 1. ESRB: E.
With both two- and three-dimensional aspects, this is an action-packed adventure (in which Princess Peach must be rescued by Mario) that requires problem-solving skills.
♟ YALSA Top 50 Core Recommended Collection Titles

1043 🎮 **Super Smash Bros. Brawl** (8–12). 2008. Nintendo. Wii. Players: 1–4. ESRB: T (cartoon violence, crude humor).
An action-packed, combo driven fighting game in which players compete as favorite Nintendo characters. The most recent release in a series that included the popular *Super Smash Bros. Melee*, launched in 2001. (Rev: SLJ 10/06)

1044 🎮 **Viva Piñata** (3–12). Microsoft Game Studios. Windows, Nintendo DS, XBox 360. Players: 1–2. ESRB: E.
Create your own piñata (brightly colored pony) and give it a pleasant environment and social life.
♟ YALSA Top 50 Core Recommended Collection Titles

1045 🎮 **We Love Katamari** (K–6). 2005. Namco. PlayStation 2. Players: 1–2. ESRB: E (fantasy violence).
An interesting and entertaining game of strategy, a successor to Katamari Damacy, in which players roll around katamari (sticky balls) seeking to increase their size until they are big enough to become planets. Players can compete or cooperate. (Rev: SLJ 2/07; CTR Summer 05)

1046 🎮 **Wii Play** (1–12). 2007. Nintendo. Wii. Players: 1–2. ESBR: E (mild cartoon violence).
Billiards, fishing, table tennis, and tanks. These are just four of the nine games included in this collection that comes with an extra Wii Remote. (Rev: CTR 3/07)

1047 🎲 **Zoombinis Island Odyssey** (3–6). 2003. The Learning Company/Riverdeep. Windows, Macintosh. $19.99.

Zoombini Island is threatened with destruction by ecologically unsound Bloats. Can the Zerbles be saved? Players face math and logic problems as they also learn about a wide array of scientific topics. (Rev: SLJ 6/05; CTR 9/03)

🏆 ALA Notable Children's Software 2003

Collections

1048 🎲 **Atari Anthology** (6–12). Atari Interactive. PlayStation 2, Xbox. ESRB: E (simulated gambling).

This is a collection of 18 classic arcade games — including Asteroids and Pong — and dozens of classic Atari 2600 games. Great for gamers who were around in the 1970s and 1980s and for newcomers interested in the history of gaming. (Rev: VOYA 4/07; CTR Winter 04)

1049 🎲 **Midway Arcade Treasures** (9–12). 2004. Midway Entertainment. PlayStation 2, GameCube. Players: 1–2. ESRB: E (blood and gore, violence).

A collection of classic games including *Joust, Paperboy,* and the gory *Mortal Kombat.* (Rev: VL 3–4/07)

1050 🎲 **Namco Museum 50th Anniversary Arcade Collection** (6–12). Namco. Windows, PlayStation 2, GameCube, Xbox. Players: 1–2. ESRB: E10+ (cartoon violence, mild lyrics).

A collection of 14 of the most popular (and easy to learn) arcade games — from PacMan and Space Invaders to Galaga and Pole Position. (Rev: SLJ 6/06)

🏆 YALSA Top 50 Core Recommended Collection Titles

1051 🎲 **Sonic GEMS Collection** (3–8). Sega. GameCube. Players: 1–4. ESRB: E.

A collection of Sonic the Hedgehog games. Play as Sonic through many exciting levels to save the planet.

🏆 YALSA Top 50 Core Recommended Collection Titles

1052 🎲 **Xbox Live Arcade Unplugged** (8–12). 2006. Microsoft. Xbox 360. Players: 1. ESRB: T (mild cartoon violence, mild fantasy violence, comic mischief, simulated gambling).

This compilation allows players to enjoy a range of games that otherwise require Internet access: Retro Evolved, Bejeweled 2, Hardwood Backgammon, Outpost Kaloki X, Wik: The Fable of the Souls, and Texas Holdem Poker. (Rev: SLJ 2/07)

Party

1053 🎲 **Carnival Games** (K–12). 2007. Global Star Software. Nintendo DS, Wii. Players: 1–4. ESRB: E (comic mischief).

Step up and enjoy any of the 25 carnival games — Test Your Strength and Dunk Tank, to give just two examples. Unlock more mini-games and win prizes along the way. (Rev: CTR 9/07)

1054 🎲 **Mario Kart Wii** (1–12). 2008. Nintendo. Wii. Players: 1–12. ESRB: E (comic mischief).

Great for single players and even better as a party game, this exciting, 32-track racing game can be played with the Wii steering wheel or the Nunchuk and features choices of cars and Super Mario Brothers characters. (Rev: CTR 5/08)

1055 🎲 **Mario Party 8** (2–12). 2007. Nintendo. Wii. Players: 1–4. ESRB: E (mild cartoon violence).

This party game is similar to a board game. Guide your character of choice through one of six playable maps. Roll the dice, use special abilities, and compete in mini-games on your way to victory by collecting the most stars. (Rev: CTR 7/07)

1056 🎲 **Muppets Party Cruise** (3–6). 2003. TDK Mediactive. PlayStation 2, GameCube. Players: 1–4. ESRB: E (comic mischief).

Players — Animal, Fozzy Bear, Gonzo, Kermit, Miss Piggy, and Pepe (the Prawn) — compete against each other as they move up the decks of a cruise ship, playing mini-games — shuffleboard, a crab toss, and so forth — and collecting money as they progress. (Rev: SLJ 2/07; CTR 1/04)

1057 🎲 **One Piece Pirates' Carnival** (3–9). 2006. Namco Bandai. PlayStation 2, Game-

Cube. Players: 1–4. ESRB: E (cartoon violence).

In Board Game mode, players, who can choose among seven characters, compete for tiles, each one representing a mini-game; strategic thinking is beneficial. VS mode allows players to play the mini-games without the board game. Based on the anime/manga series. (Rev: SLJ 2/07)

1058 🎲 **Super Monkey Ball 2** (3–12). 2002. Sega of America. GameCube. Players: 1–4. ESRB: E (violence).

An addictive collection of games — billiards, bowling, golf, tennis, and so forth — with an additional story mode. (Rev: SLJ 10/06; CTR 11/02)

1059 🎲 **WarioWare: Smooth Moves** (6–12). Nintendo. Wii. Players: 1–12. ESRB: E10+ (crude humor, mild cartoon violence).

A series of minigames require the player(s) to use the Wii remote in varied ways and complete multiple objectives for victory.

♉ YALSA Top 50 Core Recommended Collection Titles

Simulation

1060 🎲 **Animal Crossing** (3–12). Nintendo. Game Boy Advance, GameCube, Nintendo DS. Players: 1–4. ESRB: E.

Interact with fellow villagers to gain items that will improve your house.

♉ YALSA Top 50 Core Recommended Collection Titles

1061 🎲 **Monster Rancher Evo** (8–12). Tecmo. PlayStation 2. Players: 1–2. ESRB: E10+ (alcohol reference, fantasy violence).

Face many new challenges as you teach your very own monster while your circus moves from town to town.

♉ YALSA Top 50 Core Recommended Collection Titles

1062 🎲 **MySims** (1–12). 2007. Electronic Arts. Nintendo DS, Wii. Players: 1. ESRB: E (comic mischief, mild cartoon violence).

Players create their own Sim and then work to build up a town, collaborating with the residents, finding out about the community, and helping to expand and improve it. (Rev: CTR 10/07)

1063 🎲 **1701 A.D.: Discover, Build and Rule Your New World** (5–12). 2006. Aspyr

Media. Windows XP. Players: 1–4. ESRB: E10+. $39.99.

In the 18th century, colonize an island and work to develop trade with the rest of the world while maintaining a healthy economy and happy population.

♉ ALA Great Interactive Software for Kids Fall 2007

1064 🎲 **The Sims 2** (8–12). Electronic Arts. Windows, Macintosh. Players: 1. ESRB: T (crude humor, mild violence, suggestive themes).

Create characters, build houses and neighborhoods, and attempt to satisfy aspirations as the characters aim to progress toward success in a virtual life. (Rev: SLJ 6/06)

♉ YALSA Top 50 Core Recommended Collection Titles

1065 🎲 **The Sims 2: Castaway** (5–12). 2007. Electronic Arts. PlayStation 2, PSP, Nintendo DS, Wii. Players: 1. ESRB: E (animated blood, comic mischief — DS version); E10+ (crude humor, mild violence, suggestive themes — PSP); T (crude humor, mild violence, suggestive themes — PlayStation 2, Wii).

The player's Sim has been in a shipwreck and it is up to the player to cope with continuing challenges and make sure his Sim survives, both healthy and happy. This will require food and housing, but also art and entertainment. (Rev: CTR 11/07)

1066 🎲 **The Sims 2 University** (7–12). 2005. Electronic Arts. Windows, Macintosh, PlayStation 3. Players: 1. ESRB: T (crude humor, sexual themes, violence).

This expansion pack (you must have Sims 2 on your computer to install it) allows players to send their Sims to college, choose their majors, create dorms, and determine the course of their social and academic life. (Rev: CTR 3/05)

1067 🎲 **Thrillville** (8–12). 2006. Lucas Arts. PlayStation 2, PSP, Xbox. Players 1–4. ESRB: E10+ (fantasy violence, mild lyrics, mild suggestive themes).

Players create an amusement park, playing arcade and puzzle mini-games along the way. Players must build rides, train staff, maintain the park, plan games, and interact with guests. (Rev: SLJ 2/07; CTR 11/06)

Football

1068 ♟ **Madden NFL 07** (3–12). EA Sports. Windows, PlayStation 2, PlayStation 3, PSP, Game Boy Advance, GameCube, Nintendo DS, Xbox, Xbox 360, Wii. Players: 1–2. ESRB: E.

Play through many different games and seasons with real players, teams, and playbooks. (Rev: CTR PSP: 4/07, other platforms: 10/06)

⚉ YALSA Top 50 Core Recommended Collection Titles

1069 ♟ **NFL Street 2** (6–12). 2004. EA Sports. PlayStation 2, GameCube, Xbox. Players: 1–4. ESRB: E (mild violence).

Players in this "street" football game choose between straight scoring or gaining style points. *NFL Street 3* was released in 2006 for the PlayStation 2 and PSP platforms. (Rev: SLJ 9/06)

Golf

1070 ⬤ **Golf Magazine Top 100 Teachers: The More Series** (9–12). 2005. 3 discs. 192 min. Shout! Factory. ISBN 978-0-7389-3388-7. $49.98.

Expert golf instructors give a wide range of advice on everything from equipment to attitude in three sections: "More Power," "More Consistency," and "More Up and Downs." (Rev: VL 1–2/06)

1071 ♟ **Hot Shots Golf Out of Bounds** (5–12). 2008. Sony Computer Entertainment. PlayStation 3. Players: 1. ESRB: E (mild suggestive themes).

The most recent addition to this popular series features six courses, choices of players or customizable avatar, and five modes of play. (Rev: CTR 4/08)

1072 ♟ **Tiger Woods PGA Tour 2006** (8–12). 2005. EA Sports. PlayStation 2, GameCube, Xbox, Xbox 360. Players: 1–2. ESRB: E.

Choose to be a well-known golfer and select the level of play at any of six golf courses that host PGA championships. *Tiger Woods PGA Tour 08* is available for Windows, Macintosh, PlayStation 2, PlayStation 3, PSP, Nintendo DS, Xbox 360, and Wii. (Rev: SLJ 9/06; CTR *Tiger Woods PGA Tour 08*: 10/07)

Horse Racing and Horsemanship

1073 ⬤ **Sitting Right on Your Horse** (6–12). 2006. 46 min. Series: Simplify Your Riding — Ride Like a Natural. Trafalgar Square Publishing. PPR. ISBN 978-1-57076-351-9. $29.95.

The first in a three-part series, this video demonstrates how to sit and breathe properly, making the journey much easier for both horse and rider. (Rev: VL 11–12/06)

Olympic Games

1074 ♟ **Torino 2006** (4–12). 2006. Take 2 Interactive (2K Sports). PlayStation 2, Xbox. Players: 1–4. ESRB: E.

Participate in downhill skiing, speed skating, bobsledding, and other events of the 20th Winter Olympics in Italy. (Rev: SLJ 9/06)

1075 ⬤ **Watermark** (8–12). 2006. 46 min. Cinema Guild. ISBN 978-0-7815-1106-3. $175 (Rental: $85).

Following five swimmers who trained for the 1996 Olympics, this documentary newly released on DVD gives viewers a good feeling for the dedication required and the strains placed on personal relationships, not to mention the pain of losing. (Rev: VL 5–6/97)

Running and Jogging

1076 ⬤ **Runners High** (9–12). 2007. 86 min. Jacob. $100.

A documentary following four ethnically diverse teens who are part of the Students Run Oakland (SRO) volunteer program, in which inner city teens train to compete in the grueling 26-mile Los Angeles Marathon. (Rev: BL 11/15/07)

Sailing, Boating, and Canoeing

1077 ◆ **Sea Kayaking: Getting Started** (9–12). 1995. 83 min. Moving Pictures. PPR. $29.95. History, equipment, clothing, navigation, paddle techniques, and safety are all covered in this introduction to this demanding sport. Also available: *Sea Kayaking: Beyond the Basics*. (Rev: VL 11–12/96)

Skateboarding

1078 🎮 **Tony Hawk's American Wasteland** (8–12). 2005. Activision. PlayStation 2, GameCube, Xbox, Xbox 360. Players: 1+. ESRB: T (blood, crude humor, language, suggestive themes, violence).
This sequel to *Tony Hawk's Underground 2* is set in Los Angeles. It allows a choice of modes — "Story Mode," "Classic Mode," "Create-a-Mode," "2-player," "High Score/Freeskate," or online play — and gives the player the opportunity to ride a BMX bike. (Rev: SLJ 6/06)

1079 🎮 **Tony Hawk's Underground 2** (8–12). Activision. Windows, PlayStation 2, Game-Cube, Xbox. Players: 1–2. ESRB: T (blood, crude humor language, suggestive themes, use of alcohol, violence).
Play as one of many popular professional skateboarders. Complete objectives and unlock special boards, tricks, attributes, and characters.
🎲 YALSA Top 50 Core Recommended Collection Titles

1080 ◆ **Yeah Right!** (8–12). 2003. 74 min. Rhino Records. $19.95.
A documentary displaying the skateboarding skills of two Los Angeles teams. With little narration but lots of music, the focus here is on the action. (Rev: BL 4/1/04)

Skiing and Snowboarding

1081 🎮 **SSX Blur** (3–12). 2007. EA Sports — Electronic Arts Canada. Wii. Players: 1–4. ESRB: E (comic mischief).

Great music and even better graphics make this snowboarding game an instant favorite. Using both the Remote and the Nunchuk, compete against the computer or against your friends in this fast-paced race. (Rev: CTR 6/07)

Soccer

1082 ◆ **Backyard Soccer Drills** (4–9). 2004. 34 min. Youth Sports Club. $24.95.
A useful review of soccer moves that can be practiced in limited spaces. (Rev: BL 12/15/04)

1083 🎮 **FIFA World Cup Germany** (6–12). 2006. Electronic Arts. PlayStation 2, Xbox, GameCube. Players: 1–2. ESRB: E.
Players choose their soccer team and starting lineup before selecting among three modes of play. Difficulty levels are amateur, semi-pro, professional, and world class. (Rev: SLJ 9/06)

1084 ◆ **Soccer Shooting Drills** (3–8). 2006. 34 min. Youth Sports Club. PPR. ISBN 978-0-9748517-7-8. $24.95.
Some 30 drills, shown with a coed group of players, become progressively more complex; coach Marty Schupak also provides 10 key tips. (Rev: VL 7/06)

1085 🎮 **Super Mario Strikers** (3–8). Nintendo. GameCube. Players: 1–4. ESRB: E.
Play soccer against the computer or friends with the classic Super Mario characters.
🎲 YALSA Top 50 Core Recommended Collection Titles

1086 🎮 **UEFA EURO 2008** (3–12). 2008. EA Sports — Electronic Arts Canada. PlayStation 2, PlayStation 3, PSP, Xbox 360. Players: 1–4. ESRB: E.
Play soccer as one of many favorite teams from all over the world as you work your way toward the European championship. (Rev: CTR 6/08)

Tennis and Other Racquet Games

1087 🎲 **Sega Superstars Tennis** (4–12). 2008. Sega of America. PlayStation 2, PlayStation 3, Nintendo DS, Wii. Players: 1+. ESRB: E10+.
Play tennis as one of 16 classic Sega characters. The player can unlock extra characters, levels, and mini-games in this great party game that features 10 courts. (Rev: CTR 6/08)

1088 🎲 **Table Tennis** (4–8). 2006. Rockstar Games. Xbox 360, Wii. Players: 1–2. ESRB: E.
Players can choose between training, tournament, and exhibition modes in this realistic game. The Wii version, released in 2007, uses the remote in Standard mode and the nunchuk in Sharp Shooter and Control Freak modes. (Rev: SLJ 9/06)

Wrestling

1089 ⬤ **Girl Wrestler** (6–12). 2004. 53 min. Women Make Movies. $89.
Texas 13-year-old Tara loves wrestling and is really good at it, but the law prohibits 14-year-old girls from wrestling with boys. Should Tara be allowed to continue? (Rev: SLJ 9/05)
⅄ YALSA 2005 Selected Videos and DVDs

1090 🎲 **WWE Smackdown vs. Raw 2008** (8–12). 2007. THQ. PlayStation 2, PlayStation 3, PSP, Nintendo DS, Xbox 360, Wii. Players: 1+. ESRB: T (alcohol reference, blood, mild language, suggestive themes, violence).
Wrestle against friends or create your own character and start a career. Compete as any of the WWE wrestlers as you work your way to a WWE Championship.

Reference

General Reference

1091 ⌐ᵇ **Advanced Placement Source** (6–12). EBSCO Publishing.
www.ebscohost.com/thisTopic.php?
marketID=7&topicID=198
An advanced placement source Web site for students containing more than 6,000 titles from popular magazines and specialized and professional journals.

1092 ⌐ᵇ **Ancestry Library Edition** (6–12). Pro-Quest.
www.proquest.com/products_pq/
descriptions/ale.shtml
In addition to investigating their family history and looking for family members, users can research the origin of their names, geographical distribution of their last name, and interesting facts such as average life span. (Rev: BL 4/15/05)

1093 ⌐ᵇ **Cosmeo** (K–12). Discovery Communications.
www.cosmeo.com
A site for K–12 students to use at home with features such as video clips, images, teacher-selected Web sites, an online encyclopedia, and math problem solvers and tutorials. (Rev: SLJ 8/07; MM&IS 7–8/06)

1094 ⌐ᵇ **Encyclopaedia Britannica Online: School Edition** (K–12). Encyclopaedia Britannica Online: School Edition.
www.info.eb.com/Product_OSE.htm
Students using this service can search four complete encyclopedias plus an atlas, time-lines, journals and magazines, Learning Materials (study guides and activities), and other resources. Also includes nearly 40,000

graphics, images, and video clips plus "Biography of the Day" and "This Day in History") features. (Rev: BL 9/15/06; LMC 8–9/05)

1095 ⌐ᵇ **Gale Virtual Reference Library** (6–12). Thomson Gale.
www.gale.com/gvrl
Provides access to more than 1,000 electronic reference titles in all disciplines. (Rev: SLJ 12/06)

1096 ⌐ᵇ **Grolier Multimedia Encyclopedia** (5–12). Scholastic.
http://teacher.scholastic.com/products/
grolier/program_GME.htm
This up-to-date, comprehensive encyclopedia is full of videos, animation, and sound, providing students with lots of information and incentives to explore further. (Rev: BL 9/15/04)

1097 ⌐ᵇ **Grolier Online** (K–12). Scholastic.
go.grolier.com
This rich resource includes two learning environments — Grolier Online *Kids* for elementary students and Grolier Online *Passport* for older students — plus eight curriculum-aligned databases and many resources for educators. Among the best-known products available here in addition to three encyclopedias are *Amazing Animals of the World, Lands and Peoples, New Book of Popular Science, Nueva Encyclopedia Cumbre,* and *America the Beautiful.* Throughout there are fact boxes, images, videos, maps, and time-lines; projects; puzzles and games; quizzes;

and Spanish-language features. (Rev: BL 9/15/07; LMC 3/06; SLJ 10/04)

☒ ALA ALSC Notable Subscription Service 2006; ALA Notable Children's Software 2007

1098 ⌖ **Kids InfoBits** (K–5). Gale Cengage Learning.
www.gale.cengage.com/InfoBits/
Kids InfoBits provides easy access to periodicals, reference materials (maps, flags, charts, and so forth), and newspaper articles for young children who are still learning Internet and research skills. (Rev: BL 11/1/04; LMC 11–12/04)

1099 ⌖ **Marshall Cavendish Digital** (K–12).
www.marshallcavendishdigital.com
An online, customizable collection of Marshall Cavendish products that have previously appeared in print, with lots of helpful functionality. (Rev: BL 11/1/07; LMC 10/07; SLJ 4/07; PL 9–10/07)

1100 ⌖ **NetLibrary** (2–12). NetLibrary/OCLC.
www.netlibrary.com
NetLibrary provides access to an online collection of more than 170,000 titles. Students can search or borrow a variety of reference, professional, and fiction ebooks. (Rev: SLJ 12/06)

1101 ⌖ **The New Book of Knowledge Online** (2–6). Scholastic.
http://go.grolier.com
An appealing resource offering lots of material for reports. (Rev: BL 9/15/07)

1102 ⌖ **Oxford Digital Reference Shelf** (7–12). Oxford University Press.
www.oxford-digitalreference.com
The Oxford Digital Reference Shelf allows you to purchase and own any of their 30 online reference titles, each sold separately, in the areas of history and culture, literature and language, arts, and science. A companion product, Oxford Reference Online contains more than 130 reference titles on subjects such as science, business, and medi-

cine and more. The premium collection subscription offers access to an even larger collection. The Oxford Digital Reference Shelf and Oxford Reference Online are cross-searchable and bibliographic references are OpenURL compliant. (Rev: BL 6/1–15/05; SLJ 12/06)

1103 ⌖ **Oxford Language Dictionaries Online** (6–12). Oxford University Press.
www.oxfordlanguagedictionaries.com
Oxford offers bilingual dictionaries in the following languages: Chinese, French, German, Italian, Russian, and Spanish. Spellings, pronunciation, synonyms, antonyms, and usage examples are included. This easy-to-use site also offers free tools and resources. (Rev: BL 2/1/08; SLJ 11/07)

1104 ⌖ **Quia Web** (K–12). Quia Corporation.
www.quia.com
Tools and templates are provided for educational games and activities (such as word searches and flash cards). This low-cost site is divided into zones for teachers, students, and shared resources. (Rev: SLJ 7/07)

1105 ⌖ **SIRS Researcher** (6–12). ProQuest.
www.proquest.com/products_pq/
descriptions/sirs_researcher.shtml
Students can access age-appropriate, Lexile-ranked content on topics ranging from politics and economy to science and health, drawing on sources such as *Maclean's, National Geographic, Newsweek,* and *Time.* Maps are also included.

1106 ⌖ **World Book Online Reference Center** (3–12). World Book.
www.worldbookonline.com
The content of the 22 volumes of the print encyclopedia is included here, enhanced by a dictionary, pictures and maps, videos and animations, audio files, links to Web sites, a Spanish-language encyclopedia for elementary students, and of course age-appropriate searching and browsing. (Rev: BL 9/15/07)

Art and Music

1107 〽 **Art Museum Image Gallery** (6–12). H. W. Wilson.
www.hwwilson.com/Databases/artmuseum. htm
Provides access to and copyright clearance for the educational use of art images and related multimedia from the collections of more than 1,800 museums around the world. Includes more than 155,000 images of works dating from 3000 b.c. to the 20th century. (Rev: LMC 2/06; SLJ 6/07)

1108 〽 **Classical Music Library** (3–12). Alexander Street Press.
www.alexanderstreet.com/products/clmu.htm
From Gregorian chants to modern compositions, this database offers a streaming classical music service that can be searched by artist, composer, instrument, genre, period, work or opus number, soloist, ensemble, key, and so forth. (Rev: BL 4/15/04; SLJ 2/05)

1109 〽 **Naxos Music Library** (9–12). Naxos of America.
www.NaxosMusicLibrary.com
An extensive archive (more than 322,000 tracks) of music — classical, jazz, folk, world music, and so forth — available in streaming format, plus a spoken word library and a large sheet music collection. Useful features include opera synopses and libretti and composer and artist biographies. (Rev: LMC 11–12/06; SLJ 4/04)

Biography

1110 ⌐ **Biography Reference Bank** (6–12). H. W. Wilson.
www.hwwilson.com/databases/biobank.htm
Provides information on more than 500,000 individuals from all fields and nationalities from ancient times to the present. Periodicals, current books, more than 50 Wilson titles, and biographical information from the WilsonWeb databases are among the sources included. (Rev: BL 6/1–15/08; SLJ 6/05)

1111 ⌐ **Biography Resource Center** (6–12). Thomson Gale.
www.gale.cengage.com/BiographyRC/
Gale's online reference database of biographical information includes more than 440,000 biographies on more than 340,000 prominent individuals from around the world in all disciplines. In addition to full-text magazine and newspaper articles, photographs, and a Recent Updates section, it features a new interface and enhanced functionality. (Rev: BL 6/1–15/08; SLJ 6/05)

1112 ⌐ **Current Biography Illustrated** (6–12). H. W. Wilson.
www.hwwilson.com/Databases/cbillus.htm
A database of more than 25,000 biographies and obituaries that have appeared in *Current Biography* since 1940, as well as updated biographies and articles not in the print edition. The profiles are written in an entertaining and informative style. (Rev: BL 6/1–15/03; SLJ 6/05)

Literature

1113 🖳 **The Everyman Millennium Library** (8–12). 2005. 8 discs. Tool Factory. Windows. ISBN 978-1-84050-410-1. $359.95.

This set provides students with historical background, plot summaries, extracts, and readings on seven centuries of English-language literature, enhanced by excellent graphics and audiovisual segments plus a powerful search ability and master classes that point the way to topics of interest. In addition to an installation disk, the set includes: "The Age of Chaucer," "Shakespeare and the Elizabethan Period," "Restoration to Revolution," "The Romantics," "The Victorian Age," "Modernism and the Great War," and "The Late 20th Century." (Rev: SLJ 3/06)

1114 ⁀ **Literary Reference Center** (9–12). EBSCO Publishing.
www.ebscohost.com

Contains information on thousands of authors and their works from a variety of sources such as reference works, books, literary journals, and general periodicals. Some statistics: 27,500 plot summaries and work overviews; 140,500 author biographies; nearly 1,000,000 articles of literary criticism; more than 560,000 book reviews; 4,700 author interviews; plus classic texts, classic and contemporary poems and short stories, a glossary of literary terms, and a timeline. (Rev: BL 11/1/06; LMC 10/06; SLJ 7/06)

1115 ⁀ **Play Index** (6–12). H. W. Wilson.
www.hwwilson.com/databases/playindex_e.htm

An online version of the print product that makes it easy to find information on classic and contemporary plays and playwrights through its enhanced search options. Users can search for plays suitable for grades PreK–6 and 7–12, as well as plays for adults. (Rev: BL 4/15/06; LMC 1/07)

1116 ⁀ **TumbleBooks** (K–12). Tumbleweed Press Inc.
www.tumblebooks.com/

TumbleBooks offers three distinct services: TumbleBookLibrary, animated, talking versions of existing picture books that users can read themselves or have read to them; TumbleReadables, read-along titles — chapter books, early readers, YA novels, high-low books, and classics — that feature adjustable online text and complete audio narration; and TumbleTalkingBooks, an online collection of streaming audio versions of classics, plays, and children's books. Spanish titles are included. (Rev: LMC 8–9/07; SLJ 10/07)

1117 ⁀ **Twentieth Century North American Drama** (10–12). Alexander Street Press.
http://alexanderstreet.com/products/nadr.htm

Contains the full text of 2,000 plays written by American and Canadian playwrights, as well as selected playbills, and information on characters, productions, and theaters. (Rev: SLJ 4/05)

Science, Medicine, and Health

1118 Access Science (9–12). McGraw-Hill.
www.accessscience.com
Science and technology are the focus of this Web site that draws on the McGraw-Hill print collection. Students will find news, encyclopedia entries, biographies, images, helpful tools, and a useful study center. (Rev: SLJ 11/06)

1119 Current Issues in Health (7–12). H. W. Wilson.
www.hwwilson.com/Databases/current_issues_health.htm
A Topic Finder helps researchers who are unsure of specific search terms to use in this full-text database of information on contemporary health topics.

1120 eLibrary Science (6–12). ProQuest.
www.proquestk12.com/eLibrary_Science.shtml
This ProQuest service gathers information from more than 400 worthy science publications and provides continually updated science news links, facts on well-known scientists, and educator-approved Web sites. (Rev: SLJ 11/06)

1121 New Book of Popular Science (7–12). Scholastic.
http://go.grolier.com
This is an online version of Grolier's *New Book of Popular Science*, covering science, medicine, and technology. In addition to text, images, and maps, it provides biographies, information on careers, science projects, current events (including a skywatch), a table of elements, and other helpful tools.

This database is part of the overall Grolier Online research database. (Rev: LMC 10/06; SLJ 11/06)

1122 ProQuest AP Science (10–12). ProQuest.
www.proquestk12.com/productinfo/pq_ap_science.shtml
A database of higher-level materials to support advanced placement and college-level studies in the areas of earth, life, physical, medical, and applied sciences. There's content from more than 500 magazines, full-text from scholarly and professional journals, and images. (Rev: SLJ 11/06)

1123 Science Full Text Select (10–12). H. W. Wilson.
www.hwwilson.com/databases/sci_FT_Select.htm
Offering full-text articles from more than 350 science journals, this easily searched database will benefit Advanced Placement students. (Rev: BL 2/1/05; SLJ 10/04)

1124 Science Online (6–12). Facts on File.
www.factsonfile.com
A broad-based science database providing essays (many of them from Facts on File print products), news articles, biographies, diagrams and illustrations, videos, science experiments, a science timeline, definitions, and so forth. (Rev: BL 4/15/08; LMC 2/08; SLJ 11/06)

1125 Science Reference Center (9–12). EBSCO.
www.ebscohost.com

A virtual science reference library for middle and high school students that contains encyclopedias, reference books, periodicals, biographies, images, and videos. (Rev: BL 12/1/06; SLJ 11/06)

1126 **Science Resource Center** (9–12). Thomson Gale.
www.gale.cengage.com
Students can search full-text or browse by topic in this digital library of everything scientific, including more than 50 reference titles, 270 full-text journals, nearly 15,000 multimedia records, and links to carefully evaluated Web sites. Content level indicators guide students to appropriate information.

1127 **Search It! Science: The Books You Need at Lightning Speed** (K–8). Heinemann.
searchit.heinemann.com
The affordable Search It! Science database of recommended nonfiction science books for K–8 students incorporates an interface that allows users to do a fair amount of searching by clicking on icons or selecting from drop-down menus, eliminating some of the frustrations of keyword searching that young users can experience. Once a topic has been selected, users can view covers, annotations, reviews, and bibliographic information, making this good for collection development as well as bibliography compilation. (Rev: SLJ 12/04)

1128 **Teen Health and Wellness** (8–12). Rosen.
www.teenhealthandwellness.com
This Rosen Publishing database draws on the company's print series (Coping, Need to Know, Drug Prevention Library) to provide teen-friendly information on the topics of health, mental health, fitness, nutrition, alcohol, drugs, family life, and so forth. An "In the News" feature, Dr. Jan's Corner, quizzes, and personal stories add interest. (Rev: SLJ 3/07; PL 7–8/07)

1129 **Today's Science** (6–12). Facts on File/ Infobase Publishing.
http://factsonfile.infobasepublishing.com/
Connects students with the most important developments in science and technology. (Rev: SLJ 11/06)

Social Studies

1130 ⌐ **The African American Experience** (7–12). Greenwood Publishing.
http://aae.greenwood.com
A comprehensive research database that provides reliable information on African American life, history, and culture. Users can browse a wide range of subject areas, from "Arts and Entertainment" and "Business and Labor" to "Sports" and "Women." The Resources section includes the following headings: Title List, Timeline, Image Index, Primary Source Index, Landmark Documents, Slave Narratives, Classic Texts, and Audio Files. (Rev: BL 11/1/06; LMC 4–5/07; PL 11–12/06)

1131 ⌐ **American History Online** (7–12). Facts on File.
www.factsonfile.com
An attractive source of information on more than 500 years of American history, with easy access by browsing (choose among biographies, timelines, images, maps and charts, and other avenues of access); by exploring Learning Centers; and by advanced searches. Videos, a dictionary tool, and other features make this a useful virtual library. Also use *World History Online.* (Rev: *American History Online:* BL 6/04; LMC 1/05; *World History Online:* BL 6/04; LMC 11–12/04)

1132 ⌐ **Cobblestone Online** (K–8). Carus Publishing.
www.cobblestoneonline.net
This database — which is especially strong in the areas of history, geography, and social

studies — includes the full text of articles from periodicals including *Cobblestone, Faces, Calliope, Classical Calliope, Odyssey, AppleSeeds, Dig,* and *Footsteps.*
⅋ ALA Notable Computer Software for Children 2004

1133 ⌐ **CountryReports.org** (5–12).
http://CountryReports.org
Provides information on more than 260 countries, with links to facts on each country's history, people, government, economy, and so forth. Users can also compare countries and categories.

1134 ⌐ **CQ Electronic Library** (9–12). CQ Press.
http://library.cqpress.com
American government, politics, history, and current affairs are the principal strengths of this substantial collection of reference resources, including *CQ Researcher Online, Political Handbook of the World,* and *The Contemporary Middle East.*

1135 ⌐ **CultureGrams** (3–10). ProQuest.
www.proquestk12.com/productinfo/culturegrams.shtml
Explore customs, traditions, and daily life around the world with this rich database with many points of access. The World Edition is for junior high and high school students and the Kids, States, and Provinces Editions are for upper elementary students. Biographies of famous people, a photo gallery, and recipe collections add interest. (Rev: BL 3/1/07; LMC 4–5/08; SLJ 2/04)

1136 ✒ **Current Issues: Reference Shelf Plus** (7–12). H. W. Wilson. www.hwwilson.com/Databases/RS_plus.htm Offers full-text articles, editorials, scholarly papers, and content from WilsonWeb's online journals, for more than 90 different current issues and topics for student researchers. Also covers the annual U.S. National Debate topic for students preparing for debates. (Rev: SLJ 9/07)

1137 ✒ **Daily Life America** (6–12). Greenwood Publishing. www.greenwood.com/dailylife/america_info.aspx Daily Life America is a database of more than 100 different reference sources focusing on the lives of ordinary Americans from pre-Columbian times to the present, among them *The Greenwood Encyclopedia of American Regional Cultures, The Uniting States: The Story of Statehood for the Fifty United States, Encyclopedia of American Holidays and National Days,* and *Famous American Crimes and Trials.* There is lots of information on cultural topics such as housing, clothing, food, and celebrations. State-by-state resource guides give easy access to state songs, mottos, and other key pieces of information. The ability to browse — by subject, time period, region — and the primary documents, maps, and photographs make this a useful resource. (Rev: BL 1/1–15/08*; SLJ 12/07)

1138 ✒ **Daily Life Online** (6–12). Greenwood Publishing. www.greenwood.com/dailylife/ This suite of databases offers various combinations of access to a wealth of materials on history, culture, religion, economics, people, and so forth. The main components currently are Daily Life Through History, Daily Life America (see also entry 1137), and World Folklore and Folklife. (Rev: BL 11/1/05; LMC 3/05; SLJ 12/07)

1139 ✒ **History Reference Center** (9–12). EBSCO. www.ebscohost.com This extensive full-text history resource includes reference works, nonfiction books from a variety of publishers, and journals, plus documents, photographs, maps, and videos. (Rev: BL 1/1–15/05; LMC 11–12/03)

1140 ✒ **Issues: Understanding Controversy and Society** (9–12). ABC-CLIO. www.abc-clio.com/schools/ A rich database that enables students to look at controversial contemporary issues with a greater understanding of historical and social context. (Rev: BL 8/07; SLJ 9/07)

1141 ✒ **Issues and Controversies** (6–12). Facts on File. http://factsonfile.infobasepublishing.com Provides information on more than 800 hot topics, with timelines, primary sources, newspaper editorials, statistics, discussion questions, and so forth. Ideal for debaters. The "Need a Research Topic?" area provides good ideas. (Rev: LMC 1/03; SLJ 9/07)

1142 ✒ **Issues and Controversies in American History** (7–12). Facts on File News Services. http://factsonfile.infobasepublishing.com/ Covers American history from colonial times to the present with regularly updated links to overviews and background articles as well as special features to enhance research such as timelines, captioned images, full-text primary documents, facts and figures on a wide range of topics, biographies, and so forth. It also provides discussion questions and activities that assist students in understanding the issues, as well as arguments for and against. (Rev: LMC 1/07; MM&IS 9–10/06)

1143 ✒ **Latino American Experience** (8–12). Greenwood Publishing. www.greenwood.com/mosaic/lae/ Encompassing the content of more than 200 volumes — from encyclopedias to biographies — this wide-ranging database focuses on all aspects of Latin American history and culture from pre-Columbian times to the present day. (Rev: BL 9/1/07; LMC 10/07; SLJ 12/07)

1144 ✒ **Modern World History Online** (7–12). Facts on File. www.factsonfile.com Covering world history from the mid-15th century to the present, this is a useful database offering the ability to search the full text and to browse events, topics, biographies, and timelines. Learning Centers give access to key information about specific eras.

1145 🖰 **Opposing Viewpoints Resource Center** (7–12). Gale.
www.gale.cengage.com/Opposing
Viewpoints/
An excellent site for researching important social issues; providing full-text resources, thousands of topic overviews, pro and con viewpoint articles; statistical tables, charts, and graphs; and links to reviewed Web sites. (Rev: BL 11/1/02; SLJ 9/07)

1146 🖰 **The Oxford African American Studies Center** (9–12). Oxford University Press.
www.oxfordaasc.com/public
Includes research materials on the history, contributions, and achievements of African Americans, with primary source documents, biographies, images, maps, charts, and tables plus helpful thematic timelines and browse/search features that allow users to pinpoint eras or subjects of interest. (Rev: BL 7/06; LMC 3/07; SLJ 7/06)

1147 🖰 **Points of View Reference Center** (7–12). EBSCO.
www.ebscohost.com/pov
A full-text database that presents multiple points of view on more than 200 current issues. It also helps students with the skills they need to develop persuasive arguments and essays, and analytical thinking skills. (Rev: BL 4/15/08; LMC 1/08; SLJ 9/07)

1148 🖰 **Pop Culture Universe** (6–12). Greenwood.
www.greenwood.com/PCU/default.aspx
Icons, Idols, Ideas is the subtitle of this digital library of American and world popular culture that supports the history, literature, and social studies curriculums. It contains more than 250 volumes, lots of images, and Decades Pages that give instant access to important news items, movies and TV shows, fads, fashion, and so forth.

1149 🖰 **ProQuest Historical Newspapers** (6–12). ProQuest.
www.proquestk12.com/productinfo/pq_
historical_newspapers.shtml
Users can search the full text of a number of important newspapers, mostly from the sec-

ond half of the 19th century to the later years of the 20th century, including *The New York Times, The Wall Street Journal, The Washington Post, The Christian Science Monitor, The Los Angeles Times, The Atlanta Constitution, The Boston Globe,* and *The Chicago Tribune.* Access by topic is a particularly helpful feature, and there are useful timelines. (Rev: BL 9/15/07)

1150 🖰 **Rand McNally Classroom** (K–12). Rand McNally Education.
www.randmcnallyclassroom.com
Online maps and globes, country facts, current events, games and quizzes all support the curriculum and are supported by teacher resources. (Rev: SLJ 4/08; MM&IS 1–2/07)

1151 🖰 **United States at War: Understanding Conflict and Society** (10–12). ABC-CLIO.
www.abc-clio.com
An excellent site for students to research 14 wars involving the United States from colonial times to the present. For each conflict, there is an overview that discusses causes, opponents, consequences, and so forth. Timelines are provided, as are government documents, photographs and other images, video clips, and maps. Primary and secondary sources include biographies and discussions of key aspects. (Rev: BL 6/1–15/06)

1152 🖰 **World Data Analyst Online** (9–12). Encyclopedia Britannica.
http://world.eb.com
Offers statistical data (demographics, economics, and so forth) on countries around the world and also allows the user to make customized comparisons between countries and across time in the form of tables, graphs, and charts. Users can also see maps and access information on geographic features.

1153 🖰 **World History: Ancient and Medieval Eras** (7–12). ABC-Clio.
www.abc-clio.com
Covering the whole world from prehistoric times through the end of the Middle Ages, this rich database offers primary and secondary sources, maps, timelines, audio and video segments, photographs, and graphics. (Rev: BL 4/15/05; LMC 8–9/05; SLJ 12/04)

Spanish Language

1154 Enciclopedia Estudiantil Hallazgos (7–12). World Book.
www.worldbookonline.com
Useful for both native Spanish speakers and those learning the language, this online encyclopedia is an adaptation of the English-language Student Discovery Encyclopedia. (Rev: BL 11/1/03; LMC 11–12/06)

1155 La Nueva Enciclopedia Cumbre (7–12). Scholastic.
http://teacher.scholastic.com/products/grolier/program_LNEC.htm
This Spanish-language encyclopedia is not an import from Spain but reflects the Latin American point of view. It is useful for Spanish speakers and for students learning to speak Spanish. In addition to standard encyclopedia entries, it includes many timelines, maps, and a useful events calendar. (Rev: BL 2/15/05)

1156 Spanish Reference Center (K–12). Encyclopedia Britannica.
www.spanish.eb.com
Two separate Spanish-language databases — the Enciclopedia Juvenil for children in grades K–6 and PlanetaSaber, a comprehensive encyclopedia for older children — can be bought separately or as a package, combined with a dictionary, atlas and timelines.

Title Index

This index lists titles in alphabetical order followed by media type in parentheses. References are to entry numbers, not page numbers.

Subject Index

This index lists entries by subject and then alphabetically by title followed by media type in parentheses. References are to entry numbers, not page numbers.

H

About the Author

CATHERINE BARR is editor of the Libraries Unlimited Children's and Young Adult Literature Reference series and author/coauthor of numerous guides to children's and young adult literature, including *Best Books for Children*, *Popular Series Fiction*, *High-Low Handbook*, and *From Biography to History*.